Walking with Aletheia

by

Jean Hargadon Wehner

LOGOSOPHIA LLC   ASHEVILLE, NC

WALKING WITH ALETHEIA
By JEAN HARGADON WEHNER

LOGOSOPHIA LLC

Logosophia LLC
90 Oteen Church Road
Asheville, NC 28805
https://logosophiabooks.com
logosophiabooks@gmail.com

First Edition

Library of Congress-in-Publication Data available upon request.

Non-fiction

Wehner, Jean Hargadon
Walking with Aletheia

ISBN 978-1-7350432-4-1

Original cover art and interior illustrations by Maria Staub Goebel.
Cover design and interior layout by Susan Yost.

Dedication

With gratitude, I dedicate my memoir to the caring souls who have walked, and continue to walk, with me on my health path. Their love helped me find myself, which gave me the courage to accomplish my dream to write this book. Their example has awakened in me a desire to share my journey with other survivors of trauma and their loved ones, with the hope I might be of some help.

My late husband, Mike, was so loving and generous; he was my rock. My family and my friends have shown so much support for which I am eternally grateful.

The survivors of abuse at Keough and all the alumni who have supported us, have bonded like the fierce sisters we have become. I am especially grateful to Teresa Lancaster, Abbie Schaub, and Gemma Hoskins.

There are a variety of advocates working to help children who have suffered child sexual abuse. They support my belief that no child should ever be sexually assaulted, and it is always the adult's fault. Thank you for your dedication.

Finally, my older brother, Bob, who died in April of 2020, supported my effort to work through my past so I could move forward. His advice, from the Rolling Stones' "Sweet Virginia" was "You've got to scrape that shit right off your shoes." Bob, you are remembered with love and gratitude!

To My Readers   1

Introduction   3

Part One: Childhood   9
Chapter 1: Innocence Abducted   11
Chapter 2: The Keough Years   17

Part Two: Adulthood   31
Chapter 3: Matthew   33
Chapter 4: My Spiritual Path Begins   36
Chapter 5: Brother Richard   44
Chapter 6: Little Jeannie (Vignette)   47
Chapter 7: The Pressure Rises (Vignette)   53
Chapter 8: Traumatic Memories and Shattered Faith   62
Chapter 9: Strider and Velvet   71
Chapter 10: My Support Network (1992-1997)   75
Chapter 11: The Legal Battle (1993-1996)   85
Chapter 12: The Silent Years (1996-2014)   93
Chapter 13: The Great Mother (Vignette)   101
Chapter 14: Lantern in the Bowel (Vignette)   108
Chapter 15: On the Wings of an Owl (Vignette)   114
Chapter 16: Finding My Voice (2014-Present)   120
Chapter 17: The Gift of Aletheia (2016)   135
Chapter 18: Weapons   141
Chapter 19: Piecing Cathy Together   152
Chapter 20: Mediation—or Nothing Changes   161
Chapter 21: Forgiveness   171
Chapter 22: Mom   178
Chapter 23: Meeting Jeannie (Vignette)   184
Chapter 24: Birth of a Warrior (Vignette)   188
Chapter 25: Jeannie Returns (Vignette)   193
Chapter 26: My Inner Garden (Vignette)   197

Chapter 27: The Council Gathered in the Cellar (Vignette)   202

Chapter 28: Girl with the Long Black Hair (Vignette)   207

Chapter 29: The Lightness of Love (Vignette)   217

Chapter 30: The Council and the Mandala (Vignette)   226

Chapter 31: Going Back for Frances (Vignette)   230

Chapter 32: Leaving the Cellar (Vignette)   237

Chapter 33: Buried in Despair (Vignette)   245

Chapter 34: Fear and Courage   253

Appendix   259

Acknowledgments   273

Resources   275

Foreword

Walking with Aletheia is about Jean Hargadon Wehner's
most credible journey dealing with the sexual abuse she
received, first by a great uncle and then by a network of
pedophile priests and others from her Catholic high school
in Baltimore. Her dissociation from this horrific sexual
abuse lasted until the age of 27, when she gradually began
to remember the repressed memories, thus beginning the
slow healing journey that continues even now as she ages
into her late sixties. This story of emotional terror and pain
describes her ways of finding the strength to deal with these
emotions. She is now writing and speaking out, offering
support to others in their remembering and healing as she
educates therapists and other professionals about her journey. Her exceptionally strong support system included her
loving and patient husband Mike, several of her siblings,
and eventually her parents, her two children, and her many
counselors, therapists and her spiritual guides. Her story
becomes a very powerful example from which others who
have been abused can find strength, and for therapists to
find deeper understanding of the therapeutic process. I am
honored to write this foreword to Jean's book.

Most important in uncovering and healing her abuse and
pain is her continued practice of a personal quiet time of
meditation and prayer, quiet time that was shared, listened
to, and supported by her support group and therapists.
Though I have worked as a psychologist with many victims
of sexual abuse, helping them uncover and heal fragments
of their uncovered memories, Jean brings together a much

broader and more complete picture of her journey. Writing her story is so important in her personal healing, but also for others recovering from sexual abuse, freeing them from the feelings of guilt and responsibility of victimhood, and finding support in coming out of the emotional prison of the abused.

Her process of uncovering and healing includes the value of her time in quiet meditation, identifying her protective dissociated personas or aspects of herself as a young girl, and calling upon her spirit guides as they arise both from within her protective dissociation from the abuse, and also from her strength in facing the abuse. The final step in healing is for the integration of these personas with her 'self'.

Walking with Aletheia is the story of uncovered repressed abuse, forgotten due to the self-protective mechanism of dissociation. Uncovering the abuse allows her to begin on the journey of healing. Included in the book are vignettes that have given her direction in healing, most that flowed from her time of 'quiet', from her unconscious, many in the powerfully deep language of metaphor. This healing was led or supported by her numerous spirit guides, in the forms of humans and animals. Though this journey took her away from the Catholic Church and her loss of faith in the church, it took her into a deeper spiritual place of healing.

Jean's sexual abuse began at the age of three years at the hands of her great uncle with whom she interacted with while spending overnight weekend visits with her great aunt.

Jean entered Archbishop Keough High School in 1967 when she was 14. There, three more years of abuse occurred, only this time at the hands of clergy. Her vivid description of her feelings of fear and pain that explains her dissociation from this sexual abuse can best be described only by her in her own words.

Uncovering Repressed Memories and Healing

Though her sexual abuse ended upon graduation from high school, Jean's memories of this abuse did not start to return until 1980 when she was 27 years old. From 1996 to around 2014, Jean, following the loss of a legal case against the archdiocese because of a statute of limitations failure, and the untimely death of her husband, withdrew from any public exposure, but continued her personal journey in silence. In 2014, she was approached by Tripod Media to participate in a documentary called *The Keepers*. It was about the murder of Cathy Cesnik, a teaching nun at Keough, and about accusations of sex abuse of the students at the high school. In this documentary, released in 2017, Jean was publicly able to fully emerge as 'Jean Hargadon Wehner'. While participating in this production, Jean continued to recover memories and heal. Since *The Keepers'* release, she has been frequently asked to speak to various groups, and she testified in the Maryland legislature regarding the issue of the statute of limitations.

Jean reports, "For many years, my practice was to sit quietly in prayer and meditation, including some journaling and dialogue with Jesus. I did not have a special physical, prayer space; I just took time to sit with my journal and follow my heart. Many times, my heart would lead me to a period of reflection and meditation; I would quiet down and let myself be still. Of course, the normal chatter was in my brain, and the thoughts seemed like they would not stop, but with time I got beyond that." During this time of quiet, her memories of the abuse continued to surface.

Many of the vignettes were of recovering memories, memories that sometimes took weeks if not months for completion. These vignette experiences were most powerful in her healing process, especially when she shared them with her therapists and support group, those who wisely supported and encouraged her in this process. These experiences were often dreamlike visions in the language of metaphor, the language experienced when going beyond the rational mind and into the unconscious.

Spirit Guides & Integrating Her Personas

Jean relates her experiences during her quiet with spirit guides, who were protectors. Imagination comes from beyond the five senses and thus comes from within the person; it reflects an important personal dimension. Therefore, all images that arise in her quiet are parts of her and are spirit guides. Such visions often open the door to the past or are predictors of the future, but the visions frequently reflect progress in working towards some goal. Certain spirit guides provided Jean with protection and strength, guides that rose above those other guides she experienced in her recovery of memories. Many of the ones that arose in her experiences of quiet were specific to the struggles she was going through at the time.

Many of the guides are protectors of Jean's personas. Each persona is an aspect of Jean that separated from her in the protective process of dissociation in her struggle with the abuse. They need to eventually be reincorporated within her for healing.

As her experiences unfolded over time, and some took weeks and even months for resolution, they followed no logical linear timeline. She never knew what experience or fragment of an experience might arise next. The unconscious mind is not logical but time-free as nighttime dreams are free of time, e.g. in a nighttime dream you may find yourself as an adult in your childhood home or visa-versa. The time-free nature of these visions from the unconscious is the power of these visions in healing. Each vignette opens new doors in the process of healing, and with her extensive support group listening to her visions, healing progressed.

In the process of therapy, Jean's protective personas were separate from her, created in her dissociation from the abuse. For healing, these personas need to again become one with her. This reintegration reflects the final step to wholeness, of becoming one within herself. Only with time can these personas dissolve into Jean. The healing of the adult Jean continues with the integration of each of her personas that has provided her with protection and growth since her teenage years.

Jean's vision experiences while in her quiet may seem quite strange to many readers, but these experiences of connecting with her unconscious are very central and important in healing. They may arise in many different ways. In my book, *Applying the Constructivist Approach to Cognitive Therapy: Resolving the Unconscious Past*, I attempt to summarize many of these ways: dreamwork, hypnotic and ecstatic trance, guided-imagery, free-association, waking morning reverie, and self-hypnosis. Jean's quiet opens for her the door to her unconscious, uncovering unconscious repressed memories and providing a map for healing. As mentioned earlier, the metaphoric nature of these experiences is the typical language of the unconscious. Apparently, Jean on her own, from within herself, discovered and learned to value the power of these self-hypnotic experiences for healing. She has exhibited in her quiet practice an exceptional personal strength, that she is teaching others in her writing and speaking engagements, that can benefit all. *Walking with Aletheia* is a most important book of healing.

– Nicholas E. Brink, Ph.D., author of:

Applying the Constructivist Approach to Cognitive Therapy: Resolving the Unconscious Past

Grendel and His Mother: Healing the Traumas of Childhood Through Dreams, Imagery and Hypnosis

Ecstatic Soul Retrieval: Shamanism and Psychotherapy

Loki's Children: A Healing Story of Antiquity, Shamanism and Psychotherapy

To My Readers

To understand the real crime against children when adults invade their personal boundary and sexually abuse them, some of the raw traumatic events need to be shared. That, along with the impact the abuse has on one's psyche makes an individual's health walk that much more amazing.

I have survived the atrocities I will write about, but it has been a meticulous process deciding which experiences to share and why. Because of this content, some of what I share in this book is difficult to read and may be triggering for other survivors. For those individuals, I encourage you to ask your therapist or trusted confidant to read my book first and then work together from there. If you choose not to read this book because it may be triggering, I support your decision.

I continue to find ways to deal with the trauma I endured and its impact on me. Through my ongoing inner work, I discovered there is more to living than just focusing on my survival of painful experiences. Surviving is critical, but I am working on what it means to thrive by taking conscious steps to relax and have fun.

By sharing my experience, I hope you can appreciate that you are not alone. There is a community of supporters all around us ready to help. I know how hard it is to ask for help while feeling such fear and distrust. What I have found helpful for me is to: decide if I really want what lies ahead, cautiously face my fear, label the fear, tell myself to stop expecting that fear to go away, then with my supports in place I lean into the fear while moving forward. I then surprisingly find the courage to take the next step, e.g., asking for help, talking to a friend, wearing a colorful piece of clothing, giving a talk, or even writing a book. It is hard, but I find it gets a bit easier the more I practice.

Introduction

I have lived with the reality of having been sexually abused from the ages of three through 17. The abusers included a relative, clergy, and other adults in positions of trust and power. The trauma I endured was so severe that my first task was to survive. I had to sever myself from that young victim and bury her deep within my subconscious. This book is about how I both survived the terror of child sexual abuse as a young victim, and the terrifying memories which began to surface within me in 1981 at the age of 27. I will be focusing on what I had to do over time to retrieve and face those repressed memories, or what is currently called dissociative amnesia, in order to reconnect to that severed part of myself.[1] (For purposes of consistency, I will use the term 'repressed memories' throughout this book.)

I am amazed not only that I have not killed myself, but that I am able to live a seemingly normal life, even as I continue grappling with my past. I spend much of my time dealing with an always present, yet thankfully decreasing, sense of fear.

It is ironic that even though I am no longer a member of any one religion, I have used my periods of quiet meditation

---

1   "There is a large body of research, conducted over the last century, that provides evidence that dissociative amnesia is a common reaction to trauma. There are now hundreds of studies in lots of different populations showing that people forge trauma," said psychiatrist Bessel van der Kolk. "We see it in victims of sexual abuse, natural disaster, torture, rape, war, and kidnapping. And research also shows that delayed memories of abuse are as reliable as continuous memories." *Mad in America: Science, Psychiatry and Social Justice*, "The False Memory Syndrome at 30: How Flawed Science Turned into Conventional Wisdom," by Joshua Kendall, February 7, 2021.

and my journaling to remember and deal with the memories of what the priests, other clergy, and adults in my Catholic high school did to me. I developed these self-awareness skills through my religious training as an adult, although I found similar therapeutic techniques are available in other spiritual traditions and secular modalities.

One of the ways I get in touch with my memories is through quiet, deep reflection. Some may call this meditation, and some may refer to it as contemplative prayer. I learned this method of deep reflection, which I call 'my quiet', from the Catholic community, including clergy, both before and while I was learning to be a spiritual director. I have also been able to access some of the emotions and memories of what happened to me through the technique of journaling, a form of dialoguing with one's inner self, which was introduced to me by a priest. The journal mirrors myself back to me.

I can remember only as much as my mind is able to handle at any given time in my life. Often during my quiet, I experience a spontaneous form of 'active imaging' that flows naturally throughout my inner journey. New memories reveal themselves to this very day. And just because I write about my experiences does not mean I always understand their deeper meaning at that time. However, one of the benefits of writing this book, similar to journaling, is that the process of writing has brought about more clarity. The inner work needed for me to accept, understand and integrate these memories which make up my past is ongoing.

To cope, I continually rely on my support network, including my adult nuclear family, my birth nuclear family, my confidants, and my therapists. As I continue to integrate and become healthier, I need their assistance less and less.

My purpose in writing this book is not just to tell my story, although that is part of it. I hope that others who have gone through traumatic, abusive situations, will be inspired to look around for similar supports, whether those are family, friends, therapists, and/or spiritual advisers. I also want to support therapists who work with individuals suffering the impact of trauma in their lives. It is my further hope that others may find the power of reflective prayer and a variety of journaling techniques as valuable in dealing with past trauma, at times with professional guidance. These journaling techniques may include free flow writing from the heart, creating mandalas for a sacred space to contain thoughts and emotions to gain clarity, and dialoguing with oneself and others.

While these supports allow me to handle my trauma from day to day, I find that equally important is the wisdom I have discovered in myself. Other people would speak of observing or being drawn to this wisdom in me. However, I was slow to understand that the feeling I was experiencing was a deep spiritual awakening, connecting my body, mind, and spirit, which helped me cope with what happened to me. By opening myself in an honest fashion, and relentlessly struggling to make difficult choices, I have found that realizations and understandings come to me in ways I would not expect.

This wisdom spawned the meditative vignettes I will present in this book.[2] The vignettes involve my memories, along with my spiritual process and growth. My meditative periods may occur anywhere I feel moved to be still, breathe, and reflect. When the memories begin to surface, I feel very vulnerable, so I am usually by myself. The intensity of the experience can be shocking, causing me to feel totally out of control. Once the innermost movement begins, whether it be the beginning of a memory or an ongoing spiritual quest, I allow what comes up to just do so.

Sometimes, there are personas who emanate from my heart and mind. These are subconscious aspects of myself, created by me as a young girl, which held the trauma I experienced.[3] The personas are my coping mechanisms

---

2   A chapter which presents a meditative vignette will be indicated as 'vignette' in the chapter's title.

3   I also refer to persona as 'aspect' or 'part' and will use those terms interchangeably.

which have developed organically. While working with these personas in these meditative vignettes, I understand who I am, where I am, and the plane I am living on as an adult.

Other times, experiencing a type of spontaneous spiritual imagery, I am assisted by guides who take various forms, including a tiger, a snake, an owl, and individuals.[4] I believe these symbols, guides or images, similar to the cross for Roman Catholics, are understood within a deep spiritual dimension of our beings. One such guide, the Greek goddess, Aletheia (pronounced uh-LEE-thee-uh), is the namesake of this book. She is the goddess of truth, holding a mirror out for us to see our truth.[5]

The memories I have are rooted in and percolate throughout my body as if they are imprinted on my very cells. They are painful and evolving to the point that I may never really know when the memory has reached some form of completion. At times, the healing impact, which comes about through my inner work, may be accomplished without my needing to remember the full experience.

The vignettes may also include spiritual reflections about the significance of the images and the communication with myself which arose during my meditation. The reflections will at times delve more deeply into the facts of what occurred during my time as a child, particularly as it relates to the sexual abuse I experienced. Some of the vignettes also focus on new spiritual insights that unfold.

My life history will give context to the reflections and vignettes I describe. However, this is not a full biography of

---

4   "Deep imagery refers to inner journeys in which you interact, while awake, with the other-than-ego inhabitants of your psyche. With deep imagery the images come from the depths of your own unconscious, and the guide (when there is one) doesn't know any more than you what will take place on your journey. Among the most effective methods for cultivating deep imagery are those that involve *power animals*, inner guides to healing, growth, and soul work." *Soulcraft: Crossing into the Mysteries of Nature and Psyche* by Bill Plotkin Ph.D., New World Library, 2003.

5   I was introduced to Aletheia by my son, Greg, when he presented his carved gift of the goddess' image to the crew of *The Keepers*. See "The Gift of Aletheia," page 135.

what happened in my life or a full account of what happened at my high school.[6] I am just one of many girls who had this experience at my school, and it is not my place to speak for them. I will not be going into the detail of all the experiences we had, many of which have been shared in past journalistic articles and *The Keepers*, an Emmy-nominated Netflix documentary series.

My life's history will lay the groundwork for how I was able to handle the horrible memories which would arise. I will describe how my spiritual journey, my psychological self-awareness, and my emotional maturation saved my life.

Coping with the trauma of child sexual abuse is difficult for any adult. Remembering it for the first time as an adult creates a second layer of trauma—the shock of remembering it and experiencing it as both the child/victim, and the adult who desperately wants to protect that child within.

This book is my opportunity to share how I lived through and dealt with the trauma I experienced in my life. This process has helped me realize the courageous power of the human spirit which continues to move me toward wholeness. That spirit helps me see that I am so much more than the abuse.

Here is what happened to me.

---

6   I will not be sharing all the details of my abuse at Keough, only those which have relevance to my explanation of how one can heal after such experiences.

PART ONE

Childhood

I was born in Baltimore in 1953, the first girl in what would become a family of seven boys and three girls. We were an Irish Catholic family. My father was a policeman, and my mother, a homemaker. We always had enough to eat, but there were no frills. My parents had three priorities: family, church, and school.

There was little extra money, and with ten children, not much time to devote to any one child's whims or wishes. I am not complaining. We had more than enough kids to hang out with, both within our family and in our neighborhood. Growing up, we spent one week a summer at the same shore house, which was owned by our neighbors, and had frequent camping trips to the local state park. We were not only siblings, but friends as well. If there was no game to be played, we would go exploring in the neighborhood's small, wooded areas, or hang the hose off the back porch and run under the water.

We had a family structure that was set by my parents and essentially enforced by my mother. Every evening, many of us sat at the dining room table for dinner, and we all had chores. There was discipline and love. After dinner, we sat at the same table and did homework. All ten of us attended a Catholic elementary school named St. Benedict's, the local Catholic school affiliated with the church by the same name. At St. Benedict's there were lots of nuns, all members of the School Sisters of Notre Dame (SSND). They kept order and discipline just like my mother.

The school and my parents also instilled in us a faith in God and Jesus. We prayed every day in school, and every day at home. We had masses during the week and faithfully went to mass every Sunday. We did not eat meat on Friday. And it was not uncommon for us to be summoned on a balmy evening, while enjoying a game of hide and seek, to get on our knees and, begrudgingly, say an entire rosary.[7]

---

7   A rosary is a Roman Catholic devotion to the Blessed Mother Mary using a string of beads to count prayers.

CHAPTER ONE

Innocence Abducted

Starting when I was three years old, my great aunt, Kitty, who was my maternal grandfather's sister, and who was close to my mother, would have a bunch of us kids over for a weekend two or three times a year. While there were still a few children at home who were too young to go to my aunt's, the weekends were a gift to my parents, intended to give them some space for a few days. These weekends were also special for us kids. We got to eat big bowls of ice cream, watch 'shoot 'em up' cowboy shows, stay up late, drink coffee, sleep in the living room if we wanted, have lavish bubble baths, and gamble with pennies playing a board game called Pokeno. These were activities we seldom engaged in at home; that's why the weekends were so special.

Kitty was an executive secretary at a law firm. Once she came home from work or church, she would change into her housecoat and, still wearing her pearls and lipstick, go about her house chores throughout the day. Her husband, Tom, worked in a large grocery store. He was a big man who usually wore work pants and a white shirt.

Kitty and Tom had no children of their own. I was their goddaughter, and I would receive special gifts from them for my birthday. For most of the time I visited, I was the only girl in a sea of boys. On Saturdays, Kitty would have the boys do yard work while she took a nap. I did not go with them. I was teased at the time for not working and for being special; my brothers would call me 'Queenie'. My aunt and uncle even made me a shirt with that name. I did feel special.

On Sundays, Kitty would escort all of us kids to church and we would pile into the pews at Saints Philip and James. When we left her house at the end of the weekend, she would give each of us money to go along with our 'gambling winnings'.

While on one level, we thought these weekends were a vacation, the fun and games were overshadowed by a darker reality. Tom was an ex-Marine, well over six feet tall, and broad shouldered. He was an alcoholic who would terrify the children if angered, occasionally displaying an old revolver from World War II if he wanted to intimidate us. Kitty was a recovering alcoholic. Years later, my mother told me she felt that since Kitty was sober, she would take care of us and be able to protect us from Tom if his drinking got out of hand.

But it was more than just Tom's drinking. He would not only have a pile of *Playboy* and detective magazines in their bedroom, where some of the kids would sleep, but they were also visible to the children aside his easy chair in the dining room, where he would always relax.

On Saturdays, when the boys would be working in the yard and my aunt was napping, Tom would take me to the basement to sexually abuse me. He would also do so at night when he would wake me and cart me to the cellar. Their family dog, named Queenie, was always with him, including these trips to the basement.

I remember taking dishes into the kitchen after dinner one evening. My siblings were sitting at the dining room table when Tom came in behind me in the kitchen and pressed me up against the sink. Looking around his side, I saw Kitty enter the kitchen and look at what was happening. Cornered in that tiny kitchen, I already felt small and alone. Then, in a matter of seconds, my heart sank into what I can only call despair, as I watched my aunt turn her back on me and walk out of the kitchen. She affirmed what I had come to believe—I deserved what Tom was doing to me. From the age of three, with no one saying differently, I would not have thought that any of my uncle's perverted activities were anything other than normal behavior for his home.

Looking back, it is clear I was being groomed by Tom.[8] He understood the psychology of what fear can do to intimidate children. When I was around eight, I remember telling Tom that I did not want to go down to the basement with him anymore. Shortly after, he stood at the bottom of the basement stairs coaxing me down by holding a beautifully wrapped package. When I got downstairs, he handed the present to me. Sitting on the floor, I felt the box move and immediately thought it was a puppy. When I took the top off, I was shocked to find myself staring at a white rat. My joy turned to disgust in a heartbeat. Tom then molested me on the basement floor, holding the rat over my bare belly. He said afterward that if I did as I was told, he would not have to pull the rat out again. I do not remember ever telling him "No" again.

He intimidated me in even more insidious ways. Sometime after the rat incident, my younger sister, Kass, came with us to Tom and Kitty's. She was at least three since we had to be that age to spend a weekend there. At times, my uncle would threaten that if I did not do as I was told he would bring other siblings down into the basement. As the oldest daughter, who for six years was the only girl to visit Kitty and Tom's with my brothers, I naturally felt protective of them. Now, with my little sister also visiting, Tom's threat intensified within me, piling tremendous responsibility on my young head.[9]

---

8   "One tool common to those who sexually abuse kids is grooming: manipulative behaviors that the abuser uses to gain access to a potential victim, coerce them to agree to the abuse, and reduce the risk of being caught. It is usually employed by a family member or someone else in the victim's circle of trust, such as a coach, teacher, youth group leader or others who naturally have some interaction with the victim. Though grooming can take many different forms, it often follows a certain pattern: Victim selection; Gaining access & isolating the victim; Trust development & keeping secrets; Desensitization to touch & discussion of sexual topics; Attempts by abusers to make the behavior seem normal." RAINN—Rape, Abuse & Incest National Network: https://www.rainn.org/news/grooming-know-warning-signs.

9   Thankfully, Kass has no recollection of ever being abused by Tom.

On our drive home on Sundays, Tom would take all the children to a bar called The Green Door. He did so despite my aunt chiding him to "not take them to that place" as we were leaving. The bar was dark and smelled like stale beer and cigarettes. There were a few tables and a scattering of people sitting at the bar. The boys and I would be situated at a table. For us, this was one of the weekend's adventures. A friendly barmaid would give us cokes with maraschino cherries.

At some point, Tom began taking me to a back room and allowing other adults to molest me. I remember his large figure standing by the door, listening, and watching. At first, I looked to Tom, hoping he would make the smelly man stop. When Tom did not stop the abuse, I began looking to him for protection in the event the stranger began to hurt me in even more serious ways. But now I am sure he was keeping a lookout so that no one walked in on us. When leaving the bar, Tom would purchase a six pack of beer and situate the beers, one at a time, between his legs on the drive home. I always sat in the middle on the front seat.

I did not remember being sexually abused by my uncle until I was 27 years old. By then, Tom was dead. I understand now that these sexual violations were so difficult for me as a child, that all I could do was dissociate from them. Initially, I was shocked and confused when disgusting memories of Tom sexually abusing me began to surface in my adult mind and body. It was hard to know where these disturbing memories were coming from and what to believe. As I continued to work at uncovering and connecting to this young victim within me, my memories were affirmed when my siblings remembered, and my aunt later did not deny, facts that supported what I was recalling as an adult.

Years later, one of my older brothers told me he remembered waking up one night because I was not in my sleeping spot. He went to the hall and saw that the basement door was open. I was walking up the steps in my nightgown, followed by the family dog and my uncle. He said I looked like a zombie. I went to bed, but my brother followed my uncle into the dining room and confronted Tom. My brother told Tom that my father, a policeman, had a gun. Tom countered by pulling out his World War II revolver and bullets to intimidate my brother. On the ride home that weekend, my brother was positioned in such a way in the back seat that Tom could stare at him the whole way through the rearview mirror.

My next youngest sister recalled a memory from when she was three or four and I was nine or ten. She was standing at the top of the basement stairs, crying, and clutching my aunt's housecoat; I was at the bottom of the steps with my uncle. My sister wanted me to come back up, but Kitty just closed the basement door, leaving Tom and me there alone.

I believe I stopped going to my aunt's when I was 12. I had my first menstrual period at Kitty and Tom's house. I was so upset and wanted to be home with my mother. I tried to cope with it, and hide it, by stuffing tissue between my legs. When my uncle got into my bed that night intending to abuse me, he found the bloody toilet paper between my legs and said, "You've ruined everything!" He told me to sleep on the floor with the dog, while he stayed in the bed. I was upset and confused. I could not understand what I did that was wrong. I felt guilty, rejected, and paralyzed. (As an adult when I remembered my uncle's words "You've ruined everything!" I understood what he meant: I could now get pregnant.) I laid there all night, listening to the ticking of the clock. Lying next to his dog on the floor was the only comforting and strangely normal experience I was having.

The next morning, I could not stop crying. My aunt, apparently not knowing what had happened the night before, thought I was sick and had my dad pick me up early. That evening, while doing laundry, my parents discovered that I had gotten my first period. Having a daughter of my own, I can imagine they thought my earlier tears were just the result of their little girl in the throes of pre-pubescent emotions. I have no memory of ever returning to Kitty & Tom's for an overnight visit.

CHAPTER TWO

The Keough Years

When I was in the eighth grade and ready to graduate, I told my parents I wanted to go to a public school in northeast Baltimore. It was a trade school and I wanted to learn cosmetology. They would not hear of it, and insisted I attend Archbishop Keough, the new Catholic all-girls high school within walking distance of our house in southwest Baltimore. What I appreciate now is how hard my parents worked to give their children all they could. They wanted us to have a good education, which to them meant a Catholic one.

They also wanted their growing family to have more living space in a safer neighborhood. I spent my early years living in an end rowhome with a small yard. My Mom and Dad had exhausted all ideas for expansion. As the kids got older, my parents became concerned with some of the unacceptable behaviors of our neighborhood friends. They could see those behaviors beginning to influence their own children. They needed to move.

My Mom and Dad became aware of the opportunity to swap houses with one of our neighbor's parents. They had a single-family house with a big yard and were willing to trade for our small rowhome. Their house was within walking distance of Keough and the new all-boys Catholic high school, Cardinal Gibbons. There was a straight up swap, and all parties were pleased.

In 1967, at the age of 14, I began attending Keough, which was run by the same order of nuns (SSND) who ran St. Benedict's. It was reassuring for my parents to have nuns and priests working at Keough. In that way, important Catholic traditions like mass, celebrating liturgical feast days, and confession would be honored. Confession is one of the cornerstones of Catholicism; it is frequently intertwined with guilt. The priest is the person who hears the confession of the Catholic layperson. Throughout grade school, we went to confession weekly with our list of sins or wrongdoings. Most times I just went through the motions.

We were taught that we needed to make confessions to a priest, who was the only one who could forgive sins on behalf of God. This normally took place in a confessional, where the priest and the person could hear one another, separated by a screen. At Keough, priests had specific hours during the day when students could go to confession. In fact, students could be excused from class to go, showing how important confession was at that school.

In my freshman year, I went to the chapel with the intent to relieve myself of my guilt related to certain behaviors. As a 14-year-old Catholic teenager, masturbation would be seen as wrong in the eyes of the church, even though it was not abnormal. Since these types of things were never talked about within our faith and my family, all I felt was guilty about my actions and I was looking for forgiveness from God. (Years later, I understood that this particular masturbatory activity was something that had been used by my uncle in his abuse of me during my childhood.)

The shame of confessing this behavior to a priest was overwhelming. This felt quite different than any grade school confession when I recited sins by rote. I tried to go inside the confessional five times. Each time I went closer to the curtain, but my feelings held me back. Finally, I was able to enter the confessional and began whispering my guilty secret to the priest on the other side of the screen. His name was Father Neil Magnus. It was a relief to say what I had done, regardless of how hard it was to admit. If I was ultimately forgiven, I was more than willing to recite as many prayers as he assigned, the normal practice or penance given for forgiveness of my actions.

But then, the priest asked if he could look directly at me and asked me my name. I was shocked by his request. At that time, the priest normally sat with his ear to the anonymous layperson kneeling on the other side of the screen. We were taught that when you confess, you are speaking directly to God. The screen helps you focus less on the priest, creating a sense of anonymity.

The mere thought of looking Father Magnus in the eyes after what I had confessed was devastating. I hit a brick wall. What horror had I committed that this priest had to talk directly to me, and see who had told him what now seemed to be this vile and dirty thing? I felt I had no choice. I hesitantly told him, "Yes, you can look at me," and "My name is Jeannie."

This was virtually the last thing I remembered about my experiences in Keough until I was 38 years old. From this point forward, the information I am conveying to you about the balance of my tenure at Keough is either information I remembered when memories started returning to me, or facts that were elicited during future investigations. When I remembered the experience in that confessional, I understood why my mind buried the memory.

Father Magnus turned to me, looked me in the face, and began asking me about the behavior I had just confessed. I could not believe what was happening, nor could I process all my emotions. He sat so close, and yet the priest must have always been sitting that close. Why hadn't I noticed it before? Why was he looking at me that same way my uncle used to look at me? I felt the red cheeked shyness of a little girl being asked embarrassingly intimate questions by a 'man of God'. l was mortified! As I answered his questions, which felt like an eternity, I became aware that he was masturbating. He made me feel like I was dirty and disgusting. To this day, when I think of this experience, I feel like I am shrinking back into the corner of a coffin, which over time has become riddled with holes, each one large enough to fit an erect penis. I was now his captive. We ended with the priest telling me he would have to pray about whether God could forgive me.

I left still seeking forgiveness, totally stunned, and even more guilt-ridden than when I entered the confessional. As an adult, I understood that while I did not go into the confessional to talk about the abuse by my uncle, this priest's actions had reinforced what my uncle had said to me as a little girl: "You make men do these things. It's all your fault." From that time on, I would think of myself as 'bad and dirty'.

A couple of weeks after my confession, I was approached by Magnus at my locker. This was unnerving and humiliating. Magnus was the Director of Religious Studies at Keough. He was 30 years old when I went into that confessional. He was tall but not heavy, and I remember him as always wearing a black suit. As a freshman in high school, Magnus was an important person, like the pastor of a Catholic parish. To me, that place of power was intimidating. Just his standing by me in the hallway made me feel uncomfortable, as if all my classmates knew my dirty little secret. For this priest to approach me publicly meant I was probably in trouble. I wished I could crawl into my locker. He said he wanted to see me in his office.

When I went to his office, Magnus told me he did not know if God could forgive me for the things I had done. He had me sit on his lap while he prayed over me in Latin. He said that one way for me to cleanse myself was to perform fellatio on him and swallow the Holy Spirit upon his ejaculation. He referred to his semen as the eucharist, or Body of Christ. I was naïve, terrified, indoctrinated as to the godliness and superiority of priests, and conditioned due to past abuse. So, I did as I was told. I assumed I deserved this since I felt guilty about the information I had shared with him, intensified by his condemnation. He began summoning me on a regular basis, and I was told to comply in a similar fashion.

Sometime after that encounter, Magnus invited Father Joseph Maskell into his office. I was immediately afraid of Maskell. He was a little younger than Magnus but seemingly larger, at least in terms of his thickness and presence. He entered the room in a hurry, as if he were doing Magnus a favor, consulting with him about me. He appeared to be bothered with the request and disgusted by my presence. With time, Maskell became progressively meaner and more hateful toward me than Magnus had been. He would call me a whore, cow, slut, and a sinner, saying he and Magnus would have to work hard for me to be forgiven for who I was. The 'work' he referred to always resulted in me being raped.[10] These two grown men dressed in black loomed over me, a young, terrified girl sitting in a chair.

I am not sure how long these joint 'spiritual counseling' sessions went on, but at some point Maskell told me to meet him in the Chaplain's Office, which was adjacent to the chapel on the first floor. I was told to meet him there on a set day during my free period for regular counseling appointments. I now understand that this was different than some of the other girls, who experienced being called over the loudspeaker to Maskell's office, thereby alerting classmates and teachers. It seemed for a long time no one even knew I was seeing Maskell on a regular basis. My parents were never informed of these sessions.

During these meetings, I was sexually abused and otherwise terrorized into silence. At one session, Maskell appeared to be frustrated with my lack of participation. He said it was time for me to become a participant in my therapy. He went to the file cabinet and took something from one of the drawers. He demanded I take my underwear off and proceeded to use a vibrator on me. I cried for him

---

10   Throughout this book, I use the term 'rape' to include any forced, non-consensual sexual acts forced on me, including but not exclusively forced sexual intercourse. I do not think any word but rape comes close to what those perpetrators were doing to our souls.

to stop. My crying did stop when the weapon in his hand took effect. This tool was deliberately used to induce an unwanted, involuntary sexual response.[11] While calling me hateful names, I then was forced to do fellatio on him. When I was leaving his office, he told me if I did what I was told he would not use that tool on me again. As I reached for the door, I could feel him come down to my ear and whisper, "You hated that, and I'm glad." Later, I began to find other adults with him in his office, and if I appeared scared or not agreeable, he would walk toward that file cabinet. When he saw me responding in a way that satisfied the stranger, he would stop moving toward the cabinet.

Maskell used tools like this vibrator, a dog collar and leash, enemas, a pen knife, a gun, and a wooden paddle with holes. He also used catholic rituals, drugs, hypnosis, and brain washing techniques on me. He recited hypnotic phrases like, "I only want what's best for you—just what's best for you." He planted suggestions in my mind, like the sound of the click of his door closing as I left his office, which then caused everything to go blank. He would sit across from me and quickly flip through pictures of deformed individuals, like a woman with leprosy, a young boy without a penis, and a person without a tongue. He would repeat, "You see what happens when you say bad things about people?" I remember Magnus taking pictures of me with my blouse unbuttoned, and Maskell and Magnus showing me albums of children dressed in adult lingerie, in very suggestive poses.

Maskell invited other teachers, police officers, a politician, and other adults from outside the school into this environment. He took me and other students to a local gynecologist. Maskell had connections throughout the Baltimore community. He was the chaplain for the Baltimore County Police, the Maryland State Police and the Air National Guard. In 1972 Maskell received a master's degree in school psychology from Towson State University followed by

---

11   "Sexual Responses to Sexual Assault," by Dr. Lacter, *End Ritual Abuse*, February 21, 2019; https://EndRitualAbuse.org.

a Certificate of Advanced Study in Counseling from Johns Hopkins University.[12]

In 1992, when I began remembering the abuse in Maskell's office, the memories would drop into my conscious mind. They came in bits and pieces. As each new memory unfolded, I felt as if the experience was happening for the first time. However, the memories were so horrific and outside of my present reality that I have had to be meticulous in my efforts to detect if each memory was true.

As a result, I had questions about how all this activity could have happened without detection by other staff members. How did the abusers just walk through the halls to get in and out of that room? How could I go in and out of the chapel, where some of the abuse occurred, without someone seeing? How could I go into a bathroom every time after being violated without someone questioning?

After hearing other survivors' accounts of abuse, it became clear to me that the layout of the chaplain's office was an ideal setting to move adults and girls into and out of the school. The office had a small bathroom, a door into the chapel, and a door that exited to the front breezeway. Some survivors remember a fire door from the breezeway exiting to the far-right side of the school property. The door faced the convent.[13]

A number of alumni remember seeing police cars parked on the front driveway adjacent to the end of the breezeway where the side doors of the school, and the chaplain's office door were located. One of those alumni, Abbie Schaub, said "My memories are not strong or detailed about my Keough years. I do remember staying after school since they had a late bus. I often saw a marked police car parked on the circle over by the convent area when getting on the school bus out front. I can't remember anything specific about the

---

12 Since Maskell would have been in graduate school during the time these abusive, predatory acts occurred, was he using us girls for his own personal 'research' projects?

13 See picture of school building, page 263.

markings or colors though. Never thought anything about it at the time."[14]

These abusers from outside the school could easily enter Maskell's office without ever having to pass any of the administrative offices, which were located at the main entrance of the school.[15] The privacy and layout of the Chaplain's office makes it obvious why he centered the sex trafficking activity there.

Maskell was the leader of a sex ring which was exploiting young girls. I was one of a number of girls who were subjected to sexual assault at the hands of adults within and outside Keough. While I do not intend to go through all the sordid details laid out in the investigations and *The Keepers*, I can say that I and the other girls trapped in this ring felt abandoned, helpless, and doomed.

Sister Cathy Cesnik

The scope of this criminal syndicate was wide, with numerous victims, but to this day I do not remember, and I will not allow myself to remember, any of the other girls involved in the abuse. It is my dreaded fear that as I became brainwashed by Maskell into submission, I introduced other girls to his office, and I am not sure how to handle that. The blanket of guilt, shame and responsibility still lays heavy on my heart.[16]

At some point after the abuse started, an English teacher named Sister Cathy Cesnik began asking me and others about what might be happening in the chaplain's office. Cathy was in her mid-twenties, a vibrant nun who was a member of the SSND order. She clicked with all

---

14 Abbie Schaub was one of two women who sparked the readdressing of the cold case murder of Sister Cathy Cesnik, whose murder was the focus of a Facebook group.

15 See pictures of front of school building, pages 263-264.

16 See "Weapons," page 146.

the students who knew her. She was like a mentor or big sister to many of the girls at Keough.

I first remembered Cathy in early 1993 after I was shown a yearbook picture by a classmate and recognized her on some level. I remembered that on the last day of my sophomore year, I went to retrieve a book from her classroom. She was the only other person in the room and began talking with me.

As I walked toward her, standing in the front of the room, she started asking me how I felt being at Keough. I told her, "I don't really like Keough." I was very aware of what I was saying, and that she was listening. That felt very good. Looking me in the eyes, Sister Cathy sat down and asked me what could be so bad. I responded, "I can't talk about it." As I stood facing her, she said, "Fine. You don't need to talk about it. I'll ask questions and you nod your head yes or no." Sister Cathy then asked me, "Is someone doing something to you that you don't want them to do?" Looking at the floor, I nodded yes. She continued, "Is someone hurting you?" I nodded yes. She then asked me, "Is it someone I would know or be acquainted with?" I shook my head yes. "Jeannie, is it the priest?" I looked up into her eyes and made a slight nod yes. She said, "Jesus, I expected as much."

Sister Cathy hugged me and assured me that I was not to worry. I can still feel her warm embrace. She told me to enjoy the summer and she would take care of the situation. I felt as if I had just bared my soul in the light of day and I was drinking in warmth and joy and hope for a better year ahead. I felt accepted and free.[17]

That September, when I returned from my summer vacation, I found Sister Cathy was no longer at Keough. She had begun teaching at Western High, an all-girls public school in Baltimore. She did so while remaining a nun. When Sister Cathy did not return to Keough, my young, vulnerable 'teenaged-self' felt confused and scared. I had nodded my

---

17 Journal entry dated February 7, 1993.

secret to her and now I felt abandoned and fearful that I had been duped.

Shortly after my return from vacation, Maskell called me to his office, which was different then our previous, regularly scheduled counseling arrangement. I had let myself believe that Sister Cathy had taken care of this, and that these appointments were over. I cautiously entered Maskell's office.

He was furious. He said someone approached him during the summer saying he was hurting the girls. As I sat in his office chair, looking at the floor, I felt his anger penetrate my whole body. Then he walked over to me and asked, "You didn't tell anyone that I'm hurting the girls, did you?" Looking up at him, I felt terror creep over me. He knew!

Feeling like a deer in headlights, totally alone and cornered, I denied that it was me. As I sat shaking in his office chair, with him towering over me dressed in black, he said, "You don't seem to understand that you're the one who is doing things in this room that shouldn't be talked about—not me." Maskell went over to the drawer and pulled out the vibrator saying, "I think it is time to reacquaint you with our little toy." Turning my head away I began to cry, saying, "Please don't use that. I promise I won't tell. Please don't do that." He put his hand under my chin, turned my face toward his, looked me in the eyes and said, "It's too late. You already did tell. Now you have to be punished." He then raped me with the vibrator and forced me to perform fellatio on him. (When I was remembering this experience, I heard that young girl within me, wrapped in palpable despair, saying, "I hate him, and I hate me.") As I was leaving his office, he said, "Now remember not to let any lies come out of that whoring mouth. I'll see you later." Our regular counseling sessions resumed.[18]

Two months later, in November of 1969, Cathy Cesnik was reported missing by the police. It was a widely reported missing person case in Baltimore; her whereabouts remained a mystery for two months.

---

18 Journal entry dated February 10, 1993.

To this day I have no idea to what extent I was aware of Cathy's abduction and murder other than what I have remembered as an adult since 1993. For example, many former students commented that they remember Sister Cesnik being missing, and the anxiety they felt because of that. My siblings remember hearing about her disappearance. It is like I have this black hole into which all my Keough memories were buried, with each memory surfacing only when I am ready. It could be triggered by a photo, a smell, a person, or a place. And many memories are still in there. As one of my therapists, Dr. Norman Bradford, would suggest, "Don't go deep sea diving. Just wait for the memories to come to you."

One day, during the time Sister Cathy was missing, Maskell requested that I come to his office after school. Once there, he said he knew where Sister Cathy was. I felt shocked and extremely anxious. He said he would take me to see her, leading me to think she was alive.[19]

He then took me off the school property and drove several miles to a wooded area. While driving, Maskell spoke nonstop as if he were giving a sermon. As we drove through the woods, and believing Sister Cathy was alive, I wondered why she would be here, where there were no houses or people around. I was confused.

When we came to the end of the road, I saw a long brick wall which looked to me like the side of a factory building. In 1993, I told the detectives it reminded me of the Calvert Distillery, a landmark building in southwest Baltimore County. Maskell stopped the car, and we got out and began walking. Slightly to the right front of that wall was a clear piece of property.[20] To our immediate right, as we faced the clearing, was a dumpster which sat back, possibly in front of another structure.[21] Maskell walked ahead a short distance

19 Journal entry dated February 14, 1993.
20 See picture of Majestic Distillery Co. Inc., page 263.
21 I realize the description of this area does not precisely match the area where Cathy was later found on January 3, 1970. In 2015, I saw the area I was shown Cathy's body by Maskell. See "Girl with the Long Black Hair (Vignette)," page 207. That

then moved to the side. I kept thinking 'Where is she?' And then I saw her.

Cathy was lying on her right side in a heap. I ran over to her, and when I saw maggots on her face, I fell to my knees and began wiping at her face and pleading with Maskell to please help me. At that point, Maskell leaned down and whispered in my ear, "You see what happens when you say bad things about people?"

I sat back, staring at my hands in shock for what seemed like an eternity. Suddenly, from far away, I heard Maskell ordering me in a dismissive tone, "Get in the car."

As a 16-year-old, I had not seen much of death. When I did, it was neat and tidy—a loved one lying in a casket at a funeral home while family and friends stand around. But never one so shockingly real and unreal at the same time. One so violent! I do not know how I ever got up off the ground after touching Cathy's face. Eventually, after many years of intensive work with these memories, I was able to bring the paralyzed part of myself, that frozen young girl, away from her vigil over Cathy.

Following Maskell's demand, I managed to get up, and I walked like a zombie to the car. After getting in, he gave me a napkin to wipe my hands. I then placed it in the bag hanging off a knob on the dashboard. This is one of only two times that I remember Maskell giving me anything with which to clean, especially after a sexually abusive interaction with anyone.[22] As he drove, he began his brainwashing story of how terrible I was for doing this to Sister Cathy. That rhetoric went on throughout the rest of my time at Keough.

I was clearly in shock at this point, so Maskell took advantage of the situation and had me believe that he was the only one in my life who could protect me. I now knew that he could kill me. I was terrified, but I subconsciously

---

location is just a few hundred yards from where the two hunters discovered her before they called the police.

22 See "Weapons," page 144-145.

understood that the only way to leave the school alive was to submit to the power Maskell wielded. So, for the last year and a half of high school, I did what I was told, effectively living two lives. One life was a traumatized, almost mummy-like sex slave to this man and the other people he subjected me to, and another life was going through the motions of being a teenager without any emotional or spiritual connection to, or memory of, my school and my classmates.

I left Keough, graduating in 1971. I still do not remember much of my senior year, although some memories have begun to surface.

Early in my memory recovery process as an adult, I recalled an experience during the last days at Keough. I entered a room and sitting at a desk was some priest who seemed to be in a position of authority higher than Maskell. This person told me that Maskell had advised him of all the work he had done to help me obtain forgiveness. This was the same forgiveness I sought in my freshman year in that confessional. He said that Maskell told him that none of his efforts could penetrate my bond with the devil.

This priest then spit in the palm of my hand, likening his spittle in my hand to that bond. He said I was not to wash my hand until I decided to leave my wayward ways behind me and go down a new path of goodness. This was the only way God could truly forgive me. He then gave me absolution, forgiving all my sins, but it was conditional. It was conditioned on the fact that I could never speak of what happened at Keough. I went right to the bathroom, washed my hand, thereby leaving a large part of myself behind, buried within the walls of Keough and my psyche. I headed down a new path of goodness. After Cathy's death, I had vowed to do what I had to do to survive and get the hell out of that school, no matter what the cost.[23] And I did.

---

23 See "Birth of a Warrior (Vignette)," page 192.

After graduating from Archbishop Keough High School, the wonderful Catholic school that my parents spent hard-earned money to send me to, I buried my experiences, severing virtually all my connections with my classmates.

PART TWO

Adulthood

When I left Keough, I moved on to become a licensed cosmetologist, which was my original professional goal before going to Keough.[24] In many ways, it was as if those four years never happened.

While I buried the horror of what I experienced at Keough, I also buried all memories of my time there, in more ways than one. My body held the secrets, and I became bulimic both while at Keough and after graduation. Two years after leaving Keough, my girlfriend's mother said that I would get cancer from abusing laxatives; I slowly stopped this masochistic physical abuse.[25] But the memories stayed buried.

Now I see that by submitting to Maskell's demands after the threat of seeing Sister Cathy's dead body, I realized that I stood more of a chance of not being murdered. And that by severing from that part of myself and leaving behind the memories, I was increasing the chances that I would not die at my own hands through suicide, whether that be suddenly, or slowly through alcohol or drug abuse.

---

24   I was a full-time cosmetologist for one year after becoming licensed, then practiced part time while taking a full-time clerical position in a shipping company for a year.

25   This disorder was spurred on by Maskell's distorted use of enemas with statements about cleaning out the evil within me, always followed by a sexual act. Besides laxatives I ingested Epsom salts, raw eggs, diet pills and spent a lot of time hanging over a toilet with my finger down my throat. Through the years I was always constipated, but never felt any pain. I remember in 1992, when the abuse at Keough was stirring within me, I had a normal bowel movement and was surprised to immediately think the stool looked like an erect penis. Years later I realized that reaction was a foreshadowing of what I was about to uncover. I am glad to say that while I need to always be attentive, my digestive health is better.

I am not professionally qualified to explain how repressed memories work. But I will tell you that forgetting my experiences at Keough and the abuse by my uncle saved my life. I did not begin to remember what happened until I had developed a support system to allow the memories to slowly reveal themselves. By then I was 27 years old.

My primary support was my husband, Mike, who I met at the end of my senior year. Mike was a fun-loving guy with long blond hair. He was funny, could sing you any song by the Rolling Stones, played a mean air guitar, and had a passion for softball and golf. Mike loved to work with his hands, so it was no surprise that he would become a professional carpenter and home remodeler/builder. After a couple of years of dating, we were married in 1974 at St. Benedict's Church.

Meeting Mike was the luckiest thing that would happen to me. He would be my strongest support when I later began remembering the horrible memories of my childhood. But he was initially my support when we lost our first son, Matthew.

CHAPTER THREE

Matthew

In 1975, I became pregnant with Matthew. We anticipated his birth with meticulous preparations and great joy. Matthew was full term when he let Mike and me know he was ready to enter the world. My five-hour, non-medicated labor and delivery were preceded with laughter as Mike and I entered the delivery room.

Amidst all the excitement, as Matthew slipped from my body, I became like a homing device listening for my baby. It was as if everyone else in the delivery room melted away and we were instinctively attached on a new level. When he did not make a sound, I felt dread. My whole being vibrated with a sense that he did not love me. I felt so sure of this rejection, that I clung to Mike, looked him in the eyes and said, "I love you." It was a cry of desperation.

In the first couple days as Matthew was surviving on life support, as if to protect myself, I disconnected from the idea that I had just had a baby. I would not see Matthew, I would not speak of him, and I would not give him the name we had agreed to before his birth, Matthew Eric. The trauma created by this unexpected outcome caused a shock-like feeling within my body. Years later, I thought that my immediate dissociation from the fact that I had had a sick baby was intensified by a sense of unworthiness as a mother, ingrained in me by Maskell.[26]

My maternal grandmother, Mary, called the hospital to suggest we baptize the baby. Baptism is an important sacrament in the Catholic faith, preferably performed by a priest, and done to cleanse an individual's soul of original

---

26 See "The Great Mother (Vignette)," page 101.

sin. Not being affiliated with any church, Mike contacted the nearest one to the hospital, St. Ambrose, and requested that a priest come to perform the service. Father Art Valenzano responded to Mike's call. Since in my mind, this was not my baby, I did not want him baptized with the name Matthew Eric. Mike told me later that he stood with Father Art while our baby was baptized Edward Brent, a name that was on our list of possibilities before our baby's birth.

When the babies were wheeled out to greet the mothers, I became hysterical. The floor nurse got permission from my doctor for me to go home. She then pulled the curtain, sat on my bed, and said, "If you do not go and see your baby before you leave, you will never be able to live with yourself." As Mike and I were preparing to leave the hospital, I was too depressed to muster the energy to put on my shoes, so I slipped on paper booties to walk out into the November morning. I started shuffling down the hallway, when I told Mike I wanted to take a slight detour. I ventured into the Intensive Care Unit to see the baby, and I was so grateful I did. I realized that this full term, beautifully formed baby, with a 'nice head of hair' as his dad liked to say, was my Matthew Eric. When we arrived home, we called Father Art and had him change the name on the Baptismal certificate from Edward Brent to Matthew Eric. During the last three of Matthew's five precious days of life, Mike took me to see him in the ICU and showed me how to gently touch, softly whisper, and basically love our little boy.

Even though I felt that I was of no help to Mike, I was intensely aware that he was not only exhausted, but also devastated by what was happening to me and Matthew. He told me the night Matthew was born, he stood alone looking through the ICU viewing window. Watching a large group of medical staff surround his tiny baby, he said he felt helpless and overwhelmed. Although he could not lean on me, Mike was able to get support from his childhood friends and our families. He was especially pleased when his father was able to see Matthew, after he innocently entered the ICU where visitors were not permitted.

Matthew died on November 14, 1975. He was our first son and my parents' first grandson, and he was deeply missed. I was always struck by how immediately convinced I was that Matthew did not love me and was rejecting me.[27] The doctors' comments, and the testing results did not shake me from that belief since they could not determine the cause of death, calling it 'one in a million' and 'a freak of nature'. Because nobody could tell me why he died, and I caused him to come into this world, I felt that his death was my fault.

---

27   See "The Great Mother (Vignette)," page 102.

CHAPTER FOUR

My Spiritual Path Begins

Prior to Matthew's birth, Mike and I were enjoying our lives and looking forward to the changes our baby's birth would bring. After Matthew's death, we were deep within the throes of grief. Not understanding this, and not getting the therapeutic support we needed, we decided to follow our doctors' advice, and within three months I was again pregnant.

To say the least, that pregnancy was riddled with anxiety. I was afraid we were headed for the same experience as with Mathew, and it would somehow again be my fault. Throughout those nine months, I tried to pretend I was not pregnant. I not only got angry when people asked how I was, but I also got angry when they did not. I felt vulnerable and out of control.

The difference between these two deliveries was striking. This time, I was terrified as we headed to the delivery room. On the way, a nurse held my hand and told me she was present a year earlier with the delivery of our first baby. She said she felt everything was going to go well this time. There was no laughter as we entered the delivery room. Once again, I was leaning on Mike's strength as he stood beside me. Our baby slipped into the world with a cry. As Mike and I looked at each other, he said, "It's a boy!" and I simultaneously said, "It's a baby!" He was healthy.

Any sadness or fear that I felt upon entering that delivery room was erased by the cheers of a nursing class that was in the back of the delivery room observing our baby's birth. Some of those students approached me in the recovery room in tears, saying that was the most beautiful thing they had ever experienced. Knowing how heavy the emotions were for Mike and me going into this birth, we needed that burst of joy to help escort our second son, Gregory Alan, into our lives. We immediately contacted Father Art to see if he would consider baptizing Greg, which he was more than happy to do.

Even with this positive experience, we were aware that we were still raw from the grief over Matthew's death. The events of the prior year were affecting our marriage.

In 1977, a friend kindly asked me to come to Emmanuel Prayer Group. This group was from the same church we had visited right after Matthew's death. It was made up of men and women who wanted a deeper understanding of their Catholic faith. I discovered at this time in the Catholic Church that words like 'wisdom', 'healing', 'miracles' and 'mystic' were becoming commonplace. Also, personal bibles and little books like *God Calling* were individual treasures.[28] Many of my faith companions strived for the insights and wisdom that sprung from having conversations with God.

Going to that group was the first step of my spiritual health walk. Here I began to wonder what love was. The more I read, reflected, and discussed this with others, the more I became aware that I did not feel love. There was a void. One day, sitting on the stairs in our redbrick rowhome, I told God, "I don't feel love. If I'm not supposed to, then help me feel at peace. But if I should be experiencing love, I want to. I need your help to make it happen."

That desire in my heart was the beginning of my inner journey to find love, to find me. Throughout the coming years, I discovered a fundamental truth, or an answer to my simple prayer: the more I learn to love myself, the more I can feel love for others.[29]

At Emmanuel, I also relearned how to pray. The experience of praying as part of an open and enriching prayer group showed me two things: (1) I could have a relationship

28 *God Calling*, A. J. Russell, editor, 1963; original edition 1935.
29 "You shall love your neighbor as yourself." Mark 12:31.

with God and Jesus different than my experience until that point in my life; and (2) the act of praying is a completely open and a total mind/body/spirit experience.

Through much of my youth, my relationship with God had always been conceptual, detached, and based on fear. During my experience at Emmanuel, through prayer, contemplation, and deep reflective conversation with others, I came to know God in a different way. My relationship with Jesus, as the Son of God, was more intimate. He was my counselor, my friend, my spiritual guide if you will, and he was also God. While today I no longer view Jesus as God, and while our relationship continues to evolve, I do trust that he, as my spiritual guide, will usher me through some of my most trying times.

I also learned during my prayer that it is possible to be totally open to the deeper wisdom emanating from that experience. These insights and reflections come from the depths of my being, simmering as nothing more than vague feelings—sometimes for months. Other times, the insight, image, or vision can be immediate. Either way, these prayer experiences made me feel uplifted and brought deep healing.

The first person to help me with the process of discerning spiritual gifts and experiences was Father Blair Raum.[30] We became acquainted when my Emmanuel community began interacting with his parish's Catholic charismatic prayer group. Eventually, he not only provided counseling for me and Mike after Matthew's death, but he guided me in understanding what was beneficial and what was harmful in the insights and conversations I was having during my quiet time.

There were dangers in spiritually opening myself without a mature discernment process. During times of prayer in 1979, I apparently became open to a presence that I mistook

---

30 "Discernment is a quality of attentiveness to God that, over time, develops into the ability to sense God's heart and purpose in any given moment. We notice how God is present for us in the moment." "Discernment as a Way of Life," by Ruth Haley Barton, *Christianity Today*, June 28, 2012.

as Jesus. While the insights and inner stirrings I would normally experience were clarifying and helpful, I began following directions that were powerful and confusing at the same time.

An example of this would be while praying and working in my mom's garden one day, 'Jesus' told me I was pregnant. He said if I trusted him, I would get a pregnancy test. I argued that there was no way this could be, but the encouragement was becoming persistent, almost demanding. To prove I trusted him I had my urine tested. My doctor called and said it came back positive. I was shocked. He asked how many periods I missed, and I told him none. He then asked what made me think to be tested. Here was the real challenge—what would I say? I told him God told me to. He recommended I wait two weeks to have my blood tested. During that time, I had more conversations with 'Jesus'. He continued giving me loyalty tests which I took as ways for me to demonstrate my belief in him. So, when I found out that my later blood test came back negative, that did not dissuade me from believing that I was talking with 'Jesus'.

Another time, after this relationship had gotten even stronger, 'Jesus' told me he wanted to speak at one of my prayer meetings. Hesitantly, during an Emmanuel meeting, I found myself asking if Jesus could speak. I then sat in the middle of the prayer group and spoke words from 'Jesus'. The words I was saying had an underlying air of judgment toward the group, but as the vessel for Jesus, I did not feel that it was my place to end it. Someone in the group did ask me to stop. I was relieved, exhausted, and embarrassed.

My lifestyle was also changing because of this shift in my spiritual path. I went from no religious path to leaning into a more fundamental Christian direction for practicing my newfound faith. I was not brought up reading the Bible, but within the Catholic Church there was a growing interest to read and reflect on bible verses. I found myself inspired, uplifted, and excited by what I was reading. With time I began to feel spiritually guided to

Old Testament passages, with a strong inclination toward literal interpretation, rather than my usual personal interpretation. Examples would be: I was to wear long skirts rather than pants or shorter skirts, drink no alcohol, and evangelize and preach God's word. Toward the end of this spiritual whirlwind, when I visited Father Blair, I would carry a large, oversized white bible given to me and Mike at our wedding by my mother and father.

Some Emmanuel friends, including some family, became concerned. At one point I met with a friend from my prayer community. She asked me, "Have you considered this might be of the devil?" Immediately, I had a visceral reaction of blinders being ripped away from my eyes. I felt the full impact of this truth. This controlling, confusing and exhausting experience was not of God. At that moment I decided to stop interacting with the presence I mistook for Jesus.

Shortly after, I became fearful with the realization that this was not something I could just walk away from. Mike and I went to my sister-in-law's house to pray because I trusted her. She was also a member of Emmanuel. We sat together, praying that whatever had hold of me would be lifted and with it the fear and anxiety it brought. As we prayed, I could feel what I can only describe as a powerful presence which I felt had taken control of my body. Like sitting in the center of the prayer group, another force was using my body and words.

My sister-in-law later relayed her experience that early summer evening:

> [In] the course of our praying a deep dark voice came out of you that was otherworldly. It was terrifying to hear it. I thought that some dark spirit had taken you over. It had a gruff, groveling demonic sound. I felt afraid and didn't know what to do. So, I prayed to God and said, "Satan be gone in the Name of Jesus Christ." The room felt like we were in a refrigerator. You started

shaking and crying. Then there was quiet. You looked exhausted and drained. I felt like you were coming back to yourself, but somewhat unaware of what exactly had happened...I thought that you were being possessed. I knew it was important for you to see Father Blair because of his knowledge and background of possessions.[31]

Leaving my sister-in-law's home, I felt calmed by the powerful prayer that had occurred, while Mike remained concerned for me.

By the time we got home, anxiety had overtaken me. Mike contacted Father Blair while I lay on the couch. Mike was told to take a vial of holy water and a vial of holy oil from the tiny case in the back of an old crucifix my parents gave us. As I laid on the couch, clutching a rosary to my heart, Mike repeated certain prayers while sprinkling the water and oil on me. We both felt complete resistance and were once again surprised at the level of strength and aggressiveness that was coming from me. Mike told me later he felt like he was fighting another man. At some point the fear, anxiety and feeling of being out of control ended, and we were left with an unexpected calm.

I realize it is difficult for many who have not gone through something like this to understand and accept this account. Was this a psychotic break? Maybe. Could I have felt like I was 'freed' because of the power of suggestion? Yes. But all I know is that with my sister-in-law's prayers, Father Blair's assistance and the transformation within my being, Mike and I believed that we had experienced an exorcism.

Having experienced this first-hand, I can also tell you that I now believe in hindsight that while in high school, any spirituality I had when I entered Keough was sucked from my body by Maskell and the other abusers. My soul was barren. Without any sense of spiritual grounding,

---

31   In 2021, while writing this book, my sister-in-law added, "In later years when I was teaching religion to teenagers, the subject of Satan came up in discussions. I spoke from a lived experience that I could tell them that God's Spirit was stronger and more powerful than any darkness."

boundaries, and discernment, I opened myself to spiritual forces I mistook as God.

After this spiritual assault came to a sudden end, it was as if my brain had melted over my eyes; I felt physically bruised. But I also felt a simple inner calm, and a deep awareness of how different this felt from the past months. For days afterward, Mike and I moved around in a cloud of disbelief and wonder. I went through our home removing many of the religious pictures and icons I had placed there during that confusing time. One day, Mike came home and half-joked, "Thank God, I was beginning to think I was living in a convent."

Even though I felt more peaceful, I was embarrassed at being so open about this in front of my prayer community. I was confused because now I did not know what the nature of my relationship was with Jesus. I felt lost, now thinking my spiritual path might have been completely misguided.

I wanted to understand why this happened and what I could do to keep it from happening again. So, I made an appointment with a priest from the prayer group who was a pastoral counselor. As he and I talked, I realized and conveyed to him that I had an awareness of a person—a little girl—who was within me. He began to ask me questions about this little girl which helped me begin my own process of discovering who she was. Through our session I learned that her name was 'Beth'.[32] This priest suggested that I write down my feelings and thoughts about what the child looked like, and that I begin dialoguing with her. I followed his suggestion and began to dialogue, through writing, with this unknown part of myself. I was surprised when I felt as if I knew Beth before words were even used, and how easy it was to flesh her out.

I see now that this and other young aspects of myself were waiting for me to notice them. This was the start of my inner journey to discover the amazing ways that I survived

---

32 Undated journal entry, January 1980.

trauma in my life. This one meeting, which was intended to deal with my confusion, would be the beginning of my path toward spiritual direction, journaling, and dialoguing with the child within.

Even though the experiences of the previous months had me questioning my spiritual path, Mike and I were glad it was over as we continued our couples counseling with Father Blair. In 1980, we welcomed our baby girl, Sarah Elizabeth, into our family and she was baptized by Father Blair.

So, after Matthew died, and indeed because of his death, I developed five ways to work with some of the terror that would later emerge with my recovered memories. These were: (1) being willing to be cautiously open during my prayer time, (2) journaling and dialoguing with myself as a young child, (3) relying on a spiritual guide such as Jesus to help me with the pace of my recovered memories and the ability to discern which paths were healthy, (4) trusting some friends and family, and (5) working with my counselors and therapists. These five legs toward survival would stay with me to this day.

CHAPTER FIVE

Brother Richard

During this period, I was interacting with three male figures who played a powerful part in my deep healing, and who showed me how to trust myself: Mike, Jesus, and Brother Richard Breese. They saw something in me that I would not see for many years to come, but their faith in me prepared the way for deep healing.

Mike showed me what unconditional love was all about. He had a faith and unshakable trust in me.

Jesus had become a heart friend and spiritual guide. His consistent love and care for me contradicted old messages I was conditioned to believe as a teenager. One day, while sitting in my quiet, I felt a warm connection which expanded to encompass something greater. It became a magnificent scene; I was wide-eyed and wrapped in an awesome sense of wonder, as I looked out into multiple universes. It was an explosion of love that took my breath away, but my human heart could not contain it, so I returned to my quiet. After catching my breath and settling back into my body, I wanted to know what I was to do with this, how to share it, what was expected of me. Jesus simply said, "Can it just be for you?"

At first, I could not accept that answer. I had too many experiences where a gift was given with an explicit or implicit condition. The feeling of waiting for the other shoe to drop was just a part of my inner process. But with time, I discovered that nothing was expected of me in payment for these soul-stirring occurrences. Because they were causing a positive shift within myself, I began to believe these gifts were for me.

Brother Richard Breese

I met Brother Richard Breese, a cleric of the Christian Brother order, at a retreat in 1981. He was a spiritual counselor at Adamstown Retreat Center and agreed to be my Spiritual Director after hearing about the death of Matthew and my confusion caused by the 'spiritual possession'. I needed someone to help me understand the breakthroughs and insights that continued to occur during my quiet time. I also needed someone who could help me go past the mere perception of something, to be able to make subtle judgments about its meaning. For the next decade, Brother Richard would help me navigate some of the most treacherous waters of my life, help me understand what it was like to have a healthy spiritual relationship with myself and Jesus, and teach me what my personal boundaries were within all relationships. Working with Brother Richard would forever change my life.

It was because of Richard that I was able to attend a week-long retreat at Adamstown on journaling, taught by Brother Joseph Schmidt. This form of writing is non-conceptual, free flow dialoguing with spirit and self, allowing the words to come from the heart more so than the brain. It can be insightful, affirming, challenging, and clarifying. Over time, this practice can take you into a deeper part of your being. Journaling became immensely powerful in my health walk.

Brother Richard also helped me through the period when I began remembering being abused by my uncle. Those early memories came while I was alone and in prayer, so Richard's presence in my life, and spiritual support at that time, was instrumental to my inner health walk. This was the first time I was able to remember abusive situations while connecting with a part of me as a young child. This child, or persona, was 'Little Jeannie'.[33]

I continued with Brother Richard in the early to mid-1980s. I was trying to understand and hopefully heal the wound that was caused by past traumas on a psychological, spiritual, emotional and physical level. Richard asked me to assist him with retreats. He saw things in me I could not see in myself. I had no confidence to do as he asked, so I decided to seek certification as a spiritual director. In 1986, I entered a four-year spiritual formation program at Our Lady of Guadalupe Renewal Center. The program was based on Jungian psychotherapy founded by Carl Jung.[34]

Those four years of study and practice at Guadalupe were powerful. The work I did on myself while learning how to work with others was self-healing and invaluable. While with Guadalupe, I learned in depth the workings of the tools that Brother Richard was already using with me. This was an important time as I continued connecting to the young part of myself who was deeply wounded by Tom and later confused by the false messages I believed to be coming from Jesus in the late 1970s.

---

33 See "Little Jeannie (Vignette)," page 47.

34 "Jungian therapy...is an in-depth, analytical form of talk therapy designed to bring together the conscious and unconscious parts of the mind to help a person feel balanced and whole." See *Psychology Today*, https://www.psychologytoday.com/us/therapy-types/jungian-therapy; also, "...Jung's view of the psyche was that the mind and the 'unconscious' could largely be trusted, and that it was all the time attempting to assist the individual; in this way he saw the psyche as self-regulating." *The Society of Analytical Psychology*, https://www.thesap.org.uk/resources/articles-on-jungian-psychology-2/about-analysis-and-therapy/analytical-psychology/.

CHAPTER SIX

Little Jeannie (Vignette)

After the birth of our second son, Greg, I began working with the death of our first baby, Matthew. I was finding support and comfort from friends and family, members of the Emanuel prayer group, and fellow parishioners at St. William of York. I also found comfort in my personal prayer time, and I began seeing Brother Richard for spiritual direction.

One day, during a meditation, I had an image flash before my mind, something I had never previously experienced. A clear image of an erect penis, unattached to anything I was contemplating, broke through my quiet. I did not know what to make of this experience. I could only assume it had some connection to my uncomfortable feelings with intimacy. I wanted its imprint upon my brain to go away. However, that image stayed with me, and about a year later another disturbing image flashed before my mind. That one was of me strangling a skeleton, which was extremely upsetting since I could sense intense rage going into the strangle. At that time in my life, I did not really think I was angry at anyone. I also felt a new sensation that something was coming. I did not understand this, so I ignored it. With time, these images began to be absorbed on many levels—body, mind, and spirit. I eventually began sharing the impact of these experiences with Brother Richard, considering that they arose from my prayer.

In 1983, while in my quiet, I had a breakthrough memory. I remembered being on my uncle's lap on one of the weekends my brothers and I stayed at Tom and Kitty's house. This was surprising since I had very few significant memories of those visits. I always remembered the incessant ticking of the clock in their middle room and doing fun things like playing Pokeno or having bubble baths. Even though I could not see his face, I knew it was my uncle. We were sitting in the easy chair in his dining room; I was three. Unlike the earlier images, this memory was an experience I was remembering with all my senses as an adult. I was not sure what this meant, but I felt as if this upsetting memory was not complete.

With Jesus as my companion in prayer and the direction of Brother Richard, I trusted I had support with whatever was happening. During a later memory, I experienced my uncle asking me to touch his penis, which caused me great discomfort, both as the little girl and as an adult. I refused. My saying "no" seemed to end things. My mother always told me not to touch any of my brothers' 'stingers'. I was grateful that I had learned my mother's lesson well.

I now thought I understood what the images of the erect penis and the skeleton were about. My uncle had died many years earlier, so I figured my strangling rage was aimed at Tom. I told Mike what I remembered. It was an 'Aha' moment for us. We talked about how it made sense of some of my previous behaviors. For example, I was not able to feel more than friendship for Mike. Also, I would pace outside of my daughter's bedroom when Mike would fall asleep lying next to her after he read her a nighttime story. This realization became a positive development in our relationship.

Sometime later, Mike and I found a reason to make a visit to Kitty's home. I slipped into her bedroom to look for a picture of my uncle. I thought I could put these memories in some manageable context and wrap this up if I just saw a photo of him. Instead, by looking at his picture, I found a door opened to more painful memories. I began to remember the behaviors that went on in that house during our weekend visits.

I felt as if I had met this three-year-old within myself, but I wondered, "How do I talk with a three-year-old?" Unfortunately, even though I wanted it all to go away, I slowly began remembering another time sitting on my uncle's lap and then another. I was sickened to see that there were more experiences, but thankful that we only visited a couple times a year.

As I continued to work with Brother Richard, I attended a weeklong silent retreat in 1985. While I was sitting in prayer within my retreat room, I remembered my uncle molesting me as a five-year-old. I continued with the memory, trusting that Jesus was protecting me. But it was like I was experiencing this assault on my body for the first time. I was effectively transported to another time, laying on the floor of my uncle's basement, doubled over with fear and pain. I lay totally alone within this agonizing experience.

Slowly, I began to calm down, unfolded from my fetal position, and found myself on the floor of my retreat room. I felt as if I had just been attacked, feeling exhausted, panicked, cornered, and ready to run. The emotions of the child mingled with my adult feelings of horror, pushing me through the corridors of the retreat house, franticly looking for Brother Richard. I wanted answers. I wanted to feel safe. I wanted to leave the retreat house never to return.

Instead, Richard helped me catch my breath and regain my composure. Then I began the hard work of uncovering what happened to me as a child and learning what to do about it.

After that retreat, I went to my mother to tell her what I was remembering. This was hard for me. I knew my mom needed to know in case any of my other siblings told her something similar, but this was my mother's favorite aunt. She assured me that I was not responsible for my brothers and sisters and that she would take care of this.

Sometime later, I became aware that although my uncle was dead, I carried what I thought was an unrealistic fear of my aunt. My mother went with me to tell Kitty that I remembered her husband sexually assaulting me. Kitty did not argue or deny it. Instead, she said, "He always said he'd provide for me, and he did."

Mom got up and walked out of my aunt's house with me that day. I know how hard that was for her. At the time, I did not fully understand the gift my mother had just given me. She was telling me by her actions that she not only believed me, but she would stand by my side no matter what.

I was proud I had confronted not only my aunt, but my fear as well. So proud that I pulled over to the side of the road, got out of the car, and shouted, "I did it!"

As I continued to work with this new revelation in my life, I was seeing both Brother Richard for spiritual direction and a therapist, Carolyn, for psychological counseling. I only saw Carolyn for a short period of time, but she became the bearer of a great gift for me.

I thought if I could talk with the young girl within me, I could remove her from my uncle's basement. During three sessions with my therapist, I was surprised to find a way to finally communicate with this young girl, Little Jeannie.

In one of the sessions, I went into my quiet and found myself, as Little Jeannie, on the floor of my uncle's basement, in the throes of that terrifying experience I remembered at the retreat house. As the adult quietly observing my uncle coming closer, looming over this five-year-old, I watched as a beautiful white mare galloped out of a blue sky with big puffs of clouds. As this powerful horse came closer, Little Jeannie got on its back, held on to its long mane, and rode off into the clouds. The white mare took me away from the full impact of what my uncle was doing to me.

What was most defining about this experience was the beauty of the mare and the freedom she provided me as a little girl, rather than what Tom did to me. I could see how I was able to cope with an abusive and awful situation as a child. I was so terrified I felt as if I was pushed into another dimension of myself.

For the first time, I experienced the sudden presence of a 'spiritual guide' who would protect me. I call the White Mare a spiritual guide since I can feel my spirit on the back of this beautiful creature, soaring beyond my abused mind and body. I am also aware that Little Jeannie could call upon, and depend on, the White Mare to take her out of that basement. I was discovering that I too could call upon the spirit of the White Mare and my other spirit guides when I remembered and experienced difficult times throughout my life's journey.

Seven years later, when I began to remember being sexually abused by Magnus and Maskell, I went to my parents' house, and as the three of us sat around their dining room table, I told them how these memories arose on the tail end of a stream of memories about abusive experiences by Tom at a bar he frequented called The Green Door. Again, they offered me their love and support.

As I started conversations with representatives of the Catholic Church about Magnus and Maskell, I was asked to itemize what I had paid for therapy, along with what I thought a fair compensation would be. I spent time reflecting on this, trying to be truthful as well as fair.

I thought that before I could ask for anything from the church, I had to first ask Aunt Kitty. I wrote her a three-page letter telling her of the living nightmare I was experiencing, and how it cost our family emotionally, spiritually, and financially. I told my aunt I believed if her husband had kept his hands off me, the sexual abuse at Keough would never have happened. Then, I asked her for compensation and itemized my therapies to date.[35]

35　When I gave the representatives of the Catholic Church my six-page letter regarding compensation, I included the same payment statements from the therapists that

I received a note from my aunt explaining how hard things were for her and she enclosed a check for $500. Although I was at first offended by the amount of the check, when I later thought about it, I realized that check was her way of affirming the truth of what her husband had done to me.

Kitty never corresponded with me again. A year after that interaction, my aunt died. For a long time, I felt responsible for her death. But I eventually came to understand that whatever my aunt chose to do, or not do, with that painful information was not my responsibility. My responsibility was to Little Jeannie.

I sent Kitty, along with what I thought was a reasonable amount for my mental, emotional, and economic suffering. I was disappointed, and not for the last time, to discover the Archdiocese did not care about the pain and suffering I endured. They just wanted to know how much I had paid for therapies until that point—period. They reimbursed me $5,500, I gave Brother Richard $2,000 of that since he provided me with 11 years of free pastoral counseling, and my mom added $500 to the gift in appreciation for the pastoral support he provided me. The Archdiocese stopped payment for my therapies in February of 1993 when I could not give them the names of any other women who had been victimized by Maskell. (See Brother Richard's Thank You Note, page 260).

CHAPTER SEVEN

The Pressure Rises (Vignette)

In 1986, I entered the four-year spiritual formation program at Guadalupe.[36] Also, throughout the 1980s, I continued to work therapeutically and spiritually with repressed memories of childhood sexual abuse by my uncle, and the loss of our first baby.

At that time, our family lived in a wonderful old end-rowhome which we renovated to suit our needs. Our youngest child, Sarah, had made friends with our next-door neighbor's daughter who was her same age. Unfortunately for the girls, Mike and I were not comfortable with the activity that went on within our neighbor's home. We spent many years trying to regulate what the girls could do together. This was a real effort since they were becoming such good friends, and we knew it would only get harder to say no to sleepovers, dinner invitations, etc. Along with my upcoming graduation from the spiritual directing program in 1990, we began making plans to move to a new home.

The realtor we contacted, Kathy Smith, turned out to be a classmate of mine from Keough. If I had heard her maiden name, Bianco, I know I would have found a good reason not to contact her. However, once committed, I did not think it mattered.

Until that time in my life, I primarily had one Keough classmate, Maria DeiSvaldi Rauser, who I stayed friends with after graduation. She happened to marry a friend of Mike's.

---

36 Spiritual Direction is an inter-personal situation in which one person assists another person in growth in the Spirit: in the life of Faith (prayer), Hope (difficulties, sufferings, trials), and Love (life in the Christian community). *Our Lady of Guadalupe Spiritual Life Program Manual*, 1986.

Maria and I did not like Keough. We did not talk about those years or the school reunions. We both remembered little about our high school years, and we were fine with that. She became, and still is, one of my closest confidants.

When talking with Kathy, however, I began to feel inner pressure, and a sense that I needed to act, without knowing what to do. Generally, I would appear normal and acceptable to others. Like a chameleon, I could talk and dance my way around anything that was uncomfortable for me. If I did not want to discuss something, I usually was able to distract my company from his or her original focus. For some reason with Kathy, this was harder to do. It was as if my energy was depleted and my normal responses were not satisfying me, much less my old classmate.

Kathy was involved with Keough's fourth five-year reunion, and she understandably wondered if I was going to attend. The first time it was discussed, I brushed it off by quickly telling her I just did not care to go to reunions. I was avoiding this topic. I found myself wondering why I did not go to these reunions. Why was I dancing so frantically? Why was I so intent on ending this conversation? I had a sense in my body of being trapped and not knowing why. All these internal and external stressors were intensifying as if slowly building in a pressure cooker. When Kathy brought the reunion topic up again, I surprised myself and her, by exclaiming, "If I never set foot in that school again it will be fine with me!" There was so much activity going on within me causing me to feel hectic and strained; but I was unaware of what was causing it. Why could I not simply say why I would not be attending the reunion? My response made no sense and left me feeling unsatisfied.

Eventually, our family moved to a cute brick single home with a separate garage, which Mike loved. In addition to our physical move, I was ready to move on emotionally with handling the abuse by my uncle. After ten years, I accepted that the impact of those painful experiences would continue with me for a long time. But I felt like we were embarking into a new phase.

Our new house needed repair and we were more than ready for the job. We decided to start with the sunroom, which was designated as my treatment space for my new practice. I ended my realtor/customer relationship with Kathy, with neither of us knowing or understanding what just occurred.[37]

Then, another recovered memory of abuse by my uncle came forth. It involved my last sleepover at Aunt Kitty's when I was alone with Tom at the age of 12, the same age my daughter was when I had the memory.[38] I began to notice that simple life experiences like the smell of a cigar, looking at photos, the age of one of my children, dealing with an active dog, or getting lost going somewhere could cause a visceral reaction and could stir buried memories or throw me into a panic.

From the outside though, it looked like I was finally succeeding at what was important to me. Since the distance we moved was only a little over a mile, our family was still regularly active at St. William of York's parish. As I prepared to step out into my new profession as a spiritual director, I was being eagerly ushered along by the religious education coordinator at my church. I was ready to begin taking on clients. I was still involved with my prayer group, even though I was attending less frequently since I was spending more time working on our new home. Life looked to be rather good.

Meanwhile, Easter was fast approaching. During Lent, the six-week period of self-reflection leading up to Easter, I felt a spiritual and physical heaviness, an invisible weight on my shoulders. As I prepared to open my practice, I felt like I kept bumping into some sort of barrier within me. I could

---

37 As years moved on, Kathy and I have become friends and we have used her as our realtor when selling two other homes.

38 As painful as that experience was for me, I am glad that it has been the last memory I have had of abusive activities at Aunt Kitty's home.

not understand why I was having such a difficult time feeling excited about finally being able to help others on their spiritual paths. I found myself wondering: "Was I afraid? Didn't I want to work? Was I just spinning my wheels? Did I really want to take the next step?" The internal pressure I felt was building, but I could not pinpoint where it was coming from. Instead of feeling excited, I felt dread.

So, I turned to my therapists. I continued seeing Brother Richard on a regular basis and was having massages from my friend and colleague, Pat Gosselin. She was also a graduate of the spiritual directing program, as well as a licensed massage therapist. Her massages were quiet reflective treatments for me. Just as I did in meditation, I would go with whatever arose. I often found insight and a spiritual connection with my deeper self, both during and after these massage sessions.

During this Lenten season, I went to my massages with the intention that God would lift this heavy yoke, to be replaced with a sense of lightness. This was something I had previously experienced with prayer and reflection during times of struggle. No matter what this weight was, I was intent on letting it go.

When Easter came and went, I was unpleasantly surprised. It was Easter, the celebration of the resurrection of Jesus, a time of new life within the Catholic faith, but my internal struggle had not changed.

My treatment space was ready, and the religious coordinator at church gave me the name of a woman who was interested in spiritual counseling. I met the woman at her home. As we talked about her faith walk, she mentioned being negatively affected by a priest at her church, who inappropriately broached boundaries between them when she was a young girl. My client was unable to go outside her home, other than to commute to work. At that time this meant nothing to me, but looking back, I believe that appointment with her may have triggered my own buried abuse issues, adding to the pressure.

I went for another massage hoping for even the slightest relief. This time, as I lay on the table, I saw in my mind a man in plaid pants and a different plaid shirt. He was big and smelled of stale beer and cigarettes, and he was on top of me. This experience scared me. I had no idea what was going on since memories seldom surfaced while having a massage, but I knew I was in a safe place with Pat. It was very much like the flashbacks I had years before when I started to remember Tom abusing me. I had a deep, unsettled feeling about what happened, and I left Pat's with that sense of fear being ever present.

For the next couple of days, the pressure mounted. I took a day off work for prayer and meditation, to just let whatever was coming make its way through. At first, I again remembered that man on top of me, heavy and stinking. Then, for the first time I began throwing up more memories of other strangers touching me, petting me, abusing me. I remembered being in the back room of The Green Door, where I was fondled and molested by strangers while Tom stood listening at the door. I was looking to him to protect me, and, as an adult, I was disgusted that my uncle would let complete strangers touch me like that.

Then my memories took me back into a confessional at Keough. I was puzzled that something to do with the confessional would be on the tail end of a lot of memories from that bar, but I continued to let the memories come forward. I had always remembered that as a freshman at Keough, I had gone to confession, seeking forgiveness from the priest, Father Neil Magnus. After confessing, Magnus asked me what my name was and could he look at me. I always thought that was the end of that experience.

But now I was remembering Magnus asking me direct questions, probing me, wanting to know where I learned that behavior. He asked, "Who taught that to you? What else did he teach you?" As he asked me all these questions in this isolated wooden box, I was aware that he was masturbating. While staring at his right ear, I continued to answer his questions, and when he finished, he told me that God could only forgive me if I never said anything about this. But he said he would have to continue praying for me. I left the confessional.

After experiencing this on my day off for prayer and reflection, I was exhausted but somewhat relieved. I thought, "Now I know why I keep hitting that barrier." To fully come to terms with the abuse I suffered as a child, I needed to remember what had happened in that confessional, and I felt I had done so. I now believed I was done remembering, and only needed to put a face on Magnus similar to when I had gone to my Aunt Kitty's home to put closure on those experiences with Tom by looking at a picture of him.[39] By looking at Magnus' photo, I believed I could let go of the confessional experience and move on.

I went to my mother's attic and searched through boxes for my yearbook from Keough. As I opened it to the picture of Magnus, I knew immediately that it was the man in the confessional. But when I looked at the picture next to him of Father Joseph Maskell, I blurted out "shit, shit, shit..." and my body immediately began trembling with fear and dread. Like the involuntary flashing images which led me to remember the abuse by Tom, this was my body viscerally reacting to his image. This was not the end of this abusive chapter in my life, but a continuation.

After recognizing Maskell's picture I was thrown into a deep depression. I could not understand what was going on inside of me or what this all meant. Sometime later, during my quiet, I felt myself walking down the hall at Keough with Jesus by my side. This was unusual since I had never thought nor dreamed of being in my high school. As we came to the door of the chaplain's office I said, "I don't want to be here." Jesus replied, "If you want to move out in your life, you have to go through this door." I stood paralyzed at that door for many days. Finally, I asked Jesus if he would carry me into the room. He said he could not carry me, but

39   See "Little Jeannie (Vignette)," page 48.

that I could lean on him. I opened the door, and leaning on Jesus, I walked into the room. I was immediately engulfed in total darkness.

Weeks later, after I had remembered more disgusting things Magnus and Maskell had done to me, I again went to see Pat for a massage. I was totally overwhelmed and in need of a respite. I was under so much pressure dealing with painful memories that were assaulting my whole being. I was questioning anything and everything that had any religious or spiritual connection to it. This doubt had invaded my prayer and my meditative reflections. I was constantly aware of the heaviness around my shoulders.

At the massage session, as I lay on the table trying to relax with the help of Pat's healing hands, I became aware of Jesus standing by my side saying, "Let me have that." I realized I had a dog collar around my neck. I looked at him with tears in my eyes and asked, "Why did you put this on me?" He said, "I didn't, but I want you to give it to me." I began to unhook it, then slowly slipped it off and finally gave it to him. I watched as he took it from me, carried it away from the massage table and out of sight. I could not figure out why this happened, but when I left the table, I felt lighter. I now felt the relief I had hoped for at Easter, but by now I had no idea who I was, what I believed in, or if I would survive.

Within the months that followed, it seemed I had unleashed my past and all that entailed by unhooking that collar and letting it go. It felt like the gates of hell had opened and I was being devoured. Many more repressed memories of sexual abuse by the priests and other adults at Keough continued to surface and unfold.

One such memory was after the confessional experience when Magnus walked up to me in the school hallway and told me he needed me to come to his office. That was the beginning of the sexual abuse by Magnus and Maskell.

On another occasion, when I went to Maskell's office or residence, I found not only Maskell waiting for me, but another man as well. This was not the first memory of another adult being in the room with Maskell, but it was the first time I remembered this man being there. I am not sure if I was told his name was "Brother Bob" or heard him being called that by Maskell.

This day, Maskell stood by the door providing me with the feeling of being protected. "Brother Bob" began by putting a red dog collar around my throat. The collar had soft madras material on the inside, which laid against my skin, as if to assure there would be no chafing. He then attached a leash. This was the first time I remember this collar being used on me. "Brother Bob" instructed me to get on all fours. He said he would paddle me until I barked like a dog. The paddle was made of wood and had holes in it which made it more painful. This was not the first or last time this torturous tool was used on me in this room. I still hear that little girl in my head saying, "I won't bark, I won't bark, I won't bark," until it hurt so bad, she found herself barking like a dog. "Brother Bob" then raped me from the rear.

This was most upsetting since what originally took me into the confessional with Magnus had to do with behaviors introduced to me during abuse by my uncle, with his dog present. These 'men of god' took the thing I felt most guilty about, that information that was meant for God's ears only, and used it against me in that room. As a victim, I had the 'seal of confession', or zone of confidentiality, broken by Magnus, which lead to years of sexual assault by him, Maskell and others. It is ironic that the same rule of confidentiality protects that pedophile priest if he discloses the abuse in the confessional. As stated in a note from the Vatican in July 2019: "Priests...should therefore defend the Seal of Confession even to the point of shedding blood..."[40]

---

40 "Seal of Confession always inviolable, despite civil law," by Devin Watkins, *Vatican News*, July 2019; https://www.vaticannews.va/en/vatican-city/news/2019-07/vatican-states-cannot-force-priests-to-break-confession-seal.html.

My Reflections

I have come to believe the pressure I felt building during the years leading up to my 'letting go of the dog collar' was my buried past pushing its way out. That collar was put on me as a young girl to keep me down, to keep me quiet, to keep me beneath another, and to keep me in the dark. I now understand that I could never have moved forward in life with a part of me thought to be dead and buried. Moving forward actually meant going deeper within myself. The lightness I experienced after I unhooked that psychological and spiritual restraint was a sign I was on the right path.

Sharing this humiliating experience never gets easier. At times I feel as embarrassed as when this atrocity first broke through into my consciousness. I am still learning how not to blame myself when I see and feel my younger self responding to the degrading acts those men perpetrated on me. I tell myself that their behavior had nothing to do with me personally or with the sex acts themselves. As an adult woman, I understand that sexual assault is more about power over another then the act itself. However, it is difficult to separate myself from the disgusting activities these self-centered hateful men forced me to participate in. Unfortunately, I cannot erase the images from my brain. As I continue to work on accepting the wounded child within me, I can only hope that one day I will be able to freely place all blame and fault on the sexual predators who harmed me.

To other survivors, who also feel humiliated and embarrassed because of the demeaning acts that were inflicted on you, I hope you know you are not alone, and you did nothing to deserve what was done to you.

CHAPTER EIGHT

Traumatic Memories
and Shattered Faith

After seeing Maskell's picture in my yearbook, I was a mess! I did not know what to do or where to turn. Why and how could I remember this man in a book? I had no recollection of ever meeting him, and here I was, stunned at the mere glimpse of his face. No wonder I kept that yearbook in the bottom of a box in my mother's attic.

I had just finished therapy about my experiences with Tom and was ready to move forward as a spiritual director when I hit this barrier. Now, all hopes of stepping out as a spiritual director were gone. I was not only struggling with my Catholic faith; I was not even sure if I believed in God. I questioned everything I thought I was, the very roots which nurtured and taught me throughout my life. As my deep belief became disbelief, the very foundation I stood on was shattering. I was exhausted.

In a state of shock, memories pertaining to Magnus and Maskell began to seep into my consciousness. For the first time, I wanted to leave everyone, go away, and forget all of this. I could not balance what was going on inside of me with my family's needs, everyday chores, and work. Mike and I agreed that I would get away and he would take care of the kids. I got on a train and rode 11 hours to South Carolina to visit Marcella, a family friend and confidant, to have time to think, and begin dialoguing with Little Jeannie.

After returning from Marcella's home, I was sitting on the sofa in my quiet, when I felt as though a 14-year-old girl came and sat down beside me. She said she had something she wanted to tell me. She began to slowly reveal how she/I had been abused by two priests while at Keough. I came to know this part of myself—this persona—as 'Frances'.

In 1992, during many months of feeling overwhelmed, and trying to deal with the trauma, I was whipsawed into one unexpected memory after another. I again felt as if I were vomiting memories, the last one slowly and painfully unfolding like dry heaves. I remembered the assaults on me at Keough, as if they were happening for the very first time. They were brutal, methodical, and criminal. I was raped, or otherwise sexually abused, by several clergy and other adults, including a politician and a police officer. I discovered later that other girls suffered similar abuse.

As all of this continued to flood my mind and senses, I was still engaged with Frances, who was upset. She said that when this abuse began occurring as a teenager, I had the option of killing myself and ending the abuse. Frances told me I blocked out her voice. This thought that I was responsible for not allowing the abuse to end was haunting me. I felt it was my fault this young girl within me suffered that horror because I did not hear her request and kill myself.

These memories—the guilt of not killing myself as a teenager, and my self-loathing for believing I was a whore—was too much for me to handle. At that time, I was working at a hospital, and I volunteered to take a project of storing records in the attic of the hospital so I could be away from everyone. I also began to stockpile pills. One morning I sent a bouquet of flowers to my sister, Kass. Kass was one of my primary support persons at that time and I wanted to thank her for all she had done for me. Later that day, as I cried over files of records at work, Kass called me and told me she did not accept my flowers and talked me into telling my manager I was sick and needed to go home. I did, and while sitting on my couch trying to think through my next step, Mike, Kass, my mom and my dad came into the house. The flowers were obviously a red flag for what was left of my beaten down spirit. Unfortunately, all I could think was that everyone would be better off without me, and this unbearable suffering and pain would end.

On the couch, I was numb to Mike's and my family's presence and words. However, at one point I clearly heard my mom say, "If you do this you will put that man in the driver's seat of your children's lives forever." That was just what I needed to hear. I knew what it felt like for Maskell to have power over me. I would not do that to my kids. I was surprised when, years later, my mom said she did not remember saying those words to me; but I heard them. I never thought of suicide again even though the memories continued.

As the memories unfolded, I realized Maskell had replayed some of the things my uncle would do when I was younger. On a psychological level, it seemed to normalize the experience. The repetition of the same actions as in my pre-Keough years confirmed to me the lie that 'I made these things happen.' He would almost always stand by the door while someone else abused me just like my uncle did in the back room of The Green Door.[41] He would invoke my family members in other ways, threatening that I could not speak about what was happening lest my father, a policeman, would shoot me. He would say about my father, "He doesn't want you, but I do. Let me be your father."

When I first started remembering, I thought he was identifying abusers using my brothers' names; however, I did not know if these were their actual names or pseudonyms. It was very confusing. The first time this happened, the stranger in Maskell's room was called "Brother Ed", "Ed" being the name of one of my brothers. On another occasion, I went to Maskell's office or residence, and he identified a man as "Brother Bob", "Bob" being the name of another of my brothers.

On the day "Brother Bob" put a red dog collar around my throat, showing that I deserved to be treated like a dog, he raped me and ejaculated in me rather than pulling out first. Maskell came over, pulled him off me and proceeded to tell him, "She is one pup of a whole litter, so you need to

---

41   See "Innocence Abducted," page 14.

be careful and follow the rules." In my innocence, I misread what Maskell was doing as protecting me. As an adult, I knew he was referring to my big family. In short, he was saying my mom was a very fertile 'bitch' and I could be too.[42] "Brother Bob" would later tell me that he was the person who killed Cathy Cesnik.[43] I don't know whether he intended it as a threat, the truth, or both. He terrified me.

As I continued to remember this abusive treatment, I was having a crisis of faith. I questioned the role of priests in my life, persons I had put great trust in well beyond my high school years. These priests were the people we were taught to look toward for guidance and spiritual support. Their connection to God gave them the spiritual power to perform such things as marriages, baptisms, confirmations, and consecrating the Eucharist. Now I found myself doubting the very foundations of my faith. Who were these men of God, who would do such horrific things to a child, then go and say Mass, listen to confessions, and perform their pastoral duties?

I thought perhaps I was crazy. I hoped I was, because then none of this happened. But the memories continued to spew forth and, regrettably, I knew in my body that I was not crazy. These acts were done to me by clergy.

While remembering my experiences with the priests at Keough, I felt I needed to talk with my pastor, Father Art Valenzano. Art was the man who formed a special bond with Mike and me at an extremely crucial time when Matthew died. About ten years after he baptized Greg, he coincidentally became the pastor of our local church, St. William of York. My faith was slowly shattering, I stopped going to mass, and I was not attending to my church duties as a eucharistic minister. I felt a need to tell Art why I had been absent.

---

42 I now believe that these hateful acts were not about me personally, but about Maskell having power over me and other children. But at the same time, I still find myself wondering why Maskell hated me so much.

43 See "Birth of a Warrior," page 189.

During our initial visits which started the end of May 1992, Art prayed with me, he heard my confession, and he took the time to listen. He seemed to believe me. He told me he could find out where those two priests were. I started hoping they were dead. That thought calmed me down.

He found that Father Magnus had died an alcoholic. But Father Maskell was working as a pastor at Holy Cross parish in South Baltimore. Sometime in August, after several private meetings with Father Art, he recommended that I meet with the pastoral representative of the Archdiocese, Father Rick Woy, and report what I was remembering. He said that right after our first meeting he told the Archdiocese what I had confided to him. Hearing my disappointment that he did not ask me first, he explained that he was required by Archdiocesan lawyers to immediately report any allegations of sexual assault to Church representatives. Now knowing that Father Woy was aware of what I was remembering and had two-plus months to investigate my allegations, I agreed to meet.

Art, Mike, Kass, and I met with Father Woy two separate times at St. William of York's rectory. During the first meeting, Art told Father Woy, "You need to get him out of there." Holding up a skimpy manila folder, Woy told us I was the first to complain about Maskell. He said he believed me, but if they did not have their ducks in a row, Maskell, who was very 'intelligent', would 'slip through their fingers'.

At the next meeting, Father Woy brought with him an Archdiocesan lawyer named Kathryn Hoskins. Ms. Hoskins explained to me and Mike why we needed our own attorney. Leaving that meeting, we asked Father Woy and the Church lawyer if they could put an ad in the Keough newsletter or the local Catholic newspaper, to see if anyone else remembered similar things about Maskell. They told us that would only draw people who were just looking for money. We then hired a lawyer, Steve Tully; his fees were to be paid by the Church. I also agreed to give a formal statement to the Archdiocese pertaining to the abuse I suffered at Magnus' and Maskell's hands.

As I moved into the reporting phase of this ordeal, the Church as I knew it began to disappear. Instead of praying with me as Father Art had done, I found myself at a table with Father Woy, Ms. Hoskins, and Mr. Tully. Art slowly faded into the shadows as I gave those representatives my formal statement. I read to them my handwritten accounts of what I had recently remembered, including the painful and humiliating actions done to me by Maskell and Magnus. I felt as if I were putting my heart on the table for all to see. After my presentation, Father Woy immediately put a 1971 Keough yearbook on the table and asked me to point to any students who might know about the abuse. Feeling overwhelmingly ashamed and vulnerable, I felt as if Father Woy trampled on my heart when he made this request. Crying, I told them that I gave them what I remembered, that I did not know of other girls, and that even if I did, I would not tell them. I was in a living hell, and I would not put another woman through this. In my view, this was now their responsibility.

A month later I discovered, in a very synchronistic way, that Maskell had been removed from his position as pastor of Holy Cross taking a 'long-term medical leave of absence'. Mike and I were visiting with my brother and his wife who live in South Baltimore. They had no idea about my memories or the meetings I had with the Archdiocese. My sister-in-law told us that the priest at Holy Cross where their son went for daycare suddenly left. Mike and I were stunned to hear Holy Cross mentioned. She continued to share that her friend's mother, who was a parishioner at Holy Cross, said everyone in the parish knew the priest was embezzling money and keeping a teenage girl in an apartment down there. As I cautiously asked who the priest was, she began to go through a pile of papers to find the letter that had been handed out to the parents. The priest's name was Father Maskell.[44]

---

44 October 21, 1992, Catholic Community Daycare Letter, page 260.

Leaving, we gave some excuse for why we wanted the letter and the phone number of her friend's mother. I was excited with the thought that the Archdiocese did not need my statement. We immediately found a phone booth and called the parishioner who confirmed what my sister-in-law had said. I asked her if they thought to report Maskell. She said it would not matter, since they all knew the Archdiocese "gave us the alcoholics and priests from the bottom of the barrel. They're not fooling us."

We then called our attorney and asked if Maskell had been removed from Holy Cross and whether my accusations were the cause for his removal. Mr. Tully said Maskell had been removed based on my allegations and not because of any current behavior by Maskell. He said what Mike and I heard about his embezzlement of money and keeping a girl in an apartment was a rumor. We thought no more of it.[45]

A month or so later, because Father Woy had asked me to let them know if I remembered 'anyone else', I asked for another meeting where I gave a statement naming adults that I recently remembered abusing me as a student. Speaking beforehand with my attorney, I offered to give him the names of the individuals I remembered, but he did not think it necessary. Mr. Tully, who could not attend, had a young associate represent him, along with Father Woy and Ms. Hoskins.

I gave them the names of other adults who were part of the abusive activities. The two Church representatives told

---

45 One year later, a confidant of mine was talking to her pastor about her feelings pertaining to the sexual abuse of 'her friend', being careful not to disclose my name or Maskell's name. The priest said he knew she was talking about Joseph Maskell. He told her that everyone in the Archdiocese knew he had been embezzling money and keeping a teenage girl in an apartment downtown. When she told me this, I felt for the first time that the Archdiocesan representatives lied when they said they did not know about Maskell until I approached them. Now, I am even angrier since I know that when I disclosed my child sexual abuse in May of 1992, the Church allowed Maskell to remain as a parish priest in charge of children, including my nephew, until that October. But the parents of children in that daycare were never told the truth about why he was removed. See letter dated October 21, 1992, page 260.

me and Mike that they thought they could do something with the names. Father Woy ended the meeting by again asking me to look at a yearbook to corroborate the alleged abuse at Keough, but I had nothing to add.

Days after that meeting, as I stood at work talking with my lawyer by phone, he chastised me for wasting the Archdiocese's time. He said there was nothing they could do with names of the adults I gave them. The tone of his statement was surprising, considering I thought the second meeting ended on a positive note. He said the Archdiocesan representatives thought I had names of other girls. I asked him why they would think that, since Father Woy had asked me to tell them of 'anyone' I remembered? Mr. Tully responded that he thought I would be naming girls. I reminded him I wanted to tell him the names of the individuals, but he had declined that offer. By the end of that upsetting conversation, I found myself trying not to break down in the middle of my workplace. I contacted Mike in tears. He helped calm me down, then called Mr. Tully and fired him.

I felt like I was seen merely as the Church's route to getting rid of Maskell. I wanted the Church representatives to shore up my crumbling faith in God, the Church, and myself. I needed and expected them to take this unbearable responsibility off my shoulders. Instead of being supported and consoled, I was engaged in a strictly transactional relationship. They only wanted the names they could get to protect themselves, piling more responsibility on me. While they were willing to pay for psychological counseling, there was no compassion, and that is what my family and I needed most.

After letting our attorney go, I called Father Woy, who coincidentally was then residing at my parish's rectory. By that point Art was preparing for his transfer to another parish. I advised him I did not want a lawyer, or anything to do with legal proceedings, and asked him to meet with me in the Church sacristy to pray for guidance and direction. Woy refused to pray with me and advised me to get my own lawyer. It was all becoming a huge ugly legal mess, putting me in a state of shock. I gave them what they wanted and each time they wanted more. Led to believe that I was the only one to accuse Maskell of abusing children, I believed if I did the right thing and cooperated, the Church would take care of the situation. That never happened.[46]

I was now terrified and completely groundless. I did not know if I believed in God, and I certainly did not believe or trust in the Church. The worst part was I had begun looking at Jesus, this presence that had become my heart friend, and asked, "Where were you while they were doing those things to me? Were you just watching? Why didn't you stop them? Are you who I thought you were, or are you just a figment of my imagination?" This breakthrough of memories began the heartbreaking end of my innocent and naïve relationship with Jesus, just when I needed to blindly trust him.

---

46   Later, in 2017, I became aware that they had previously known that Maskell had abused other children. So, while I thought I was trying to help them understand what Maskell was capable of—they already knew! I thought of the Navajo Proverb, "You can't wake a person who is pretending to be asleep."

CHAPTER NINE

Strider and Velvet

I have mentioned how everyday life experiences could unexpectedly trigger memories. An example is when Mike and I owned two dogs at different times through our years together.

We got Strider, a beautiful golden Irish Setter after Greg was born and before any of my repressed memories surfaced. I always thought I was a dog person and could not wait to own one. I also believed I was not an angry person and valued the fact that I had a positive outlook on life. That is why I was upset when I found myself feeling such uncontrollable anger towards Strider. Like an addict or abuser, my wrath would explode when no one was around. Looking back years later, I realized it escalated when I started remembering abuse at my uncle's hands. When I got out of control, I became someone else. It was no longer about the actions of an innocent animal. I was lost in a flow of anger that was coming from deep within me. Once I realized what I was doing, I would pull myself together, put the dog somewhere safe and cry. I was so angry, but more confused by my feelings and actions.

Since I could not understand my unusual behavior, I felt there was something wrong with me. These guilt-ridden actions continued in secret, even as I voiced a need for help with an active dog, and now two little children. As Mike put more time into exercising Strider, he too became aware of her high energy level. Before appreciating what was triggering my impulsive reactions, a friend lost their dog and wanted a new one. They had eight acres of land for a dog to run, and Strider became our friend's loving companion.

Our second dog was a black Airedale Terrier and German Shepard mix named Velvet. She became a part of the family after I graduated from my spiritual direction program. This was in 1991, when we moved to our single home with a larger yard. Attributing my anger with Strider to what I took to be her hyperactivity, I believed this new dog, Velvet, would be different. Not only was she less active, but now that the kids were older, they would have a role in caring for her.

Unfortunately for Velvet, as the pressure of the memories about the priests sexually abusing me surfaced and mounted, Velvet, like Strider, became a scapegoat for my unrealized anger.[47] This time, after unleashing my anger for something insignificant, I would put Velvet into her doggie cage. I was terrified and confused. I would sit next to her cage, apologizing and crying. I did this when no one was around, yet I wanted someone to stop me. Why was I so angry at this innocent animal?

My life turned upside down when I began to remember the abuse I suffered at Keough. There was no way I would have survived that time in my life without a variety of therapists. Sandy, my movement therapist, was already helping me work on surfacing emotions connected to repressed memories.[48] Feeling distraught, I confided in her about my 'secret' outbursts with Velvet. We began to work with constraining my emotional outbursts and working with that disgust I felt toward myself.

First, Sandy told me the responsible thing to do was to stop my bouts of anger at Velvet. With her help, I began to understand that I was disconnected from my feelings. It would take time to work out these emotions and abusive actions but thinking I could 'will' them to stop would result in my inflicting more emotional and physical harm on my dog and myself.

---

47   See "The Pressure Rises (Vignette)," page 55.

48   See "My Support Network," page 83, and Dance Movement Therapy; https://www.sheppardpratt.org/knowledge-center/treatment/dance-movement-therapy/.

I did not want to hurt Velvet or any living being again, so I made a choice. By telling my secret to my movement therapist, I chose to protect Velvet. With the support of Mike, we moved forward knowing the best thing for Velvet would be to find her another home. Once we decided where that would be, Mike, seeing how upset I was, offered to drop Velvet at her new house. Thinking I was in control, while nursing feelings of shame and responsibility for having to give away another dog, I told him I was fine and had to do it myself. As I drove, I told Velvet how much I loved her and how sorry I was for how I treated her. I was going through the motions of being responsible, yet I felt numb to any emotion.

After I dropped off Velvet, I stopped at my brother's house. I put my head on his dining room table and sobbed. I cried for two good dogs I had to give away to protect them from me. I also cried because I did not like me. I did not like what I had done and the confusion it caused. I did not like how I felt. I did not like the thought that I would hurt something or someone. I did not understand why I could not just stop.

With time, and the help of my family, friends, and therapists, I was able to recover and heal many of these emotions connected to the wounded little girl within me. Thanks to my therapists, who helped me see why I was acting so violently, I began to understand that as a child, I had no control over the abusive situations I was forced into. Not being able to control my dogs as an adult triggered the rage I felt toward my abusers, which I had buried. Similarly, years later I realized that I had been blaming my mother and father because I was unable to feel and direct my anger at those who deserved it.[49]

I now understand the answer to the question: "Why dogs?" With the recovery of many memories, I realized that dogs were used in different ways by my perpetrators. Strider was with us when I began recovering memories of

---

49 See "Mom," page 182.

Tom's abuse, in which his dog was always present. Velvet was with us when I began remembering "Brother Bob", who attached a red dog collar to my neck.[50] I was responding to those terrifying men, who were surfacing in my adult life, by striking out at innocent dogs who had become symbols of the way those abusers had demeaned me.

I like to think my dogs forgave me when I decided to protect them from my anger by giving them away. As terrible as I feel about my behavior, I am glad that I made that choice before I did something I could not live with. I sometimes wonder where the abuse would have gone if those animals were not in my life...my children? Sadly, it was because of my frustration with those two good dogs that I was able to discover the iceberg of emotions caused by sexual abuse I endured as a child. That iceberg laid beneath my unacceptable behavior.

---

50 See "The Pressure Rises (Vignette)," page 60.

CHAPTER TEN

My Support Network (1992-1997)

Once the memories surrounding my Keough years began to surface, my support network that was forming became critical for my health walk. Many people supported me throughout those years, but there was a special network of friends, family, and counselors who were integral to my survival.

Mike was most important of all my support companions; he provided me unconditional love, trust, and advice. During our first nine years of marriage, I continued to encourage him to leave me and find someone who could love him the way he deserved. He would laugh and say, "I'll take what I can get." Later, after I began remembering the sexual abuse from Tom, we began to understand why I could not feel love; it was complicated. As memories continued to flow, I told Mike I was prepared for him to leave me, now knowing all that I had done. I cannot count the number of times he would look at me and say, "You didn't do anything, it was done to you." I could not understand his undying love and support for me.

The most exquisite example of Mike's belief in me was shortly after he was diagnosed with esophageal cancer. He walked into our living room, looked at me with tears in his eyes and said, "I can't imagine you with anyone else." By that time, I had shared with him a lot of sexual interactions I was forced to be in, not to mention a number of strangers who abused me. That was Mike, he did not see my sordid past as intimate or sexual in nature. He always saw the young girl within me, not the whore who was repeatedly sexually assaulted. His genuine care for me was transforming. He was my rock, my strength, and the mirror which constantly reflected what he saw in me and what I would eventually see in myself.

After I became certified as a spiritual director, I took on my first client, Barbara Brunk. She was a woman I knew from my days in the prayer group, so we were already comfortable with contemplation and deep prayer. Eventually, Barbara asked that I share my prayer experiences with her, since she often found insight in such exchanges. Her request would change our relationship from one of director/client to spiritual companions and confidants. As she began to hear my inner and outer struggles, she made a conscious decision to keep showing up as a spiritual support for me. This decision was not an easy one, since it would have unexpected effects on her personal faith walk. We met regularly for prayer and shared reflection. At times, it felt as if we were hanging by a thread of a belief in God. While our faith was shattering, we reassured each other that we were not alone. Barbara was an unexpected gift in the middle of a small yet instrumental network of people who helped me survive remembering and reliving the abuse at Keough.

Barbara and Mike, along with a few other members of this special network, had no problem expressing their righteous anger at what happened to me and the Church's lack of a response. I, on the other hand, was victimized and conditioned to be afraid of everything. My fear increased as my close supports expressed their anger, triggering in me a need to protect myself. The child within me likened their anger to Maskell's hateful acts toward me. In hindsight, they were mirroring back to me what a healthy reaction to torturous child abuse should be. My ability to begin to explore my own anger could not have happened without these trusted companions.

My sister, Kassy, was my link to my family roots. As a sister, she knew me and supported me as I worked through memories of abuse by our uncle. Her unwavering belief in me helped to keep me connected to reality when I thought I was crazy. Her strong, loving presence helped to provide the strength I needed to take each step.

On February 13, 1993, I asked Kassy and Mike to sit with me during my quiet. This was unusual since I was normally alone when memories surfaced. But I had just recalled Cathy Cesnik telling me she would take care of everything at the end of my sophomore year. I had also remembered that at the start of my junior year, Maskell told me that someone had approached him during the summer about hurting the girls.

I could not shake the feeling that I had loved Cathy and that I had killed her. I increasingly felt like I had blood on my hands. I sensed I was on the brink of an important memory.

The next day I journaled about how hard it was to sit with anyone while reliving past events, but I needed Kassy and Mike's support:

> Yesterday, Kassy came over. We were going to get together with Mike, sit in the Sunroom, and see if I could remember what I saw—find out if I killed Sister Cathy. All week my gut told me I saw something that was very upsetting. I want to know what that was. I knew I couldn't deal with it by myself, so Kassy offered to sit with me, and I asked Mike to be there as a support. It was very hard for me to let them be there. I realized I don't trust many people, but there wasn't anyone else I'd have there. (I was even pushing it asking Mike.) I decided to let myself fall into the 15/16-year-old. I got quiet and just let my younger self talk...

Seated as the adult between Kassy and Mike, I went into my quiet, and proceeded to remember Maskell taking me as a teenager to see Sister Cathy's dead body.[51] The next day, I journaled about this memory:

---

51 See "The Keough Years," pages 27-28.

> Suddenly all I saw were maggots Everywhere! I almost
> went through the roof. I was moving my hands trying to
> get them off her. I stood up hysterically saying, "Mag-
> gots, Maggots...get them off, get them off of her." Later
> I was glad Kassy and Mike were there to hold onto me.
> After taking a break, to cry and calm down a bit, I went
> back to the memory...

Still sitting between Kass and Mike, I was able to move
through the rest of that torturous experience. At some
point I could not go on. My brain once again felt as if it
were melting over my eyes and my head felt like it had
been split in two. I could not stop crying. I continued later
in my journal:

> Kassy had her arm around me and said, "You didn't get
> blood on your hands hurting Cathy—you were trying to
> help her." That made me feel good. Mike said he knew
> I had to be relieved to know I didn't kill Cathy. I was,
> but I could feel the 16-year-old still thought I had done
> it. That would take time.

I needed my family and friends at times to just listen,
but always for support. While immersed in painful memories, and feeling totally overwhelmed, their going into
action strengthened my understanding that I was not alone.
They hired Richard Bussey, a private detective referred by
the lawyers Mike and I retained after firing Steve Tully.
Mr. Bussey was hired once I began to remember Sister
Cathy's murder. He investigated any responses to the ads
my lawyers posted in the newspapers pertaining to abuse
at Keough, keeping me anonymous.[52] My family and friends
also organized and raised money through fundraisers and
from donors for the costs of litigation.

---

52 After the appellate court's decision (See "The Legal Battle," page 85), Mr. Bussey
    gave me all his notes and the personal responses to the ads. I think just having
    these notes in my possession helped to strengthen the truth that was taking root
    within me that I was not alone, no matter what the outcome of the case had been.

My brothers and sisters anonymously mailed inquiries about possible abuse to approximately one thousand Keough alumni.[53] This one act of support, worked on as I sat zombie-like in my brother's crowded dining room, brought many individuals forward to speak to my lawyers. Their names as well as any personal information were kept confidential, but knowing of the substance of their responses helped break through my belief that I was the only one. I was especially grateful that Teresa Lancaster, known as Jane Roe in the subsequent trial, responded to our inquiries. Her corroboration and her decision to move forward with the lawsuit gave me the courage to continue to follow my heart.

My family would periodically meet for a variety of reasons but mainly for moral and spiritual support. We came together twice, once in 1992 and once in 1993 to talk about the impact that Tom's behaviors had on us individually and as a family.

In late 1992, when the meetings with the Archdiocese were ongoing, my brother set up a visit for my mother and I to talk to Father Paschal, her pastor at St. Benedict's. My parents had been parishioners there for over 40 years. Since hearing of my abuse at the priests' hands, my mom stopped going to mass. I told Paschal I could be of no help to her since my faith was shattering, so he would need to support her. Two of my brothers separately asked him to help her as well.

"On November 20, 1993, I wrote Father Paschal letting him know how disappointed I was in his lack of support for my family."[54] Almost two years after meeting with Father Paschal, and seeing barely any movement on his part, my family met in August 1994. We learned that the priest said he was told by the Archdiocese to stay out of what was going on with our situation, and he did.[55]

---

53 See Original Drafts of Letters to Alumni and Newspaper Ad in 1993, page 265.

54 Jane Doe et al. v. A. Joseph Maskell et al., Answers to Interrogatories, November 1994: Answer to question #38.

55 "Betrayed and Abandoned by Catholic Archdiocese of Baltimore, Families of Many Sexual Abuse Victims are Still Struggling to Heal," by Tom Nugent, *Inside Baltimore*

I informed the family that my lawyers intended to file suit against Maskell and the Archdiocese. After our discussion, we said a rosary as I leaned heavily on their unconditional support.

Dr. Norman Bradford

In 1992, due to the nature of the memories that were surfacing, I felt I would need a psychologist who had a spiritual, but not a religious, modality of therapy. I was referred to Dr. Norman Bradford and within ten minutes of our first meeting, I knew he would be the therapist I would be working with. I told Brother Richard I found a psychotherapist that I felt comfortable with; we both knew I needed psychological as well as spiritual support through this nightmare.

While I was remembering the torture by the priests and as I began meeting with the Archdiocese, my sessions with Brother Richard increased, sometimes more than once a month—by phone or in person. Amidst all this upheaval, he helped to keep me focused on the remaining thread I had to God. As I realized what the priests were willing to do to wield power over a teenage girl, I found it extremely difficult to have anything to do with any religion, much less the Catholic religion. I became acutely aware that the Church hierarchy was dysfunctional, devoid of a natural balance of male and female energy. All the teachings handed down were from men's hands. Feeling so raw and violated by those 'holy men', I was losing all trust in my beliefs.

May 3, 2018; https://insidebaltimore.org/2018/05/03/betrayed-and-abandoned-by-catholic-archdiocese-of-baltimore-families-of-many-sexual-abuse-victims-are-still-struggling-to-heal/.

I told Brother Richard that I could not understand how he, who was so instrumental in my deep spiritual growth, could stay connected to the Catholic Church. The Church's priests were responsible for committing horrible acts against me in the past and Church leaders would not take responsibility for harboring those same pedophiles. Richard told me he spent a lot of time wrestling with that question. He believed there was a fundamental difference between Archdiocesan priests and members of institutions like the Christian Brothers or the Franciscans. These orders were run independent from the Archdiocese. Therefore, he felt he would not be indebted to the Archdiocese for his physical wellbeing and would not be intimidated if he started to receive pushback from what he might say. He felt he would be more helpful staying in the Catholic Church instead of leaving. I thought he was rationalizing. We discussed this at length without a peaceful conclusion, and that spiritual relationship slowly and painfully came to an end.

Many years later I heard that the retreat center where Brother Richard was the director would be closing its doors for good. I met with him to apologize for cutting him out of my life and to explain what the deeper reason was for my disappointment with him and the Catholic Church. I could now articulate what was causing some of the confusion and despair in 1993 and 1994. I told him as my faith was shattering, I was experiencing a powerful feminine presence that was totally new to my consciousness and ferociously protective. That presence contrasted with the male led faith I grew up with, which seemed to be cowering behind the legal system. I was confused, felt abandoned by my church, and unfortunately, our spiritual counseling relationship ended up as one of the many casualties caused by the Archdiocese's decision to do nothing in support of me and my family. I told Richard I thought of this experience as my awakening to the Great Mother.[56]

56 See "The Great Mother (Vignette)," page 101.

Richard said he understood and ran to retrieve something he wanted me to have. He presented me with a beautiful picture that he had received in 1968. This handmade Thai Silk picture, called "Our Lady of Siam", is one of a mother holding her baby. In his way, Richard was affirming my personal awakening to a powerful feminine presence, in the image of a mother protecting her young—protecting me. I was touched by his effort to meet me where I was and felt our paths once again merge. When I heard Brother Richard died in 2012, I was grateful that I was able to make peace with him so I could grieve the loss of a loving friend and mentor without regrets.

My work with Dr. Bradford continued. He was a deeply spiritual Jungian therapist, which was important to me since the spiritual direction program I graduated from was based on Jungian psychology. He implemented practices I was familiar with; he gave me the space to learn to trust myself.

At one point in my therapy, I was constantly overwhelmed with a feeling of standing on the edge of a black hole waiting for something horrible to emerge. I wondered if I could be hypnotized, have it all come up, thereby getting everything out. Dr. Bradford said he could refer me to a hypnotherapist, but first we went over our original agreement which pertained to my desire to follow my personal process. Because I dealt with the surfacing memories at a slow pace, and with a select group of supporters, I had never been admitted to a hospital nor prescribed medication. Knowing the intense nature of my remembering, Dr. Bradford informed me if I were to experience a flood of memories, which could occur with hypnosis, I may need to be in the hospital to function. If that were to happen, there would be an entirely different team of therapists working with me. I decided to put hypnosis on a back burner while continuing with my current therapies. I understand that Dr. Bradford's caution had to do with his concern for me and how vulnerable and fragile I was, not the practice of therapeutic hypnosis.

Sometime later, when I was riddled with fear and eager to know what else I did not remember about my past, Dr. Bradford suggested, "Don't go deep sea diving. Wait for the memories to come to you." His words have become a helpful gauge which encourages me to be still, to reflect on what is motivating my need to know the unknown, and to discern if I was prepared for what might surface. I still think of these words to this day. I saw Dr. Bradford regularly for five years, and during my intense periods, three times a week.

Through Dr. Bradford, I connected with Sandy, a marvelous movement therapist. She showed me how to engage with my inner self, my childhood self, and the trauma related to that by being in tune with my body. Through movement therapy, I was able to express the feelings that came with the newfound trauma that had been locked up in my entire being.

Sandy was especially helpful after I remembered Maskell taking me to see Cathy's body. After recalling that memory, I began to feel disgust for my hands. They seemed to be a constant reminder that I was responsible for Cathy's death, intensified by the image in my mind of me placing my hands on her dead body.

In 1993, this eruption of buried memories was too much to bear. I began to have thoughts of cutting my hands off. As I journaled on February 24th, a week after meeting with Kass and Mike:

> I just got off the phone with Sandy. I told her of the thoughts I've been having since I saw her last. I went to sleep last night with the image of slitting my wrists and the blood flowing down over my hands. It wasn't scary and it didn't seem painful. I even told Mike about

it while we fell asleep. I had the image again at different times today. I know I've struggled with the idea of suicide, but this didn't feel like that. I felt my hands had something to tell me.

I saw Sandy the next day and she had me do some work with clay. As I let go and let my hands work the clay, I felt how much the teen in me wanted to shake Cathy to get up. She was supposed to save me but couldn't laying there; she didn't. I was aware of how angry that child was at Cathy. So many tears and unexpected feelings. It was an emotionally exhausting session.[57]

My obsession with my hands calmed down after that visit with Sandy. I had much more work to do, but I now understood that my body continued to hold emotions connected to that trauma.

Sandy became an anchor for me, especially during the years of the legal battles with the Church and the year after Mike's death. She taught me to feel the ground under me, and how to trust that ground, even when I felt abandoned and lost in deep despair. She was compassionate, supportive, and always available. I saw her on and off until 2008.

This special network of supporters and others showed me there was goodness in the world at a time when I was reliving experiences of unbelievable evil that had been let loose on me as a child. They held me up when my strength was gone. Their trust in me, and compassion for me, was a healing balm for my wounded soul, as well as a powerful example of how I might be there for myself.

---

57 Journal entry dated February 24, 1993.

CHAPTER ELEVEN

The Legal Battle (1993 to 1996)

In 1993, shortly after firing Mr. Tully and being advised by Father Woy that he would not pray with me, I did as he suggested and retained three lawyers, Phil Dantes, Beverly Wallace, and Jim Maggio ("Dantes & Wallace"). I retained them to help me deal with the church, while protecting me from any legal threats by Maskell. Surprisingly, I was quite afraid of Maskell. I was surprised because since my adult self would not have known him if I fell over him, my newly found younger self seemed to know him intimately. Trying to navigate this new terrain was indeed an intense time for me and my family.

It was after I retained my attorneys that I remembered being brought by Maskell to the body of Sister Cathy. This breakthrough memory was different. I was now talking about a known murder that had not been solved.

Dantes and Wallace embarked on a two-year investigation into what happened to me while at Keough. After discovering over 40 women who had also been abused by Maskell, my lawyers filed suit in 1994 on behalf of myself and Teresa Lancaster, another student victim of Maskell who was one year behind me, and who I did not even meet until 2016. Named in the complaint were, among others, Maskell, the Archdiocese of Baltimore, the School Sisters of Notre Dame, and a gynecologist, Christian Richter. Magnus was dead by then.

The central issues in the case were whether I did or did not repress memories of the abuse at Keough, and whether that even mattered. In short, because the suit was filed so long after the period of limitations had expired, the court needed to decide if repressed memories as the cause for the delay was a valid reason to toll, or stop, the statutory period within which one must normally file suit. According to the statutory law in 1971, we would normally be looking at a period of three years from the time the abuse ended.

I went through three days of depositions and two days of hearings. During the depositions I was asked if I had any diaries. I told the defense lawyers I did not have diaries. I did have prayer journals, explaining that these books were filled with reflections on my prayer experiences and dialogues with God, Jesus, and myself. I considered them sacred which were never intended for others to read. I told the defense attorneys to check with their client about prayer journals since I was taught this form of prayer by Catholic clergy.[58]

Later, while at the depositions, I told my lawyers, in a private room, that Dr. Bradford was keeping my journals for me because I was terrified the Archdiocese's attorneys would read my writings and quote them out of context to imply I was crazy. One of the lawyers for the SSND, whom I only know as 'Mr. Harrison', was obviously listening to our confidential conversation through a closed door. He abruptly entered our meeting and insisted that if Dr.

---

58   See My Personal Journals, page 259.

Bradford could have the journals the defense could also. I was then advised by my lawyers that if I did not turn them over, the case could be dismissed. After an agonizing weekend of prayer and meeting with Sandy, I conceded.

At the depositions, I was mocked by the defense lawyers. I had my personal journals, which were so important to my spiritual walk, portrayed as gibberish and nonsense. I was embarrassed and distraught. I was still in the throes of remembering the trauma while being ridiculed for what I said. Mike sat silently because he was told that if he spoke up, he would have to leave, and he knew if he left, I would leave. I could feel him behind me seething at the questions, and more particularly, the mannerisms and the behaviors of the defense attorneys. His self-restraint was a powerful support for me.

Each day, Mike and I would leave the meeting or court hearing and walk to our car and decompress. One of my lawyers, Beverly, said she would see us in the parking lot after the depositions, and Mike would literally be holding me up while I sobbed in his arms. Then, Mike would drive me to Sandy's where I would have an intensely emotional, yet much needed, session. It was as if I were caught in a vise—terrified to be doing what I was doing yet needing to follow what my heart felt was the right thing to do.

After the depositions, I was told by my lawyers that I would only need to be in the courtroom for one day, so like an athlete, I began to prepare. I went alone to a friend's place at the ocean hoping that if I spent a weekend in prayer and meditation, the boulder of terror I felt on my chest would be lifted so I could breathe. I was not only afraid of the intimidating defense lawyers, but of the possibility that Maskell might be in the courtroom. Even though this fear accompanied me to every meeting, this felt different, more public. Unfortunately, at the end of the weekend the fear remained.

Mike drove us to the courtroom on the day of the hearing since I was too spacey to concentrate on anything other than getting through this ordeal. I kept thinking "in a couple hours this will be over." When I got to the courthouse, I told my lawyers I did not think I could do it. I was sure I would never be able to look at the defense lawyers again. Phil told me to "Look right at the judge. Don't even look at their lawyers." Some of the terror that accompanied me into that courtroom was defused by my ability to stay focused on the judge, which allowed me to think.

As the hearing came to an end, Mr. Harrison, the SSND lawyer, requested that I return the next day for further questions. I could not believe what I was hearing. I did what I was asked to do and now they wanted more. The defense lawyers had beaten me down in the depositions, interrogated me in this public arena, and now were pushing me past my limit by insisting I return. Through all these re-traumatizing interactions, the defense lawyers never once treated me like the victim of a sex crime, whether my memory had been repressed or not. I felt crushed.

At the back of the courtroom Mike once again held me up while I sobbed against his chest. Jim, one of my lawyers, asked Mike if it would be OK for a local paper to take a picture of my legs as we left the front of the building, so people could see that 'Jane Doe' was a real person. Mike looked at Jim above my head and said, "Find me a back way out of here." I was ushered out a separate exit in tears.

In the car, as I cried, I told Mike repeatedly, "I'm not going back there!" Mike said he would do whatever I wanted. Phil called that night and Mike told him he would have to wait and see what my decision was in the morning. At the end of a sleepless night, I still did not know what to do. No matter how hard my frayed nerves and overloaded brain tried to convince me that I could not go back, my heart told me I was not finished. I also knew that if I did not show up for the second day of hearings, my case would be dismissed.

So in the morning, I told Mike I would go back. I became singularly focused, walking almost without thought, and moving forward, both with and into the fear. I had to muster up the energy and courage to go into that courtroom.

When Mike and I got to the courthouse, all three of my lawyers were standing at the door to meet me. As I walked into the building, Phil said, "I didn't think you'd come." I told him, "Phil, get out of my way. If I stop, I won't go in there." I could not think nor talk about what I was about to do, I just needed to get in that room. Our lawyers moved out of the way and, numb with fear, I entered the courtroom.

Somewhere between the courtroom door and the witness chair, something was happening within me. Just as lead turns to gold in an alchemy experiment, the fear I felt when I walked into the courtroom was transforming into a feeling of courage. As I sat in my chair, looking at the judge, Harrison asked the judge if he could approach me and have me look at him, a request which was granted. I felt Harrison had seen my weak spot and was about to pounce on it. Just as he did with my prayer journals, I instinctively knew he was about to invade my personal space. Rather than waiting for him to approach to look at me, I swiveled around and looked him directly in the face. I transformed from terrified victim to a courageous survivor. My senses heightened as I was totally focused on Harrison and, staring him right in the eyes, I said, "What's your question?" Different than an 'out of body' experience, this felt more like an 'in-body' experience. I stood my ground and did what I had to do to get the hell out of there.

The lawyer asked me his questions and I gave a clarifying answer for each of them. I did not stop to talk to anyone as we left that day, through the front door of the courthouse. Mike could not stop saying how proud he was of me and my interaction with Harrison. He wanted to stand up and cheer. Here he was once again mirroring back to me what he saw, a courageous woman.

This process of the mirroring of myself through others' eyes was important to my health walk. Like the negative effects Maskell's brainwashing techniques had on me as a teenager, my support team's repeated observations began to have a positive impact on me. I began to believe I was who they saw.

At the end of the hearing, the judge found that the scientific community had not accepted repressed memories as being reliable.[59] In short, the court would not allow the repression of my memories to be the basis to toll the running of the statute of limitations. The case was dismissed.

I was then asked by my lawyers if I wanted to appeal the trial court's decision. I was exhausted, feeling as if the ground beneath me physically and spiritually was not my own; it was now so foreign to me. I told them I had to think about it. Shortly after, Mike and I went to a family function, fearful of what people thought. We were determined to act normal. Bob, my brother, came over and pulled me up to dance to Sheryl Crow's "All I Wanna Do (is have some fun)". I still remember feeling as if I were floating and free! Later, dancing with my dad, I told him of my lawyer's request for us to appeal. Dad began to say things like: "Didn't I think I had done enough? Wasn't it time to move on to other things? Wasn't it time to let everyone finally rest…?"

I had not shared the details of the abuse with my close loved ones. I was too embarrassed and ashamed and did not want to hurt them more than they already were. Dancing with my dad, by then a retired policeman, I told him about Maskell sitting across a table from me at the school, holding a gun. Maskell removed each bullet from his revolver's chambers, put the gun against my temple, and pulled the trigger. He said that if my father knew I was 'whoring around', he would do the same thing, but the gun would be

---

59   The defense offered Dr. Paul McHugh, Director of Psychiatry at Johns Hopkins University School of Medicine, as their expert testifying against accepting repressed memories as being reliable. McHugh has consistently testified for the Archdiocese and its agents against claims of the reliability of memories caused by dissociation. McHugh never met with me. In contrast, Richard Sipe, a renowned mental health counselor, former priest, and consultant for our lawsuit, told *The Baltimore Sun*, after meeting with me, that he found my story credible. He said he felt physically sick when he heard the descriptions of sexual abuse by the victims of Maskell. Sipe "believes Wehner and other victims can repress their memories of traumatic experiences for years." *The Baltimore Sun*, Dan Rodricks, May 25, 2017.

loaded. Looking me straight in the eyes, Dad said, "Appeal it!"

We appealed the decision, and two years later, the trial court's decision was affirmed by the Maryland Court of Appeals. Everyone was devastated when the Court's decision was rendered, and it set me back health-wise. As a survivor who had repressed abuse memories, I took that decision as a judgment on the legitimacy of my experiences.[60] I also was afraid that by not holding sexual predators like Joseph Maskell accountable, other like-minded predators would hear that their behavior is tolerated.

After the decision came down, I knew Mike was as distracted as I was, but his primary concern was me. How was I doing? Would I survive this? How could he keep me safe? Two weeks after the court's decision, Mike, who was a carpenter by trade and used his hands to make a living, fell off a roof and broke both wrists.

The day Mike fell, I was in the middle of staining my parent's shingled home. I was on their roof talking to myself, trying to decide if I could survive this final decree even though my entire life had changed. I had no faith, no church, and no community. I felt I had hurt Mike, my children, my parents, my siblings, and their families. At that point, even though most of the details of what happened at Keough were in the court records, only a few people really knew what I had been through. I thought I must have made too big a deal about what I was remembering, and the court's decision made me doubt myself even more. Even with all of that, I thought I could somehow move forward.

Then my dad put his head out the window to tell me to come in because "Mike had an accident". Instantly I

---

60 Since 1996, the statute of limitations for child sexual abuse in civil cases has been extended to seven years from the date the victim reaches the age of majority, or 25 years old, and 20 years from majority for grossly negligent offenses, or 38 years old. This current law applies to anyone abused from October 1, 2010, to the present. The change in the law is not retroactive. Unlike many states, Maryland courts still do not recognize repressed memories as a valid reason to toll the running of the statute of limitations.

thought God was punishing me for speaking up about the abuse at Keough. I felt as though I was being chastised for not remaining silent and my family was being hurt in the process. I had told the secret and given names of abusers, and nothing happened. They were all still out there and I was acutely aware that God was not happy with what I had done. I was terrified of the consequences. With time, I could see how my reaction to Mike's fall was rooted in the Keough priests' brainwashing of me regarding God's condemnation.

Before heading to the University of Maryland's Shock Trauma Unit, I was told Mike had broken both his wrists. Immediately I thought "Who's going to protect me now!?" I was surprised by this since I had never consciously thought of Mike as my physical protector. I now realized that the person who was my main source of protection was in bilateral wrist tractions. After an intense operation, as we prepared to head home, I asked Mike, "Who's going to protect me?" He said, "We'll put a baseball bat by the front door and use it if we have to." His response helped provide me some comfort. More importantly, the fact that he immediately replied to my unexpected question showed me that he felt the same fear. The baseball bat went by the door.

CHAPTER TWELVE

The Silent Years (1996 to 2014)

From 1996 until 2014, I was not in an emotional state to be visible. I felt I had been silenced by the response of the Church, the courts, and God. I was terrified of anyone discovering who I was and what they might do to me and my family if they found out. Throughout the court ordeal, Mike held his tongue in hopes that there would be a more positive outcome. He knew how afraid I was and how important it was not to make waves, so instead of acting on his anger, he swallowed it. He shared a fantasy with me whereby he would kill Maskell, then bury his body in the foundation of one of the houses he was building. He even knew which concrete guy he would call to pour the foundation. I begged him not to do that because, per my therapist, our family would suffer the consequences—no one else. Mike chose not to follow through with his plan. After the court's decision, with his care for me and the kids as his priority, Mike continued to swallow his anger, while working hard to provide for us.

I focused on caring for my family, and on my health and emotional wellbeing. I continued to accept emotional and psychological support from my biological family, close confidants, and multiple therapists. Even though the courts and church had silenced me publicly and stifled the pace of my inner growth, I continued to take my quiet time and struggled to retain some form of journaling, since my prior journals were exposed during the trial. These efforts were necessary as memories surfaced. My spiritual journey was far from stifled, as I continued to experience meditations that were deeply healing. For example, a meditation that unfolded in the late 1990s involved my emergence from the metaphorical tomb I was confined to upon exiting high school. This powerful interaction within my quiet was the seed for my desire to dedicate my life's work to other survivors of trauma.[61] These spiritual experiences were changing my perception of myself, helping me reconnect to my inner child, and strengthening my desire to help others realize that they were not alone and there were ways around the obstacles in our paths.

I continued my pursuit of a two-year college degree. While taking a death and dying class, I experienced a breakthrough. I realized the paralyzed teenager within me had never grieved the loss of Sister Cathy. This began a period of mourning for Cathy, someone who meant a great deal to my inner child. As the sadness decreased, I promised that little girl that, if possible, I would visit Sister Cathy's grave.

As I prepared to go to her gravesite, I felt I wanted to also visit her family, some of whom may still have been living in their hometown. I eventually decided not to do that, thinking that her family may be hurt by such a visit from me. That might remind them that I said their loved one was killed by someone who knew her, and not by a stranger.

During that time of mourning, I was also working on severing from "Brother Bob"; I felt enmeshed with him. Sandy helped me create a plan. I took a wine bottle and painted skull and crossbones on it. Having not remembered the face of "Brother Bob", I made a collage consisting of pictures that represented how he made me feel and what he did to me. I rolled it up and put it in the wine bottle. I placed the bottle behind the cat's litter box and every time I walked by, I would say, "I'm not him. He's over there."

In the spring of 2004, I took that bottle with me when we went to visit Cathy's grave. Leaving the cemetery Mike took a detour, and on that blustery day, we found ourselves on the edge of a swiftly flowing river. Together we got out

61 See "The Great Mother (Vignette)," pages 105-106.

and I threw the bottle into the water, hoping to finalize my separation from "Brother Bob".

On our drive home we both felt as if we were sitting in a bubble of peace. I believed I had finally completed my work on my relationship with Cathy and the impact her murder had on me as a child. The next day, I sent an e-mail to my family. I wanted to share this feeling of closure with them since they had helped me through some hard years. Here is what I wrote to them on March 3, 2004:

Hi everyone!
Mike and I are always thankful for the overwhelming support my family has given us throughout the years. I have experienced an exciting breakthrough in my health walk that I would like to share with you.

I was taking a Death and Dying course at [my community college] about two and a half years ago. While studying, I was surprised when one single sentence struck a nerve deep within me. This began a much needed, yet unexpected, time of mourning for me. I was, on many levels, finally able to grieve the death of Sister Cathy Cesnik. One year ago, as the grief subsided, I promised myself I would put flowers on her grave if it were at all possible. Searching for her gravesite was another experience of chiseling away at the boulder of fear, once a mountain, which can tend to rule me.

On Friday March 5th, Mike and I went to Pittsburgh and laid flowers on Cathy's grave. As we sat next to her gravestone, I realized I was simultaneously letting go of her while embracing more of me. I was ready to let her "rest in peace" and bring an end to the 35-year vigil I have been keeping for her within myself. This was powerful! Reconnecting to my truth is painfully real, extremely growthful, and incredibly liberating.

Now when I think of Cathy, I see a small gravestone on the side of a hill with beautiful flowers blowing in the breeze. This image comes with tremendous peace.

Please say a prayer that the man who killed Cathy Cesnik will be brought to justice, in this life or the next.

*I whole-heartedly share my WOW experience with you
and send it to you with joy and love.
Always,
Jeannie*

I was overjoyed with the fact that I had completed this
major step in my health walk. I seemed to think, or more
precisely hoped, that each time I accomplished a difficult
task toward integration and wholeness, my inner work
would be over. Major obstacles became accomplishments,
like making it through the court ordeal or finding a resting
place for Cathy, or believing I finally let go of "Brother Bob".
With each accomplishment, I thought that this might be it.
Unfortunately, just longing to be finished with the horrible
experiences at Keough did not make it happen. This was not
the last time I would revisit my memories involving Cathy
or "Brother Bob", but it was a significant step in my personal growth.

As time moved on, I had a growing desire to somehow
help others experience similar subtle, yet healing, shifts
within their body, mind and spirit. In 2005, I began my
initiation into Reiki, a meditative and vibrational healing
practice. This alternative therapy creates a parasympa-
thetic response that induces relaxation and supports the
body's natural self-healing ability. With my first experience
of Reiki, I knew in my heart that becoming a Reiki practitioner would be a gentle way I could energetically and spiritually support others along their journey. I then enrolled
in a reflexology program which would eventually provide
me with a national certification. Reflexology is an ancient
art and science that helps a body achieve optimal balance
and circulation. I also began a curriculum to be a certified
life coach. During these silent years, my healthcare practice
slowly began to grow as I continued to work on my fear of
moving outside of my safe space.[62] As I cautiously took these
steps, I discovered a way to support others on a one-to-one

---

62   My health care practice, "Light the Path" was drawn from one of my prayer journeys.

basis, while keeping my anonymity intact. It was at this time that I finally came to a peaceful acceptance of Jesus as my spirit guide, separate from any religious connections.[63]

In the spring of 2006, Mike was diagnosed with esophageal cancer that had metastasized to his liver. After so many years of Mike being my protector and provider, I now needed him to rest assured that I could provide for myself, so I moved swiftly through my certifications and clinical practices and created a treatment space in our home. For the next year, after accomplishing many things on his bucket list, his condition deteriorated, and we began to make final arrangements.

Years before, when Matthew died, due to a lack of money we had no place to bury him. I felt his presence in my heart and did not need a gravesite, however Mike had a desire to have a place where he could visit with his son. My parents offered their burial plot for us to bury Matthew and we gratefully accepted. Their amazing gift provided Mike a place to visit often with his little boy. Now, as Mike lay sick in bed, I told him I had made an executive decision. I was having Matthew's body exhumed and reburied with him. Mike was not happy and argued that funds were going to be tight, and I would need that money for more important things. Looking him in the eyes, I asked, "Do you want that little baby with you?" He began to cry and said "Yes." I told him to consider it done.

Mike's last words to me were, "I can't believe how peaceful I feel!" He went into a coma the same day. Two days later, as I slept beside him, I felt, on some deeper level, that he nudged me awake saying, "I got to go" as he took his last breath. Mike died in the early morning hours of May 27, 2007, at the age of 56. At his burial, our son Greg carried Matthew's small coffin, draped with one of Greg's own baby blankets, and laid his brother to rest beside their dad.

For years after, I dealt with the feeling that I was responsible for Mike's death. I would remember Brother Richard's

63 See "Lantern in the Bowel (Vignette)," page 113.

words of wisdom, "That's stinking thinking." Nevertheless, I was the one who begged Mike not to speak out against the church's cowardice or the Court's final decision. I am the one who continued to ask him not to write letters, say anything bad about church officials, or show his anger in any way, since I was now more terrified than when I first began remembering the horrors at Keough.

Richard would always say everything was 'multi-motivated', and I generally believe that. That said, while intellectually I know there were several factors causing Mike's untimely death, and he ultimately was responsible for his own choices, I still feel his bottled-up anger and disappointment at the Catholic Church was the most likely culprit causing his illness.

Of all the support I had through this ordeal, nothing compared to the loving support and encouragement given me by Mike: from listening to me talk things through for hours on end; to never doubting me no matter how horrific the nature of my experiences were; to being right there when I met with the Church in 1992, and going through the court process with me for four years thereafter; to doing double duty with our children and the house when I was too raw and wounded to be able to get out of bed; to accompanying me when I visited Cathy Cesnik's grave; to knowing when it was time to go out for nachos and red wine. He even moved me into a new home two months before he died. The condominium was closer to family and friends and had an entrance buzzer, which he hoped would mitigate my fear of strangers at my door, thereby helping me feel safe. As I said earlier, Mike showed me what love really looked like.

Mike also provided a much-needed sense of protection. His death only exacerbated my fear. Because of this, I found myself back in therapy with Sandy, my movement therapist. I was not there so much to work on my grief; I had a grief counselor through hospice for that. Without Mike's presence, I became terrified that "Brother Bob" would find me and kill me, even though I did not know if he was dead or alive. (Maskell had died by this time.) I was surprised that I felt this fear stronger than my grief, and I knew Sandy would understand and be able to help me—and she did. Due to the intensity of my emotional state, I started seeing an acupuncturist, as well as a new psychotherapist now that Dr. Bradford had retired.

In 2009, now certified as a Spiritual Director, Nationally Certified Reflexologist, Life Coach, and Reiki practitioner, I began my private practice. At the same time, I once again wanted to write about my healing process in a public forum. This would prove difficult considering I no longer had a desire to spontaneously journal following the lawsuit. Since the defense lawyers invaded my inner space by reading my journals, I felt violated and could not trust using that form of prayer. I did, however, find it less threatening to continue my inner dialogues with aspects of myself without having to write the words on paper, unless I experienced an insight or breakthrough within the interaction.

I now felt prepared to begin journaling about my experiences at Keough, and my spiritual healing process. This required me to renew my periods of quiet prayer and to be more disciplined in my writing efforts. I resolved that I was going to take a six-month period and focus on writing. I was not clear who my audience was; I just felt a need to write.

During this writing, I was shaken to the core. In one of my quiet sessions, a teenaged girl introduced herself to me. I think of this aspect of myself as 'Jeannie'. Jeannie was the persona who arose after Frances. The persona, Frances, introduced herself to me in 1992, when the memories began to surface. It was Frances who was raped by "Brother Bob" right after he said he killed Cathy. She lay motionless on the floor, and it was Jeannie who spontaneously arose when Frances could not get up.[64]

In my quiet and while journaling, Jeannie proceeded to tell me that she was in love with "Brother Bob" and to "get over it." I was horrified. I stopped writing, put Jeannie

---

64 See "Birth of a Warrior (Vignette)," pages 191-192.

back in her box, and went underground again.[65] But unfortunately, I could not forget what I had just learned about myself. It meant more years of therapy.

---

65   See "Meeting Jeannie (Vignette)," pages 185-186.

CHAPTER THIRTEEN

The Great Mother (Vignette)

Meeting the Great Mother

In 1975, when Mike and I lost our first child Matthew, the doctors called his death 'a freak of nature' or 'one in a million'. During the six years after his death, I had apparent physical symptoms that I could not explain. At times, my arms were literally so heavy I could not hold them up. My thoughts of Matthew's death were dark and heavy, as if they were a weight on me. I went for neurological testing which did not indicate any medical issues.

Around 1980-81, Mike and I decided to take an eight-week course at a local Catholic hospital to help other parents who had experienced the loss of a child. We would be equipped to help parents who had babies born prematurely, as well as those who had lost their babies at birth, or shortly thereafter like we had. This program presented a variety of professional speakers.

One evening, a psychologist spoke on grief, giving many examples of how grief plays out in people's lives. I told him I never was able to hold Matthew, before or after his death, even though I had wanted to. I wondered if that could have anything to do with the heaviness I experienced with my arms. He suggested I sit quietly with something that reminded me of that time, to be still, and see what happens. So, when I found an appropriate time, I took Matthew's little baby book, sat on the floor in our bedroom, and went into my quiet.

I immediately felt as if I was holding Matthew. My tiny baby boy was lying in my arms! I was ecstatic. To this day

I know I was holding that baby, on a spiritual, psychological, and emotional level. I can still feel the weight of his precious head in the crux of my elbow. I found myself cooing and whispering how much I loved him. I began to cry, telling him our choice to disconnect the respirator, which was a decision we were left with at the end of his life, was made with the hope that he would finally be at peace. Even though his tiny heart gave out on its own before the doctors disconnected him, I believed on some level that, by deciding to disconnect the respirator, he felt we did not want him. I cried, "It never meant I didn't love you!" Until I said those words out loud, I had no idea just how guilty and unworthy I felt.

I continued to cry, holding Matthew in my arms while sitting on the floor in the quiet of the room. I allowed the guilt of our decision and pain of not being able to hold my firstborn child wash right through me. I do not know how long I sat there. Time had no meaning, as if past, present and future all stood in that one powerful moment. Eventually a calm came over me. I instinctively knew I was now free of the pent-up heavy emotions rooted in a painful loss and longing for what could never be. I felt lighter and at peace.

Not knowing what to do, I asked Jesus, my spiritual companion at that time, what I should do. I did not want to give my baby back. This experience was so real that I could feel Matthew lying in my arms. Jesus asked me who I would want to leave Matthew with until I could be with him again.

I thought of Mary, the mother of Jesus. After Matthew's death and Greg's subsequent birth, I began to accompany my grandmother to regular Catholic novenas, which were evenings consisting of special prayers to the Blessed Mother. Because of Grandmom's deep love for Mary, whom she had been named after, I grew to love Mary also. I found myself remembering the times I watched in my mind's eye as the statue of Mary in the Church changed from a colorful, peasant girl, to a black woman, to an elegant lady, etc. I believed this amazing mother, who was in the image of me and my line of 'mothers', was teaching me that she lovingly meets people right where they are.

When I looked up within my meditative state, I saw Mary standing before me. I thought, if I were to trust anyone to care for my little boy until I could be with him again, it would be her. Feeling content, I placed Matthew in her outstretched arms, and as she gently drew him to her breast, I fell against the bed.

Within my spirit I was lying in a field of beautiful flowers, on a gorgeous spring day. The sun was shining bright, I felt the warmth of it on my face, with a breeze moving through my hair. I watched the flowers swaying in the field and I was at peace. To this day, whenever I think of Matthew, I find myself lying in a field of beautiful flowers, engulfed in peace. My arms never felt heavy again.

When my memories of Keough surfaced ten years later, I recalled Maskell showing me pictures and objects while repeating upsetting phrases. Once while flashing shocking images of what he said was a dead fetus, he told me this was what happens when girls like me try to have a baby. He was referring to girls who were, as he would say, 'whoring around'. He said that I was, "not worthy of having a child and being a mother."

With the help of therapy and loving supporters, I was able to deal with how intertwined my reactions to Matthew's birth and death were with the abuse I suffered at Maskell's hands. His hateful statements subconsciously dictated my innermost feelings through the years. I now understood why I felt unloved and unwanted by Matthew when there were complications at his birth. I believed I did not deserve a baby, and my baby left me knowing I would be a bad mother.[66] In 1981, my holding my baby boy in my arms with Mary present was instrumental in instilling in me a truth about myself—that I was a good, loving mother.

---

66 See "Matthew," page 33.

Great Mother Re-Emerges

In 1992, I was falling into an abyss, a big black hole from which all the horrible memories came. I was disconnected from my faith and the Church. I met frequently with my therapists and counselors, but the Archdiocese offered no pastoral support, despite my request. I felt confused, lost, and unimportant. I did not know what to believe and started questioning everything I was taught as a Catholic.

I needed to know how I could be in the image and likeness of this male God, something we had been taught since first grade Catholic catechism classes. After remembering what the male priests at Keough made me believe, that God wanted these abusive acts done to me through them, I could no longer relate to God as the Father. I had already agonized over how Jesus, as the son of God, could have let that horror go on, and I now wanted nothing to do with him either. Everything reeked of males, causing me to recognize the one-sidedness of my faith, which seemed so dysfunctional. Did I fit in as a woman? What other kind of God was there? I was lost.

I struggled to continue on a daily basis to rest in my quiet, to breathe, and to be open to myself and whatever guidance would come. During these contemplative prayer periods, I began to sense a woman's presence, as if she were standing nearby, yet just out of my reach. An image of her emerged slowly over time. As I remembered events from my Keough years, this woman, just like my resurfacing memories, was taking form, filling out, and becoming clearer. I saw her standing barefoot, her hair loose around her shoulders. She had a womanly form, stocky and solid, reminding me of a peasant woman. She wore a dress to the calf, with an apron.

This woman, standing with her arms outstretched, was staring at something in the distance. As that meditative experience continued to unfold, I was aware that she was intently focused on the rocky side of a mountain. Light was pouring out of her hands and her eyes as if trying to penetrate the surface of the mountain.

At some point, I realized I was not just observing. I found myself being drawn toward the light. I was now in the mountain, and I was scratching and clawing through the rock. There were pieces of rock in my fingernails and dust in my eyes, but I continued to claw like an animal, struggling with my breath as I went. I was tearing away rock and stone to get to this light, which was slowly penetrating the side of the mountain.

As I drew closer to the light, I was now aware that I was fully engaged within the experience. The object of the woman's intensity was me, and I was furiously digging toward her, and the light was helping me find my way out. As I scratched through the inside of the mountain toward that brilliant light, I had no idea what was drawing me, what was helping me, what was loving me back into life. All I knew was my whole being was instinctually moving toward that light.

I broke the surface on my hands and knees; my body felt completely sore, raw, and exhausted. Coming from the side of the mountain, I was immediately engulfed in an intense and all-consuming, brilliant light—nothing but light! It was so bright that I had to shield my eyes by turning my head back toward the tunnel of darkness which led to my tomb.

Looking down that tunnel, I could see so many other pairs of eyes staring up at me. There were others still down there!

For a number of years, I remained in a dazed state, staring back at those eyes. I felt a deep responsibility for the others down there and could not imagine leaving them behind. I was afraid if I left them, they would stay buried, and I knew what that was like. I did not know what to do. I also was afraid to move from that spot because I did not know where to go. I did not know who I was. I did not know anything about the 'Jean' that was being reborn from that horrific place of pain and suffering. This would take time and a lot of inner work. Slowly I began to realize that to truly be able to help those who were still down there, I needed to stop staring at my past and move forward, one step at a time.

While I continued to heal and process breakthroughs within my psyche, I was now aware of the intense love of this Mother presence. I needed time to integrate my experience of this spiritual awakening to the sacred feminine energy. When I found that I was finally ready to turn from the tomb's entrance, I was surprised to see the woman still standing there with arms outstretched, patiently waiting. She had not moved. I was slowly realizing, as an adult, that I had been buried alive and that this mothering presence was drawing me toward the truth of who I was. I walked into her embrace and was consumed by her love. In that moment we were pure light. Her love for me was overwhelming. Her presence was pulsing with life, love, and determination.

It took years of contemplation and therapy before I began to see that tomb as the womb of re-birth into my life. Believing my younger self was dead, I was surprised when I began to feel a tiny spark of life awaken in me. Ironically, when Maskell terrorized me into dissociating, much of me was buried into a tomb-like void; but that void became my haven. It was where I slept like Snow White in a fairy tale until this loving and powerful Mother sought me out. Because of her, I experienced a transformation within my being that would take years to articulate and understand.

It made sense when I remembered that at the end of my senior year, I met with the superior of Maskell's who said Maskell had told him how difficult I had been, and how Maskell thought I was unworthy and could not be forgiven. That Catholic cleric gave me what I had longed for, that which I had originally gone to confession in my freshman year to receive: forgiveness. I left the school, forgot everything, and sealed my metaphorical tomb—until I dug my way out of it.

These two experiences of meeting The Great Mother, which occurred many years apart, were remarkably similar. In both spiritual encounters—exiting my premature grave and finding peace with my son's death—the Great Mother lovingly reached out, took the weight of death off me, and left me with a feeling of love and lightness that to this day is indescribable.

This woman showed me over time that there is a deeper spiritual foundation, a basin of love which is ultimately true. While the terror these men instilled in me 'in the image of God' was real on one level, it was not the true reality. I had misplaced my trust in the illusion of those who professed to be holy, and the God they bantered about as all-knowing and wrathful. That illusion included the imprinting in me that I was unworthy and powerless.

The truth that was now being born within me was that the fullness of God was balanced within Mother and Father, and feminine and masculine energy. This loving Mother, whom I am in the image and likeness of, was drawing me to that realization. I was finally beginning to find my ground again.

CHAPTER FOURTEEN

Lantern in the Bowel (Vignette)

From 1992 through 1996, I was bombarded with repressed memories of sexual abuse previously suffered at Keough, causing me to feel vulnerable and isolated. My family was losing our faith and trust in the Church, and there was no life preserver to be found.

After experiencing so many powerful prayer encounters with Jesus's guidance in earlier years, I now felt extremely alone. I could not tolerate the thought that Jesus, the heart friend I came to know, did nothing to stop the sexual abuse I suffered in high school. I also began to question my need for this spiritual guide to be male. Was that just because I was taught from a young age, through words and actions, that males were more powerful than females? I became so confused and angry at Jesus that I wanted nothing more to do with him. This was a very dark and empty time for me. I refer to this period of my journey, from around 1996 to 2000, as the Artemis Years.

I was rudderless and needed something to fill the massive void in my heart when I stopped relating with Jesus as the son of God, a spiritual companion, and a friend. I certainly had outside professional, spiritual, and familial supports to keep me moving. They helped me through that next level of healing and integration, with me feeling abandoned by the Church and divorced from any concept of God, much less Jesus. I was beginning to have faith only in myself.

So, I decided to start relating with a female spirit guide. For a few years I tried to replace Jesus with the Greek goddess Artemis, who I believed was the equivalent of Jesus in many ways. Artemis is the daughter of Zeus, king of the gods. She was regarded as a patron of girls, young women and the protectress of women during childbirth. Artemis is also the goddess of hunting, so I knew she would be strong enough to protect me. I thought if I could replace Jesus with Artemis, I could continue my deep spiritual relationship with this guide. I spent several years attempting to imagine and sense this female warrior, as well as the inspiring and wise spirit guide she could be.

Amid this struggle to create an authentic relationship with Artemis, I continued to make time for prayer and meditation. Once while in my quiet, I found myself at the entrance to a dark tunnel with a lantern inviting me to follow. I cautiously began moving forward. The lantern would appear, floating up to my left, but I had a sense someone was holding it. I struggled to see Artemis carrying the lantern to guide my way, but I could not see anyone. I questioned if this was Artemis or Jesus, then realized it did not matter. What mattered was the light which was illuminating just enough space around me to see where I was stepping.

I slowly followed the lantern for a few weeks in real time, realizing as I progressed that the tunnel was my bowels. I was being led by the lantern through the depth of shit in order to find more of myself. I would encounter different things as I moved along, and then I would sit in that place for any number of days, reflecting on what I came across. One time, as I rounded the bend of the bowel, I saw myself as a young child stuck up to her waist in feces, and she could not move. I was confused, and sat contemplating, "What is this about?" and especially, "How do I get her out?" I was stuck in the experience of the abuse; this muck was paralyzing parts of myself and was suffocating me. Through this process I was becoming aware of how deeply the child within me was affected by the abuse.

I knew the healing that unfolded from my prayer experiences was multi-layered and could happen instantly or it could take months, maybe years. As this ongoing meditation progressed, I began to share this inner quest with my support network. I realized I was dealing with the self-blame, fear, and separation that the wounded child within me was still immersed in. As I worked in my therapies on this new awareness, as well as others discovered along the way, the girl eventually became free of the muck.

I see now that this psychological and sacred journey through my subconscious, which showed up in my quiet as my bowels, was like a mirror reflecting the severed child to my adult self. In the same way photos trigger memories, this process was showing me what was going on within one part of myself that I was not yet connected to. Pausing, sitting, and contemplating each finding was allowing the truth within me to surface into my consciousness.

At some point, as I continued on my inner journey, I came around another bend within my bowel and heard the most terrifying sound. It stopped me in my tracks. I thought it was a monster. I still had the lantern illuminating enough space for me to move. Consumed with fear, I sat down. Days went by, and I would not go any further because I thought this would be the end. I could feel the child fearing a monster around the corner—someone or something that was going to hurt me in some way. The monster was waiting to devour me.

I finally got up the courage and cautiously went around the bend. There before me was a cross and hanging on the cross was an old woman. She was crying out with pain. Her moans were the sound of raw suffering. I sat at her feet and sobbed.

As I reflected on this breakthrough, I began to understand who this woman was and what her pain represented.

I felt, on a spiritual plane, that there had been an intense battle which occurred at Keough between good and evil. As I remembered more horrific acts perpetrated against me, I experienced a deep despair, which accompanied an intuitive sense that my little spirit was always running five steps ahead of Maskell, staying just out of his grasp. I believed that with the death of Cathy Cesnik, he caught me.

The clergy abusers' evil actions broke me down and were an attempt to destroy my connection to that deep feminine spirit within all of us—with all the wisdom, grace, and power that that entails. And they succeeded in making me feel that my soul was dead and that any wisdom I should seek was external to me.

The atrocities that happened to me blocked my connection to my very self, separating me from my soul and causing me to suffer. I knew in my heart that the woman hanging on a cross in the depths of my bowels was Wisdom—is Wisdom.[67] She came to me in the form of an ancient grandmother who had not only shared in my suffering but was now awakening me to the truth that I am wise, I can be empowered without hurting others, I can trust my intuition, and I am lovable and loving.

I continue to get stronger in my belief of these truths. I have been able to put a stepladder against the cross, climb up, and carefully bring that weak and withered body down to the ground, relieving our pain and slowly connecting with the wisdom she shares. I am working on bringing this woman to full health and integration.

After much time and having other experiences within the bowel, I reached the end of this inner path. When I came around that last corner, I stood before an ancient stone cell with bars and a secure lock. As I got closer, I saw something in the cell. I could not tell if it was a person or an animal.

---

67   Years later, I learned that in the Bible, Wisdom is referred to as a sacred feminine presence, (Proverbs 8:1-5; 9:1-6) and that God created Wisdom first. (Proverbs 8:22). The Greek translation for Holy Wisdom is "Hagia Sophia". "Who is Sophia in the Bible?" by Joyce Rupp, *U.S. Catholic Magazine*, January 2016; https://uscatholic.org/articles/201601/desperately-seeking-sophia/. Meeting the wise old woman along my inner path was an important part of the Sacred Feminine reawakening within the depths of my soul.

I was drawn closer and closer. This thing was chained to the wall. That heavy chain was connected to an iron collar around the neck of this child/animal. It was bent over with its ears appearing to have grown shut. I saw no movement of its eyes, which also looked as if they had grown shut or were purposely plastered shut. This tiny, scaly thing was hunched in the corner of the cell with a brilliant red ruby plugging up its mouth. It pained me to look at this creature.

I sat with this experience of the bowels for a long time, but I was hesitant to return to that child/animal in the cell. Reflecting on that place made me afraid and confused. I did not want to have any part of this discovery, even though I was now aware that the creature was a child. I suspected this was the precious little girl running from Maskell, and while a part of me had been caught, this part was hidden away.

When I found the courage to reflect and move closer to the cell, I saw how still the child was. Like a chameleon she could have been mistaken for one of those ancient stones that formed her cell. Outside the cage stood a guard who was also very still and focused.

At some point I approached the guard and said I wanted the key. He told me "No." I told him, "That child is a part of me and I'm telling you I want the key!" The guard said, "She gave me the key and said I was not to give it to anyone."

I was stunned by this response. To be sure nobody got in or out of the cell, the girl gave the key to the guard. I could not imagine why she chose to stay locked in a cell, but I knew this new clue meant we were making progress. I believed if I could figure out what the ruby was, I would learn why she was there.

Meanwhile, I realized my efforts to make Artemis my spiritual guide were not going to work. My previous experiences had taught me I could not create a spirit guide; the guide needed to present himself or herself to me. These guides show up unexpectedly with their own purpose: to protect and guide me. I am often surprised by what they say or do, causing me to realize their message was far from my own conscious thought. I don't understand where the guides come from, but I know when their presence is authentic, and I can trust them.

I had to admit to myself that the spirit I was drawn to for guidance and counsel was not Artemis; it was Jesus, and Jesus was male. My dilemma was: I once thought I knew who Jesus was and now I was confused about him. Even as I worked tirelessly to separate us, I realized that Jesus was available whenever I acknowledged him. Still, for all I knew he could have been a figment of my imagination, another persona within me, the son of God or the actual spirit of a man who died. Whoever he was, I felt fooled and deceived by 'him'—or was it my own self. I now was reluctant to blindly follow Jesus as I once did, since I did not trust that he would have my best interest at heart.

So, I presented Jesus with a spiritual contract which I wrote out: He could stay as my spiritual guide named 'Jesus' and I would not care that he was male, but I could not unconditionally place my trust in him. I was going to discern and dissect everything, especially as it pertained to him. He agreed.

CHAPTER FIFTEEN

On the Wings of an Owl (Vignette)

In the year 2000, I woke one morning to find the left side of my face was paralyzed. My left eye would not close, the left side of my mouth would not function normally as I tried to eat or speak, the muscles were like mush, and I felt I had cotton stuffed in my left ear. Mike and I were terrified that I was having a stroke. Later, we discovered that I had come down with Bell's Palsy.

Within two weeks, due to my condition, I had my first acupuncture treatment. It was performed by a very compassionate and gentle acupuncturist named Tom, and I was sold. The experience was comfortable, and as I stated in my journal on February 5, 2000:

> When I woke the next morning, I felt the blanket of despair had been lifted. I felt lighter and that the situation and diagnosis was workable. Before getting up to get an MRI, I experienced a breakthrough of light in my mind. The darkness was ripped open by a splash of light—a blue tinge of color, rough like a wave. It was beautiful!

I had not been seeing any of my therapists and getting Bell's Palsy made me realize that my unaddressed stress would keep building if I did not resume working with my counselors. I knew I was playing with fire, so I began seeing my acupuncturist regularly, and I resumed a schedule with my massage therapist and movement therapist. Within four months, my facial muscles and hearing had fully recovered.

In 2004, my daughter, Sarah, began a master's degree program to become a licensed acupuncturist. I was thrilled with her decision and not just because of my positive experiences with acupuncture. Sarah had a way with people. She had great listening skills, a compassionate presence, and a natural ability to go right to the heart of what a person needed. As she moved along in her studies, I began getting auricular acupuncture treatments from her. Those sessions were great opportunities for me to relax while working on decreasing the stress in my body.

During one of those early treatments, I had a vision. As I sat comfortably on her couch, she placed the needles in certain acupuncture points, put on some soft music, and let me rest. As with my massages, I went gently into my quiet.

This time I found myself with Jesus on the edge of a mountainside facing a great vastness, as if we were standing on the edge of the world. We were discussing what it was to truly let go. As we walked a little closer to the edge, Jesus suggested I jump. I insisted that that was not in the plan. I was not going to just let myself go off the side of this mountain. As we stood there, I asked him if I jumped would he hold me. He said, "No." I had to do it myself. He said he would be with me, and I could trust he was not going anywhere.

The next thing I knew, I found myself screaming as I fell over the side of the mountain, certain that I was plummeting to my death. The anxiety and terror were so intense I was sure I would have a heart attack. Within seconds, I came up from the fall on the back of a huge bird, with Jesus lying protectively on top of me. I was literally lying flat on the feathered back of a bird, and I was smaller than the width of its warm body.

As I held on tight, my face was immersed in little downy feathers around its neck. We were flying! It was exhilarating, but I was a bit queasy. Mostly I was thrilled that I did not die when I fell. These feelings were all going on simultaneously within myself, without any real thought. Lying on that huge bird's back, we flew down toward what looked like a jungle. The bird slowed down, then proceeded to land in a forest of lush, green foliage. I felt as if we were entering a place located in the past. I got off the bird's back, and he stood, looking very majestic. By then I knew this was an owl, and I had a sense that it was male. He gracefully moved to my right side.

I was amazed by what just occurred. Yet I was fully aware that this experience was unfolding in my body and mind as I was sitting on Sarah's couch in the middle of my acupuncture treatment. I was not asleep and dreaming. As usual, if I felt that I trusted my immediate surroundings and the person I was with, I would let myself go with the experience and discern it later. I was both in this adventure and observing it while being aware of a few slight energetic movements occurring within my body.

Then out of the woods came what appeared to be a tribe of people indigenous to that jungle. They were wearing beautiful owl headdresses that looked like the bird I just flew in on. They came toward us, expressing their deep respect and love for this great big owl. I was confused and surprised when I realized this celebration was for both of us. The owl and I stood there as one being. I felt embarrassed by their praise and unworthy of such a place of honor. I did not understand anything that was happening.

I heard Jesus ask me to walk with him. As we walked, we were surrounded by colorful flowers set against a backdrop of rich green foliage, enormous trees, and babbling streams, all combined with the variety of unusual wildlife. It was breathtaking.

However, all this beauty did not bring me comfort and I was confused because I was not worthy of this. My conversation with Jesus gently guided me into some form of insight. I knew Jesus was encouraging me to let go and embrace the part of myself that was worth honoring. I was aware of my lack of confidence and low self-esteem, and how my insecurity manifested in my daily life. This had been an ongoing conversation with Jesus. Now, I felt I was being invited to go deep within myself to reconnect to my natural abilities and genuine giftedness. The two of us stayed with that experience well after that one acupuncture session ended. This vision stretched me in ways I did not yet know or understand.

This new part of my path also included this large owl that apparently was special to me. I would never lose the feel of the owl's warm body under me and my face in those soft downy feathers.

Later that week I researched whether there was such a bird; it is called the Great Grey Owl. As one author described the bird, "A great gray owl flies low across a Manitoba forest clearing—wingbeats utterly quiet, ultrasensitive ears tuned to the faintest sounds of prey concealed beneath the winter snow. For these woodland predators, survival depends on focus…Great grays make devoted parents… Snow is piling up, and the afternoon temperature won't make it above 25°F. With three owlets tucked snugly under her dense plumage—and a nearby mate that can continue to hunt by sound, however poor visibility becomes—this nesting female seems calmly prepared to ride out the storm."[68]

This encounter with an animal spirit guide was not unique to my spiritual path. Years before, I was introduced to the White Mare while working with my young persona, Little Jeannie.[69] But this experience with Jesus and the owl felt different. Through the years, guides who were

68 "Great Gray Owl Winged Silence," by Lynne Warren, *National Geographic*, February 2005. (Great Grey is interchangeably spelled as "Gray" or "Grey".)
69 See "Little Jeannie (Vignette)," pages 50-51.

connected to my personas protected and guided those parts of myself to whom I was blind. But I found Great Grey was both presently and consistently there for me throughout my day. Like Jesus, who seemed to be my present-day spiritual companion, Great Grey was my present-day spiritual guide. Jesus would challenge me, and at times frustrate me, yet he was regularly a source of support and guidance. Great Grey would be there as I leaned into my fears, whether stepping out of my comfort zone, or remembering and reflecting on something from my past. In those instances, I would find his wings wrapped around me, giving me great comfort and a sense of protection.

Shortly after that acupuncture treatment I wrote in my journal of my dialogue with Jesus, "I asked Jesus what I needed to do with the Great Grey Owl. I was wondering if it was an important piece of my inner work of accepting and sharing my gifts. Jesus said, 'Yes'."[70]

As I learned more about how to communicate with, relate to, and trust Great Grey, I discovered many of the gifts he shared with me: spiritual and intellectual wisdom; acute listening skills; the ability to pierce the darkness of the unknown to get to the heart of an issue; and the capacity to view all aspects and angles of a situation, while trusting my instincts. He became a tremendous source of strength and support.

Eventually, I began to ask Great Grey for help. At times, I could feel myself flying on his warm back, with greater perspective of the issue at hand. At other times he would lead the way as I journeyed through my inner forest toward some amazing and unknown insight.

For example, once in my prayer, I was running childlike along a path within my forest, following Great Grey. I came up short when he led me into this beautiful valley. The dark green grass and glorious flowers were swaying in a breeze, bathed by the sun. That experience allowed me to hear in my heart that the light is always one step from the heavy

---

70   Journal entry dated February 21, 2005.

darkness of my inner path through the unknown. This visual experience brought the truth of those words into my consciousness. Afterwards, I would find myself reflecting on this as I made my way through some dark times.

Mike's death in 2007 was one of those dark times. I am grateful that Great Grey had become a trusted and devoted guide by then. I journaled an example of this on May 14, 2008. Sarah and I had gone to a cabin in the woods for a little rest and relaxation. I was seeing a hypnotherapist for help dealing with intense fears that surfaced after Mike's death. The therapist was teaching me to envision a place within my mind where I felt totally safe, then make time each day to breathe and just be there. So, in my quiet I pictured Mike and I sitting on a bench overlooking a beautiful waterfall in the Big Sur, which we visited before his death. Both of us were wrapped in a burnt orange blanket with my head on his chest listening to his heartbeat. This made me feel safe, secure and at peace.

The first morning at the cabin I sat in my quiet and found myself sitting peacefully on that bench overlooking the waterfall with Mike. I was asked by Jesus to let go and fly. I felt safe and warm under that blanket, wrapped in Mike's loving embrace. Then I found myself on the back of Great Grey. I was right at home and felt fearless!

Later I reflected on this meditation, and the level of fear I felt at the time. I was surprised how the secure feeling of being wrapped in Mike's love seemed to linger beyond the bench scene; strengthening my ability to go into the unknown with Jesus and Great Grey. This lesson would become clearer in time.

Great Grey was the gift I received from Jesus to help me let go into my fear, and just allow what needs to happen to do so. With the help of Great Grey, I have learned to be more comfortable in opening myself to the love others have to share, and to generously share my love and understanding. This involves seeing and leaning into the fear that could, if left unchecked, hold me back.

CHAPTER SIXTEEN

Finding My Voice (2014 to Present)

In 2014, a writer who had been tracking Cathy's murder and the events at Keough since the 1990s, Tom Nugent, asked me if I was interested in being interviewed for an online paper he was authoring, *Inside Baltimore*.

I met Tom in 1997 when my attorneys introduced us; Tom was thinking of writing about Cathy Cesnik's cold case and the events at Keough. When I told my parents, my dad got angry and called a family meeting around his dining room table to discuss this writing possibility. That meeting did not end well for Dad and me, leaving me shaking and crying as I left his home, even though all my siblings supported whatever I decided. Now I understand that after the court's ruling, my father was left to pick up the pieces of an explosion that just occurred within his family. My mother had always been his rock, but now her faith and emotional state were fragile and apparently nothing constructive came of the ordeal our family just went through. Their church community was also gone, and he was in sheer protective mode. He was afraid that for me to publicly write about what happened while the family structure was still so fragile would tear us apart. He was left grasping at whatever was left of his spiritual and familial foundation, and he was not about to let go. My dad, who had worked so hard to raise our large family on a modest salary, did not deserve this fate.[71]

I chose to move forward with the writing, but I eventually changed my mind and decided I was not ready to go public. Tom also put the project on hold for his own reasons. But

---

71 See pictures of my family in 1997, pages 266-272.

in 2005, he wrote a piece about Cathy and Keough for an alternative newspaper in Baltimore called *The City Paper*.[72]

In 2014, Tom contacted me again and said he wanted to update the Keough events on his online paper. Tom had been approached by a group of alumni who had begun a Facebook page called, "Who Killed Sister Cathy?" I was aware of the Facebook group, but I still did not trust anyone. In 1994, I had come out to the public in court, albeit under the pseudonym 'Jane Doe'. The case was effectively buried, and I was left hanging out to dry. There was no way I was going to stick my neck out again, and this time identify myself. I told Tom I would watch to see if the Facebook folks fizzled out before I took the risk.

The Facebook group did not fizzle out. In fact, they gained strength in both followers, and in those coming out as having been victimized. While the original focus of Gemma Hoskins and Abbie Schaub, the administrators of the site, was to solve Cathy Cesnik's murder, the scope widened to include the culture of abuse at Keough. Tom first interviewed Teresa Lancaster, my co-plaintiff referred to in the court case as 'Jane Roe'. That article was positively received.

Meanwhile, I had many therapy sessions discussing why I wanted to come out from hiding considering how scared I was. As we talked about my desire to support other victims and survivors, as well as assist the grassroots investigation, I thought about how often my automatic response was to be a good girl and do what I was told. My therapist would ask me, "How will this benefit you?" This was a new concept for me, to think of myself first and choose what I wanted to do, and not necessarily what I thought I should do.

I told her that when I said yes to publicly identify myself as Jane Doe, I would also be saying yes to working on buried feelings connected to the horrible experiences of my youth. Those disconnected feelings terrified me, and I would need

72 "Who Killed Sister Cathy," by Tom Nugent, *Baltimore City Paper*, January 5, 2005; https://www.baltimoresun.com/citypaper/bcpnews-who-killed-sister-cathy-one-of-maryland-s-coldest-murder-cases-heats-up-20170504-story.html.

to lean heavily once again on my support system. But I knew this action would motivate me to go forward in the next step in my health walk.

Cautiously, I watched to see how stable and dependable the Keough Facebook movement was. I began to feel more assured that I had the strength and support to come out from hiding.

Before I did so, I contacted the Baltimore County Police and updated them as to everything I remembered about Cathy's death and the admissions made to me by "Brother Bob". I felt a need to speak to the police before I considered offering my memories to the public.

I then had to decide if I would allow Tom to interview me and use my name. What I was about to do was terrifying. I knew that making this one decision would be a huge turning point in my life. Very few people outside of my immediate family and close friends knew I was Jane Doe. It was not only scary to me, being a very private person, but it could also be scary to my support group. Being anonymous provided all of us a sense of security and safety. By going public, I was outing myself, my family, and my close friends.

I decided not to let fear stop me. I took off my Jane Doe mask of silence, identifying myself as Jean Hargadon Wehner, in an interview with Tom on November 12, 2014.[73]

Although I did not post on the Facebook site, I knew from the administrators of the Facebook page that support for me poured in after the piece was published in *Inside Baltimore*. Abbie would send me the responses from Tom's site so I could read them in the privacy of my home. I did not respond to the comments, and no one was given my contact information. (I still feel that overwhelming caution and remain very private for my peace of mind.) I remember when I read the 37th response to the article, my daughter

73 "Baltimore Witness Says She Was Shown Body of Murdered Nun by Abuser-Priest," by Tom Nugent, *Inside Baltimore*, November 5, 2014; https://www.bishop-accountability.org/2014/11/baltimore-witness-says-she-was-shown-body-of-murdered-nun-by-abuser-priest/.

said she could tell the amazing things people were saying about me were not sinking in. I admitted to her that it all seemed surreal, leaving me with a familiar feeling of numbness. It was terrifying to be suddenly seen for who I was: the woman who not only publicly accused Maskell, a priest, of sexually abusing her, but also said he took her to see Sister Cathy Cesnik's dead body. I realized I could no longer be invisible, and that exposure felt overwhelming. With time, I could feel how affirming and healing this was for me to be supported and corroborated by my classmates and fellow alumni at Keough.

In late 2014, I and several other women were interviewed for *The Huffington Post's* investigative piece on the death of Sister Cathy and the abuse at Keough.[74]

At about the same time I began speaking to *The Huffington Post*, I was approached by Ryan White and Jessica Hargrave of Tripod Media about making a documentary around the abuse at Keough and the death of Cathy Cesnik. (This series was later named *The Keepers*.) Ryan White's aunt, Trish McCabe Romefelt, had been a friend of mine in grade school and a classmate at Keough. She was surprised to discover that I was Jane Doe, and unbeknownst to me, she suggested to Ryan that he may want to talk with me. It was synchronistic that my cousin, Patty, from Redondo Beach, California, had been best friends with Ryan's mother, Peggy, since high school. Because of their friendship, Patty was close to Ryan since he lived in Los Angeles. The interrelationships, and the assurance from Patty that Ryan was a good guy, was what got him and Jess in to see me. Then it was up to them to make their case.

Our first meeting was around my dining room table with a couple of close family members in attendance. We talked for six hours. I told Ryan I could not be a party to a project that presented this crime in a sensationalizing or

---

74 "Buried In Baltimore: The Mysterious Murder of a Nun Who Knew Too Much," by Laura Bassett, *The Huffington Post*, May 14, 2015; https://www.huffpost.com/entry/cesnik-nun-murder-maskell_n_7267532.

tantalizing fashion. He ended by telling me what he hoped to accomplish with this documentary, which at that time he thought would be one hour. He said he wanted to present both aspects of this tragedy, the systematic sexual abuse that went on at Keough and the facts around Cathy Cesnik's unsolved murder; then let the audience decide if the two were connected. Ryan told me later that he and Jess knew by the time they reached the elevator to leave my building that they believed me and wanted to do this project.

It took me somewhat longer to feel I could trust them. But I am so pleased I opened my door to these two amazing and talented individuals. Their documentary team consisted of Ryan the director, Jess the producer, and John Benam, the director of photography. Over the next two and a half years, these three people became like family.

The experience of making *The Keepers* moved me into a whole other level of healing. I chose to use this next step in my life as a different, but remarkably effective, therapeutic tool. When I had gone to the Church in 1992, I wanted to be heard. The Church chose not to hear what I had to say. But in 2014, Ryan and Jess listened, and in turn I felt heard.

By finally having the opportunity to speak about the crimes that happened at Keough, and the re-traumatization at the hands of the Archdiocese and the courts during the 1990s, my healing on a body, mind and spirit level was accelerated. Ryan and Jess came to town monthly for two and a half years. I was one of the people who would meet with them during each visit.

When they came, I would have a list of two or three things I hoped to accomplish. For example, we would meet with a family member or close friend, but only if he or she wanted to meet the documentarian team and/or interview with Ryan. Now that I was taking steps to share my truth with others, they did not need to continue keeping my confidences. I encouraged them to share their feelings and thoughts with Ryan and others pertaining to my years of silence. It was important for the world to see the cruel ripple effect the Church unleashed from its until-then successful effort to squelch the telling of my experience and the experience of others at Keough.

Another example would be our stumbling around through the woods in 2015, putting flowers in areas where Cathy was possibly found. Originally, we did this following some information Abbie Schaub and Gemma Hoskins had discovered.[75] Later in 2016, one of Cathy's family members came to town and was given a map from the police marking the spot where Cathy's body was found.

When I discovered this, I went with Sarah and the film team to the wooded area, now knowing our destination. Standing in the place where Cathy's body was discovered, I was overwhelmed with bittersweet emotions. On October 10, 2016, I went back with some family members and posted a memorial plaque in honor of Cathy Cesnik, the woman who tried to protect me and other girls from harm.[76] This was a deeply healing experience for me. Before 2014, all I ever thought pertaining to where Maskell took me to see Cathy's body, was the phrase, "It was far, far away...". Now, aware of how close the location was to Keough, I believe that phrase was just another of Maskell's brainwashing efforts to block my memory.

Because I was afraid of triggering more memories, or being overwhelmed with people and inquires, I stayed private. Ryan and Jess told me nothing of what they did before or after filming with me; Gemma and Abbie said nothing of what they were discovering unless I asked. Ryan and Jess's visits motivated me to go out and explore, accompanied by them, and sometimes Sarah and John. Their presence defused my fear and allowed me the freedom to uncover more pieces of my past.

I was also able to speak honestly to the camera, letting the camera become my witness. This was important to me as the adult and as the child within me. All these

---

75   See "Girl with the Long Black Hair (Vignette)," pages 209-210.
76   See Picture of Memorial Plaque, page 261.

atrocities occurred in secret; there was no witness. Now after so many years of silence, I took the opportunity to speak my truth publicly for the victim in me and in other survivors. I hoped that sharing these horrible experiences would help me heal. That could only happen with the trust that was slowly building between Ryan, Jess, and myself. This was a major step in my health walk. My name, my face, and my story could finally be out there. My voice would be heard.

One example of using the camera as my present-day witness was when I shared how ashamed I was to admit that when I was throwing up memories in the 1990s, I remembered the humiliation and self-loathing I experienced being treated by grown men like a dog.[77] Until *The Keepers* was being filmed, I was too ashamed to speak about this self-condemning memory except to my therapists and a few confidants. Despite how embarrassed I was telling Ryan and Jess, by talking to the camera I could speak about that dehumanizing experience for what it was—violent and degrading. I was shedding some of the weight I had been carrying around for 25 years.

A second example was when I revealed that Maskell forced me to have an abortion. Three times, he took me to see a doctor. Once, he and the doctor raped me. A second time, the doctor examined me for a possible pregnancy. The last time the doctor aborted my baby without my consent. Even though in 1994/1995, I began to remember being taken to a gynecologist, my memories were faceless. At that time, I was afraid to request pictures of individuals because I considered that to be 'deep sea diving', which Dr. Bradford cautioned me against.[78] I did not remember the face of the gynecologist until I asked Ryan and Jess for a picture many years later. I looked at the picture of Richter

---

77   See "The Keough Years," page 22, and "The Pressure Rises (Vignette)," page 60.

78   The lawsuit named Christian Richter as a defendant, but he was included at that time based on Teresa's experiences. That is why I did not join Teresa in her part of the suit against Richter.

with my therapist present. I immediately knew he was the doctor Maskell took me to see on these three occasions.

I feel the abortion was a tortuous attack on my whole being. Richter aborted my baby without my consent and with Maskell present.[79] Here were two representatives of revered social institutions; how was I, as a child, expected to comprehend, much less fight that power? Reliving the abortion was devastating, but it did not compare to the deep moral and religious struggle it threw me into as an adult woman raised as a Catholic. I not only connected to that horror for the first time, but I could see the psychological manipulation and blatant disrespect for me as a person. Maskell let men rape me, and he used the abortion as the contraceptive.

Let me be clear, a Catholic priest, who preached on Sunday that abortions were the worst possible sin, and a licensed doctor, who was bound by law not to perform abortions until they became legal in 1973, took a child from my body without my consent. I had no idea what they were doing to me. I remember Maskell telling me we were going to get candy, obviously another one of his hypnotic suggestions. Once there, the doctor and Maskell were unusually serious, and the experience caused me excruciating pain.

In 2009, the young girl within me expressed the same gut-wrenching feeling. When I could finally talk about what happened in 2016, I relayed what she said to the camera:

Lying on a table,
feet in stir-ups,
legs apart.

Silent pain shrieking through me.
When did I get on this table?
The pain brings me back.
Blood warm on my leg.

---

79 While I did relay my experience of the abortion to the camera, it was edited out of the documentary for my privacy.

"Stand up!"
Pot in hands,
legs apart.
Something falling.
out of that pain-filled
silent scream,
into the pot.

Someone, far away
calls it candy.
Doesn't look like
candy.

Shortly after the abortion, I was sitting in a school office with the vice-principal and Maskell.[80] They told me the administration's rule was to expel any girl if she had an abortion. If they let me stay and were found out, the school would be shut down. They also said if my parents ever heard that I had had an abortion they would disown me. I was terrified! Already convinced that I was a terrible person, I believed I was now causing these authorities so many problems, which now included the school possibly being forced to close.

In the end, they decided I could stay in the school if I did not say a word to anybody. I was grateful to them for allowing me to stay. Years later, I realized Maskell once again was putting the blame for his actions on me. I was being asked by them to carry the heavy burden of responsibility for keeping my high school open by burying another secret. I also wondered if my mother was writing my tuition check at that very same time.

As a grown woman, reconnecting to this assault on my young body created intense grief and longing for that baby. I was sickened by the way those men treated me as a teenager,

---

80 On August 2, 2018, I sent an e-mail to the now retired vice-principal by way of her caregiver. I told her I remembered her and believed she was aware of what Maskell was doing. I asked her to call the city police task force detective, Scott Suriano, and gave her his phone number. I informed Detective Suriano in case she called him; I never heard anything from either of them about this.

allowing me no say in what was done to my body. I was also angered at the outrageousness of the Church's stance, then and now, that it is up to these men in the disguise of God's will, to tell women and girls, even those pregnant due to a rape committed or orchestrated by a priest, that they were forbidden from deciding whether to have an abortion.

It was heartbreaking to have the dehumanizing experiences I was forced to endure witnessed by the camera. However, doing this helped me feel as if I were being seen for the first time; and the healing was worth the risk.

Through all this inner and outer growth, I continued my much-needed weekly therapy sessions. During the making of *The Keepers*, I could sense myself becoming more integrated and thereby taking back my power, something I had been working on for many years. I was also aware my family and friends were experiencing this in their lives as well.

The Keepers debuted worldwide on May 19, 2017, in seven episodes. Like the Tarana Burke's #MeToo movement, which went viral in October of 2017,[81] it helped create a community of survivors who were finding their voices together.[82]

For me, the airing of *The Keepers* was both necessary as well as overwhelming. After being silent and hidden for so long, just putting my name on Jane Doe was terrifying. To be seen in the documentary and recognized on the street was at times unbearable. As a survivor, the only way I could participate in the film was by thinking my painful memories would be seen and heard through the camera, and only by the three people filming me. If I thought too long about the fact that the video was to be broadcast worldwide, I would have been unable to move forward.

I was not prepared for how scared and vulnerable I would feel once the documentary was released. I had poor personal

---

81 "Tarana Burke: The woman behind Me Too," by Andrea García Giribet, *Amnesty International*, August 21, 2018.

82 The Emmy nominated Netflix documentary, *The Keepers*, directed by Ryan White; https://www.netflix.com/title/80122179.

boundaries and being hypersensitive, the young victim in me waited for people to say what I was conditioned to expect—that I was lying. I was also afraid that now I had told my secret, 'they' would come and hurt me. That is why, with the help of others, I got off the grid—no e-mail, phone, social media, new clients, etc.

While my being recognized is at times scary, I have been encouraged by the numbers of people I helped just by telling my experience. From simple nods by women recognizing my face, to perfect strangers hugging me, sobbing, and telling me that by seeing me in the documentary, they felt empowered to speak up.

In the summer of 2019, two years after the release of *The Keepers*, while at a neighborhood festival in Baltimore, I approached a young woman serving ice cream out of a truck; I wanted to buy a treat for my grandchildren. She saw my face and began crying. She then walked away from her serving window, pulled herself together, re-approached me, and told me that after just watching me on *The Keepers*, this year was the first time she could talk about her abuse to her doctor. It was once again an affirmation of my decision to work with Ryan and Jess. I knew if telling my painful truth about the sex crimes at Keough could help one person, it would be worth it.[83]

As I carefully tried to find my footing on this new terrain, I was asked to give my first public talk, along with Ryan, at the Baltimore Shambala Center, a local meditation community. It was called Leaning into Fear and Finding Courage. When asked why he was there, Ryan said one reason was that he felt he had 'outed' me, and he wanted to support me.

I thought as an adult I should be able to do anything I put my mind to; but then the terror of my past would engulf and paralyze me. So, I continued to work on my psychological

83 In fact, the title to *The Keepers* comes from a friend's on-camera discussion about her abuse, and about how we keep it all inside because "people can't handle hearing what happened to us." We are also intimidated and bullied into keeping the secret of the abuse on behalf of the perpetrators. This discussion was edited out, respecting the interviewee's privacy.

and spiritual health while I slowly moved in my public environment. I was asked to give more talks or join in panel discussions. Making these decisions was not easy. I would talk with my therapist, and she would once again ask, "How will this benefit you?" The Serenity Prayer is a simple expression of my process, "God grant me the Serenity to accept the things I cannot change, Courage to change the things I can, and Wisdom to know the difference."

As I moved beyond the airing of *The Keepers*, I developed a routine that has helped me process this fear when agreeing to give a talk or interview:

- talk personally with the moderator or interviewer;
- get a copy of the questions;
- find out the anticipated number of participants;
- take someone with me to the talk; and
- if possible, see the venue ahead of time and know where the exit routes are.

Since I began recovering my memories, I found one of the hardest things for me to understand, much less explain, was how I could sever from a complete section of my past life. Now that the world had heard my life's story, I became afraid of similar questions from others.

Those questions did eventually come from the public. Not being a psychotherapist, my challenge was how to explain, as a layperson, the dismemberment and integration of myself to people who cannot fathom the experience. After I had spoken a few times in public, I found myself coming back to the analogy of a trash can. I explained to audiences that the trash can symbolizes the depository for the discarded parts of myself which I struggled to contain beneath the can's sealed lid.

The dismemberment of a precious part of myself began when I was very young. My emotional reactions to the abusive behavior were purely subconscious, but nevertheless totally self-destructive to me as a victim.

I was conditioned through my faith and social systems, which were led mainly by men, to believe that as a girl I was somehow inferior to a male. Sex was not talked about in our house; yet being surrounded by six boys, it was obvious to me that I did not have what they had, a penis. As a little girl, if I was told by an abusive male caregiver to do something, and after I did what I was told he said I was bad, how does one handle that message? Since the sexual perpetrators were men in positions of authority, I wonder if I subconsciously translated my being 'bad' as my being 'female' or different. Slowly something inside of me began to hide, shrink away, die off. On a psychological and spiritual level, I slowly began to separate from the 'bad' part of myself, which must have been hard, since that meant I was ultimately separating from my feminine spirit.

That is why the analogy or visual of the 'bad' part of myself as an arm in a trash can helps me explain this process. Here is a summary of how I like to relay this to help others understand:

Imagine that every time an abuser told me I was bad or made him do a bad thing, I hid my arm. Whenever a perpetrator said that my parents would be mad if they knew how bad I was, I picked at my arm. And every time I was told someone else would be hurt if anyone found out how bad I was, I picked at the wound I had created on my arm. Each time someone saw me being abused and turned away, I chewed at my shoulder joint. Each time I was called a whore, a dog, the 'Daughter of the Devil' or unforgivable for being so bad, I would bang my wounded arm against a wall hoping to disengage from it. Then, when I was shown a dead body and told in a variety of ways that it was my fault, I hit that disgusting arm against a wall until it finally fell to the ground. Totally believing that that thing was the evil part of myself, I picked it up, dropped it into a trash can, and held the lid in place.

So, after the abuse ended, I subconsciously became
hypervigilant about keeping that lid down by presenting
a pleasant and acceptable façade, hoping no one would
ever find the evil whore contained inside. This left little
capacity for learning, and healthy, personal growth.
When my repressed memories began to push their way
out, I began to understand just how exhausting my
efforts had been.[84]

When the lid finally came off and the stench of decay
filled the air, I felt a familiar terror that everyone would
find out how bad I really was and abandon me. However,
when sharing disgusting memories with others, I was
baffled to see compassion. When, after looking at what
I was led to believe was evil, loved ones cried instead of
leaving me, I found the courage to pick up and care for
the decayed flesh from the bottom of the trash can. Then
the real breakthrough began to happen; every time others
showed me they trusted I was not a bad person, I found
myself trusting that this thing was not evil; it was just
an arm.

I am proud of the work I have done to discover and reconnect with my severed child. I am happy to be rid of that
'trash can' and thrilled to feel my energy being freed up to
be used for my own self-care instead of being wasted trying
to hide a part of myself. I am encouraged by the growth and
healing my fractured psyche has experienced and believe
that fully reconnecting will help my whole being function
more smoothly.

Similarly, by finding and using my voice in interviews,
in *The Keepers*, giving talks, and writing this book, I am
finally experiencing healthy, personal growth, while helping
others. I feel the courage in me growing as I continue to
grapple with the fear.

---

84 This was a breakthrough time for me. I always thought I was stupid, only achieving
11 credits short of an Associate of Arts college degree over the years. I never had
the confidence to have a steady profession; I struggled with the fear of stepping
out and being public.

Postscript

When *The Keepers* came out, many of the statements that were most upsetting came from a few well-meaning family members, friends and/or supporters. A comment like, "I would have told him to go fuck himself and left," would feed my adult mind's self-loathing as a 14-year-old victim. I already blamed myself for what happened to me because I did not fight back. Because I had zero compassion for myself, I feared others also thought I should have fought off Magnus and Maskell. Statements like this affirmed my anger at my teenaged self and intensified my separation from her.

Another upsetting response was, "Clergy abuse has been going on for centuries. There's no stopping it." What I heard was, "You can't stop them, and it sucks to be you!" I wondered what those individuals who are resigned to this corruption in their faith system would say if a survivor who was a friend or family member disclosed that, rather than a clergy member, they were sexually abused by a neighbor or sports coach.

One of the more seemingly innocent but hurtful statements was, "But for the grace of God, that would have been me." This is so offensive to a survivor of clergy sexual abuse. Survivors deserved the grace of God. They prayed for that grace. That spiritual rape performed by religious leaders, and the absence of God's grace, is one major reason I am not connected to any formal faith system.

Innocent comments like these can be most upsetting to your friend or loved one since survivors are already filled with self-blame and endless shame. The last thing survivors want is to feel upset with our closest supports. We just need to hear that it was not our fault and that we are accepted no matter what. It is fine to just be quiet and simply be with them.

CHAPTER SEVENTEEN

The Gift of Aletheia (2016)

The following is a presentation by my son, Greg, to the production crew for The Keepers, *but it was such an incredible gift for me:*

To the Crew:

I wanted to say thank you for putting this on and doing this for my mother and for all the survivors. I wanted to come up with a gift or an expression to express this.

I have a lot of meaning that I find in totems—in objects that are charged with significance—whether it be a book that's all beaten up, but I don't want to throw it away because it's the book that my grandmother gave me, or a teddy bear I had when I was four years old that I want to pass on to my kids. I feel if that bear is in their bed, they'll be protected from bad dreams. Part of it is superstition, but it is more about connection. When I have my dad's hand tools in my hands, I feel like I'm directly connected to the time that I spent working with him; or if I've gotten bricks from my grandparents' yard that I want to put in my own garden, those objects are passing on a tradition of meaning. They allow me to focus on the people that aren't physically here anymore, and the moments that made those objects important in my life.

I wanted to find an object that represented what I felt that you three had done, and are continuing to do with this documentary. Part of it was finding an object that I could charge with significance, that I could charge with meaning, that would mean more than its own definition. I looked for things first from my own life.

When I was a kid, I used to love Greek mythology, and my children really enjoy Greek mythology. So, I started looking for the Greek god of truth. I discovered there is no Greek god of truth, but there's a Greek goddess of truth named Aletheia, She's the spirit of truth, truthfulness, and sincerity, and she opposes trickery, deception, and lies. The Roman name was Veritas.

Oftentimes with Greek mythology there will be a special symbol, like an owl for Athena, but unfortunately Aletheia has no symbol. What I did find as I continued to look is that Aletheia is also a term in Greek philosophy.

I used to study philosophy, so that jumped out at me. Aletheia is also used by Martin Heidegger, who was an existentialist in the 20th century. This was also important because I used to study Heidegger; he had an impact on my life.

What caught my attention was that Aletheia, in ancient Greek, means 'unclosedness, unconcealedness, disclosure, truth, the state of not being hidden, the state of being evident.' The Greek word means to be opposed to 'oblivion, forgetfulness, and concealment.'

I couldn't think of a better match for what I feel you all have brought to not just this particular case, but in all your work in investigative documentaries. You're not trying to just tell people what you think; you're trying to take something that's hidden, and bring it into the light, right? That idea is to disclose, to fight against concealment and forgetfulness, to witness something that is true and tell it properly. So that really is where I hooked on, and I thought, ok this is it.

I started looking for either statues or images. I found a couple, mostly in relationship to the Roman version, Veritas. One of them, painted by Gustav Klimt, who painted the famous painting *The Kiss*, is called *Veritas Nude*. There are a couple different versions of it, but I found one picture that seemed perfect, because it is a picture of a wood cutting. In the past, folks would carve a figure from a flat board and dip the carving in ink to create a stamped image.

So, I got a block of wood (unwraps carving), and I started to carve a copy of Veritas or Aletheia. I got a piece of basswood, which is a softer wood used for carving. I then laid it out (lays out carving to demonstrate), I got Veritas made to scale from a print, laid it over the wood, pinned it all out, then got a profile on the side that I drew out. I was not totally comfortable with doing this kind of carving since I don't do it regularly, but I thought back to my woodcraft days and pinewood derby days and decided I could try my hand at carving.

As I worked, I thought about what you must have to go through; you start with just the barest notion of what you might be getting into, right? That block of wood. Maybe it's got a profile on it. Maybe it's got a little bit of information that you can see: I see you saying, "There's something in there that we wanna show people. But we gotta get the stuff around it out of the way. We have to uncover what's there in order for folks to see." Right?

With this carving, I used my father's tools, and my children's pocketknives from scouting, and I slowly cut away the big parts, and started to carve out the details, until I got something that looked fairly recognizable. One of the things that I also kept thinking about was how I wanted to make one of these for my Mom. But what struck me, as soon as I had that idea, is that you all have already made one for my Mom. What you've done with this film is present her with Aletheia—with disclosure, with uncoveredness, with the opposite of concealment. You have been Aletheia, the goddess of truth, in what you've done here.

Aletheia's symbol is of a woman standing in the nude with a mirror held outward, reflecting people back to themselves. I think it is the greatest mascot. It strikes me as the gist of what I think you're doing, showing people what happened. It's going to have different impacts on different people. Some people are going to see it and they're going to find the truth, and some people are going to see it and they're going to get upset, because they don't want to see the truth. What is inside each of us as we uncover, or cover up, what's really going on, will cause different reactions to the truth. But that mirror doesn't lie, that mirror is still there. The fact that you have done such an amazing job, all of you, at bringing the truth out, is something that I'll never truly be able to repay.

It has been the greatest feeling that I've had to watch my Mom. Her entire life has changed in the process of this. It's what my father always wanted, which was simply to have her feel like she could face the world, with power, and hope. And without feeling so terrified that there was a sense of helplessness.

To Jean:

I don't know if this could've happened with Dad here, you know? You had to do this on your own two feet. It was quite powerful that, even with the people around you, you faced this by yourself, and I'm immensely proud of you.

To the Crew:

Anyway, this is for all of you. I just wanted to share the story because the story is what makes it special for me, and I hope it makes it something special for you.

My Reflections

Months before Greg presented this beautiful gift to 'The Crew,' I began to remember and explore—really meet—who I was as a senior at Keough. I had begun to have compassion for my persona, Jeannie, when she was a senior.

I was struggling with the memories of Maskell's conditioning behaviors, which had surfaced when I first began remembering abuse in 1992. Maskell instructed me to simply glance at the abusers' faces, not to look directly at them. Also, some of the abusers did not want me to look at their faces. If my eyes showed fear during a situation, Maskell would later take me by the hair to look into the bathroom mirror to remind me who the whore was in the room.

Although I was beginning to have compassion for Jeannie, I could not escape the feeling that she was a whore. But she was me, and I had my mask to cover her up. Having compassion for her drew me to look at who she truly was. But I was so afraid to look. If I went on this exploration, I might lose the mask I wore to stay safe, be good, fool others, and ultimately fool myself. I found comfort in my mask. Much of this struggle played out through the summer of 2016 before a mirror. I wrote this poem several weeks before Greg presented his gift:

Mirror, Mirror Who do I See?
I think I know who I see,
while gazing in the mirror
at this face I call
Me.
"Don't dare look too close or too long, but look."
Whose eyes are they?
Whose mouth is that?
I think I know. Do I?
I should not look too closely, but do.
Those eyes belong to one who knows
the Truth.
They scare Me...
NO—DO NOT STARE!

It's not polite.
I'm a good girl.
But, what might I see,
while staring into those eyes of Truth?
A power-filled Me,
who shatters the mirror,
destroying
Me?!
Don't look too close or too long.
That's a good girl.

CHAPTER EIGHTEEN

Weapons

Maskell had a toolbox of weapons he used to terrify his young victims. I find it particularly difficult to write about my experiences pertaining to these weapons, knowing how hard the experiences are for others to hear. So often, I fear that I am hurting people by describing what Maskell put me through. As Sarah, my daughter, would say, "You're not hurting people, Mama, Maskell and the other perpetrators are the ones who hurt you!"

Terrifying his victims was the main tool used by Maskell to assure that we would not talk about what went on behind closed doors. Maskell used drugs, psychology and the police in his criminal activities. These actions had the same effect as when he used his gun to terrify me and other girls.[85]

Each of these weapons dis-empowered us victims, threatened our lives, and caused us ongoing physical, psychological, and spiritual trauma. Maskell strengthened the effects of these weapons by intimidating, manipulating, and deceiving me, other victims, and our families.

Psychological Manipulation

Early on, when I started remembering the tortuous abuse at Maskell's and others' hands, I felt I was being hypnotized. An example of this would be realizing that at the end of each memory of abuse in the chaplain's office, Maskell would say, "…and don't be late for class." Then, as I stood on the outside of his office, I would hear the click of the closing door, and everything that went on in that room went blank.

---

85 See "The Legal Battle," page 85.

To this day I can still hear the click of the door in my left ear, and I feel the hypnotic power of the door and his voice admonishing me not to be late for class.

Similarly, Maskell would repeatedly say, "I only want what's best for you, just what's best for you," then everything would stop. He would plant phrases or words like that. He would say we were going for 'candy', a 'sucker', or an 'ice cream cone'. Then, within the unfolding memory, I found myself performing fellatio on an abuser. I felt as if I were waking up, extremely confused, and wondering what was going on, since I thought we were going for an ice cream.

As the adult, I became aware that I had different experiences on a body, mind and spirit level when remembering these hypnotic states. At one point, while I remembered what Maskell was doing to control my mind, I felt that the part of me that had dissociated from the experience was still able to observe what was happening from a distance. I could see the memory unfolding and see myself as a child responding to Maskell's brainwashing. I was observing the events from the vantage point of the third person. But I was simultaneously able to see what happened from the child's perspective, even though the child was in a trance state.

Sometimes, after Maskell gave his hypnotic suggestion, I could not remember or see anything more than what was there from my adult perspective. Then, after some blank time, the memory of what happened would pick up from the child's perspective.

Other times, I would remember Maskell frantically addressing me as if I had done something wrong and finding myself in a different position than before everything went blank. I am not sure of the levels of brainwashing that Maskell was using, but I do know I had no sense of control; he had all the control.

Shortly after I remembered Maskell taking me to see Cathy's dead body, I began a series of memories about what happened after Cathy went missing and before her body was found. As each memory unfolded, I was acutely aware that during the interaction, the persona, Jeannie, was relieved that she was not being forced to do anything sexual. As the adult, I wondered if Maskell was just laying low after Cathy had gone missing, or had he purposefully stopped the sexual assaults on me during that time so my brain would totally focus on his intended efforts to make me believe I killed Cathy.

One day, when I went to the chaplain's office, Maskell was angry and agitated, going on about a ring that apparently went missing from Cathy's body. He reached into the pocket of my school blouse and pulled out a ring. He said I must really be terrible to kill someone for their ring. I pleaded that I did not take that ring; he then said "I only want what's best for you, just what's best for you"—and everything stopped. I 'came to' with Maskell yelling "What did you do?" I looked down to see a finger in my hand. I threw it on the floor while Maskell was screaming about how evil I was to cut Cathy's finger off to get the ring. In the early months of 1994, I entered this in my journal:

> Jeannie told me "He would show me things and tell me things." I asked her what would he show me? She said "He showed me a ring that he said was Sister Cathy's. It had, 'To God I commend my heart, Love Cathy' on the inside of it." I asked her "What did it look like?" Jeannie said, "It was a gold band, like a wedding ring." Then I asked, "Why did he show it to me?" Jeannie replied, "He kept saying I was the one who hit Cathy and killed her; her ring was on me."

Another day I went to Maskell's office and found him agitated, pacing while asking me if I killed Cathy for her jewelry. He went on about how he was trying to keep me safe, to protect me from the police. He said he searched my locker and found a necklace, which he had in the palm of his hand. The necklace consisted of a chain with an Immaculate

Mary medal hanging from it.[86] He continued his endless ranting while I stood there.

My third memory involving hypnosis occurred after being shown Cathy's body by Maskell and being told by "Brother Bob" that he killed Cathy.[87] Maskell seemed intent on quickly making me believe that I was totally responsible for Cathy's death. I recalled entering Maskell's office and immediately felt his agitation and anger directed at me. I was doubly afraid because "Brother Bob" was there. Maskell repeated his trance phrase, "I only want what's best for you, just what's best for you," causing me to stand perfectly still, disengaged. "Brother Bob" came toward me asking if I knew that Sister Cathy was killed? I shook my head yes. He then pointed at Maskell and asked me if he killed her. I shook my head no. He then pointed to himself and said, "Did I kill her?" I shook my head no. He then pointed at me and asked, "Did you kill her?" I shook my head yes. "Brother Bob" acted shocked, saying he could not believe I could do such a thing.

He walked me to the bathroom and handed me a pipe. When he opened the bathroom door, I saw a rat lying on the floor, and he told me to show him how I did it. I 'came to' with Maskell yelling, "Oh my God, is that what you did to her? Oh my God!" I was beating the rat with the pipe. I dropped the pipe and sat back, looking at my hands. Maskell handed me a napkin and said he would clean up

---

86   The medal of the Immaculate Conception is known by Catholics the world over as the Miraculous Medal. The front of the medal depicts Mary, the mother of Jesus, standing on a globe, with her foot on the head of a serpent which represents evil. This medal is worn by many Catholics, so it would not be unusual for a nun to wear one.

87   See "Birth of a Warrior," page 188. Since the memories come with a beginning and an end, but they do not come with clear placement within my years at Keough, the process of putting them together to create a timeline is based on the logical progression of where the various experiences I remembered fit with one another. For example, at one point in my quiet periods, I remembered being shown Cathy Cesnik's body by Maskell; then during a later quiet period, I remembered "Brother Bob" telling me he killed Cathy. So, when "Brother Bob" showed up in Maskell's office, talking about Cathy's murder, I concluded it occurred after he told me he killed her.

my mess. He then put the napkin in a bag as I walked out of the bathroom. The two men were saying that they were taking care of me and would make sure no one found out what I had done. As usual, Maskell ended the session with "…and don't be late for class."

Maskell would take something he knew about my past and use it against me. My uncle held a rat over my abdomen to terrify me as a little girl, and there I was with a pipe, in Maskell's bathroom, beating on a rat. I wonder how much easier it was for Maskell to control my brain when he replayed parts of my familiar past, like when I knelt next to Cathy's dead body.

I discussed this memory of the rat in the bathroom with Dr. Bradford. I asked him if he could tell me whether Maskell used my memory of my uncle with the rat to terrify and manipulate me into thinking I was taken to Cathy's body. Or was it a replay of my torturous experience of seeing her body, with Maskell hoping to imprint that horror on my psyche to keep me quiet. I was always grateful for his honest assessment. Dr. Bradford told me either explanation was possible. He said with so much hypnosis being used, it could have been a way for Maskell to make me think I saw Cathy's body to terrify me.

Ultimately, I concluded that my experience with the rat was Maskell's way of making me think that I hit Cathy with a pipe and killed her. That thought was implanted by him and "Brother Bob". But seeing Cathy was real. I could not deny the visceral sensations of touching Cathy's face covered with maggots. My visual and body memory was validated when there were maggots found in Cathy's body at her autopsy, even though she was missing in the autumn and early winter. Also, my memory of the area where Maskell took me to see Cathy's body is about a couple hundred yards from where she was found by the hunters that January.[88]

---

88 See Majestic Distillery Co. Inc, page 263, and "Girl with the Long Black Hair (Vignette)," page 207.

During this period, the last two memories took place with only me and Maskell sitting in the chaplain's office. He was repeating how he was protecting me from being arrested by making sure nobody found out what I had done. Then he said he wanted to help other girls in the same way he helped me. Maskell wanted me to assure other girls that they could talk to him, that he could help them, and that they need not fear him. I fumbled around, saying I did not know which other girls were dealing with issues. He ended the session telling me to think about what we talked about.

At our next meeting Maskell had a bag sitting next to him on the floor. He asked me if I had decided to help him. I again told him I really did not know anyone who needed to talk to him. With that, he opened the bag, I looked down and I thought I would vomit. It was a piece of meat or rotten fruit crawling with maggots. Maskell looked at me and said, "You have to remember that I'm protecting you. I could get in trouble. I'm making sure no one finds out what you've done." I found myself telling him that I did not know anything about anyone. Then I heard my persona, Jeannie, begin to say, "but there was someone in the cafeteria...".

As the adult, I began crying and vowed to terminate that memory and not pursue any memories of advising Maskell about other girls. I was disgusted with Jeannie. I had no compassion for what she had been through. I had no sympathy for her having to withstand Maskell's torture and terror tactics. All I could do was condemn myself for not being stronger. I was plagued with questions like: Who did I tell him about? What did he do with the information I gave him? Who was called into that room because of me? Who might have killed themselves because I told him about them? What could have happened after this exchange terrifies me, and to this day I won't allow myself to go there.

By using his brainwashing techniques and misusing hypnosis, Maskell made me believe I killed Cathy Cesnik and that he was my protector. And he was effective; years later, not remembering anything about most of my high school years, and after seeing a picture of Sister Cathy, the first thing I felt was: "I loved her, and I killed her."[89]

Drugs

For a few years after 1992, I had no memory of Maskell drugging me. Then, after we lost the lawsuit in 1995, I remembered looking at a white pill in the palm of my hand. Maskell said it was an aspirin, and since I got headaches whenever I was in situations like the one I was walking into, I should take it beforehand. I assume these 'situations' referred to when there was a group of adults waiting on the other side of the door, like the unfolding memory. Because of the upsetting nature of this experience, I vowed never to pursue memories regarding possibly being gang raped.

I had no other memory when drugs were involved until 2017. Since 2015, I would only open an envelope of an adult's picture from my childhood with my therapist present. These photographs sometimes were of individuals I did not recognize, and at other times the photos brought clarity to my memories.

The experience I had one early April afternoon in 2017 was unlike any I had previously. I was looking at a photograph in my therapist's office. After recognizing the man's teeth, my whole body went limp. As I spoke to my therapist, my head lay on my chest. I told her I could not move a finger even if I wanted. My body was paralyzed as if I were drugged, yet I was mentally alert and aware. It took at least 15 minutes before I came out of that state.

Realizing that Maskell used drugs to force me and others to submit to his instructions, I began to experience a whole new degree of rage and disgust. During that time,

---

89 Maskell's unethical and diabolical manipulation of my mind, by using terrorizing and torturous methods, should not cloud what are the many benefits of valuable psychological tools such as hypnosis. With time I came to understand that Maskell was misusing hypnosis for his own benefit by instilling fear, intimidation, and threats. After Mike died in 2007, I went to a trained hypnotherapist to help with my serious phobia of rats. The months-long sessions were not only helpful, but the therapist was respectful and gentle.

I participated in a panel called "Women Courageously Speaking Out—Women of *The Keepers*, May 2017". I was so angry I found myself passionately telling the audience that what happened to us was a crime against humanity. These same techniques were used to beat down the spirit of people in concentration camps or to dehumanize a person in the bonds of slavery. That talk was an amazing step in my health walk, considering how for years I was afraid of expressing my pent-up anger for fear of hurting someone. Letting it go in this positive way felt right.

Years later, I continue to sit with the truth that Maskell drugged me to keep me from reacting 'negatively' to his patrons. When remembering, I not only felt present to every detail going on around me, but I am disgusted and humiliated at being physically positioned for the pleasure of Maskell's 'Johns'. I was engulfed in a terrifying feeling of being totally out of control. I am aware that my soulful plea for help which was pouring from my eyes to the perpetrator before me, was met with the man looking away. At the risk of sounding crude, I have had to accept the fact that I was treated like a piece of meat, not a human being. I have not pursued more memories of being drugged since I know in my heart that it had happened more times than I want to remember. Unfortunately, while I have not pursued further memories, a number of women recall being drugged by Maskell.

Police Involvement

At my second meeting with the Archdiocese in 1992, I presented a list of perpetrators I had remembered. I was embarrassed and ashamed, and innocent to what they expected. Apparently, the Church representatives were not pleased to receive my list of adults. When they heard the names of adults, we later learned from our attorney that they were surprised and disappointed. They thought they were going to get the names of other victims.

The list included a tall black-haired policeman, standing in uniform, while I was being forced to perform fellatio on him. I could not remember the face of the officer, probably because that memory was most disturbing considering my father was a policeman. I came to believe Maskell not only had police involved in his sex abuse ring for his protection, but he also used policemen in uniform as part of his brainwashing techniques.

I had no other memories involving policemen until May of 2017. By then, believing there were no more pictures of people who could possibly trigger any memories, I sat down for the first time to view a section of *The Keepers* with Sarah, Ryan, and Jess present. During a segment where an older man named James Scannell was being interviewed, I saw a photo of him years earlier, wearing a police uniform. I found myself sitting in my bathroom repeating, "Turn it off, turn it off!" A part of me knew that man, but my mind was blank and numb. It took a while for me to calm down. It would take weeks for the whole memory to unfold and years to work through my feelings pertaining to what that man and Maskell did to me.[90]

I remembered shortly after Cathy was found murdered, I was sitting in the chaplain's office after school. Maskell was standing guard by the door to the hall, and a man was sitting in street clothes across the desk from me. He said he was a policeman, and he did not want to wear his uniform, claiming he could get in trouble if seen talking with me without arresting me for what I had done. He showed me

---

90 "'I knew him for many years, and for about ten of them he was the Baltimore County Police Department chaplain,' says former Baltimore County Police Capt. James B. Scannell, now 73 and retired. 'Father Maskell loved to ride around in our police cars, and more than once he rode with me. He was a wonderful priest and a loyal friend.'...Retired Baltimore County Police Capt. James L. Scannell says he has never forgotten finding the nun's body on the frozen field that day. 'I remember her blue coat, and the purse nearby,' says...Scannell, who spent 37 years as a county police officer before retiring in 1992." "Who Killed Sister Cathy," by Tom Nugent, *Baltimore City Paper*, January 5, 2005; https://www.baltimoresun.com/citypaper/bcpnews-who-killed-sister-cathy-one-of-maryland-s-coldest-murder-cases-heats-up-20170504-story.html.

several 8 x 10 black and white photos. The man said I killed Cathy and caused her to look like this.[91]

At some point my attention was drawn to the breeze-way door. I saw the man I later recognized in *The Keepers* standing in his police uniform. As Maskell stood by the hallway door, the man who showed me the pictures came from behind the desk, walked me by my arm over to the policeman by the breezeway door, telling me to show him what I wanted to do to my father. He forced me to my knees before the uniformed officer. As he literally began pushing my head back and forth, physically forcing me to perform fellatio on the officer, he squatted down next to me to watch. While pushing my head he repeated in my ear, "Oh my God! That's what you want to do to your father?"

Suddenly, I collapsed on the floor and cried hysterically. Maskell came over, wanting to know what was going on. He was asking the officers what they did, but they could not get me to calm down. Maskell quickly ushered the men out the door to the breezeway, then called the Vice Principal for help.

When she came into the room I was still crying, curled up in the middle of the office floor. Maskell told her we were working on some of my issues, and it got too upsetting for me. The Vice Principal helped me up off the floor, sat me down, got me a drink of water, and helped calm me down. Once she could see I was calmer, she sent me home. I can remember the feeling of pulling myself together as I walked home late that afternoon.

What those men did that day was destroy any possibility of me ever telling my father what they were doing to me. I was disgusted and terrified when they told me I wanted to do this to my dad, another police officer. The schism between me and my father was complete. I believe that was one of Maskell's goals.

---

91   In 1993, I told the police of a memory I had of being shown 8 x 10 black and white photographs of Cathy's body when she was found, likening them to crime scene photos. The trauma of this experience has blocked any memory of the contents of what I saw in those photos. It is clear the main point of my interaction with those men that afternoon was to traumatize me by making me look at Cathy in that state.

I remember James Scannell, the policeman interviewed in *The Keepers*, being involved in Maskell's sex abuse ring on at least three different occasions. One of those times he was with two other officers. One was a policeman named Bob Zimmerman, but I have not yet remembered the other officer. I have no other memory of the policeman who showed me the 8 x 10 crime scene photos, just the sense that he was there to terrorize me. Even though I continue to remember other police involvement, I still do not have a face for the uniformed policeman I told the Archdiocese about in 1992.

Postscript

For years, I would say that Maskell was a genius. Mike would become upset when I said that and exclaim "Don't give him that power. He was not a genius; he was just a pervert posing as a therapist." (While Mike was an experienced contractor, he had a bachelor's degree, having majored in psychology.) In 2019, I learned that a project run by the CIA from the 1950s until 1975, MK-Ultra, used hypnosis, psychological manipulation, terror, and drugs to erase the memories of the subjects of the experiments.[92] The government issued grants to psychiatrists and psychologists in universities to conduct the experiments. There is no evidence that Maskell was associated with MK-Ultra. However, when I read about the project in 2019, it dawned on me that Maskell, who was a psychology graduate student, could very well have understood the ways in which mind-control techniques, hypnosis, terror, and drugs could be effective in erasing or suppressing the memories of what had happened to a victim of abuse. The techniques Maskell was using were not novel, and I began to appreciate Mike's comment that there was nothing special about Maskell as a professional psychologist, except that he was evil, incredibly unethical, and perverted.

---

92 https://www.history.com/topics/us-government/history-of-mk-ultra.

CHAPTER NINETEEN

Piecing Cathy Together

In 1992, I had two meetings with the Archdiocese of Balti-more. I was asked to give a statement of what I remembered about the abuse at Keough by Maskell and Magnus. The Archdiocese told me that unless I gave them the name of another classmate, i.e., a survivor as opposed to an abuser, there was nothing they could do but allow Maskell to resume his pastoral duties.

So, I called my friend Maria in early 1993; she was a good friend and former classmate at Keough. I wanted to meet over lunch to discuss whether anyone ever told her about inappropriate behavior by a priest at the school. Maria brought another woman who was also a classmate, thinking she might know something. I told them that I was remembering a priest abusing me in high school, but I did not give any details. We talked and they shared a few things. Our classmate remembered that it was mandatory for students to have one session with Maskell, the school chaplain. From her session, she remembered that he was creepy, and she distinctly recalled hearing the 'click of the door' when she left. I had not shared any of my memories with either of them before or after the three of us met.

Maria brought a 1969 and a 1971 yearbook for me to borrow; our graduation year was 1971. As she began leafing through the 1969 edition, she pointed out Sister Cathy Cesnik. Sister Cathy's picture was not in my 1971 yearbook since her last year at Keough was 1969.

As we were talking about Cathy and others in the year-books, I could feel something stirring in me. I did not know Sister Cathy, but I was uneasy about having viewed her photo. When I got home, I felt restless, like something was not right. I went to bed with feelings like when the memories of abuse at Keough began surfacing the year prior.[93] Looking in the mirror the next morning, I kept saying to myself, "I loved her, and I killed her."

But I did not want to explore surfacing memories on this day; this was the second day my birth family was meeting to discuss how our uncle's abusive behavior impacted our lives. My uncle was not only sexually abusive to me; he was also physically and emotionally abusive toward some of the other children. The meeting had been organized by other siblings solely to discuss the impact the abuse had on the whole family and what we wanted to do.

The feeling of dread that I had loved and killed Cathy Cesnik was consuming me. Halfway through our meeting, I could not keep my feelings contained. I went to the bathroom, broke down, and told Kass what I was remembering. When we returned, the topic of the meeting changed immediately.

For nine months, only a few of my siblings knew I was remembering the abuse at Keough. My family now learned that I was not only abused by Maskell and Magnus, but the meeting culminated with me leaning on my brother, Ed, and crying repeatedly, "I killed her! I killed her!" That was the first memory I had of Cathy Cesnik.

After that weekend, my therapies intensified, the investigation around the cold case murder of Cathy Cesnik was reopened, and more traumatic memories surfaced. These nightmarish memories came involuntarily from the depths of my being, as though I were vomiting them from my mind and body. As I became aware of the facts around Cathy's murder, and due to the intense conditioning and brainwashing by Maskell, I believed I was responsible for her death.

Shortly after seeing Cathy's picture in the yearbook, I remembered going into her classroom at the end of the school year to get a book.[94] I did not think she had been my

---

93 See "The Pressure Rises (Vignette)," page 53.
94 See "The Keough Years," page 17.

teacher, so my adult mind questioned why I was going to that room. I also could not understand how, in my memory, Cathy was so seamlessly communicating with my younger self, as though she knew me. Nevertheless, what was clear was that she cared enough to address me by saying she would 'take care of' stopping the abuse. The memory was clear, and yet it was impossible to add to it or understand it until more experiences surfaced or unfolded. My ongoing inner work, along with a variety of therapies, helped me gain insight and some clarity around who Cathy Cesnik was to me.

In 2016, many years after first seeing Cathy's photo in the yearbook, I was participating in the filming of *The Keepers*. One of the things I brought to the project were the boxes of papers I collected from when I first began remembering the abuse at Keough in 1992. For the two years I had been working with Ryan and Jess, these papers had been reviewed with a fine-tooth comb, or so I thought.

Late one evening, after filming was finished, Ryan, Jess and I were sitting around my dining room table. We were going through the papers one more time and were about to schedule another meeting.

I then noticed my high school report cards at the bottom of the box. I never noticed them before. I pulled out four original report cards, one per grade level; these were given to me years earlier by my mother. Jess asked if she could see them. While I was putting papers back in the box, Jess, who had been looking at the cards, looked at me and said, "You had Sister Joanita." I asked, "Who's that?" She responded, "That's Cathy Cesnik."

I went into a full panic attack. I could not breathe, I had to put my head between my knees. My brain could not compute how I could have had her of all people for a teacher and not known it. I understood blocking information like this before 1992, but it was 23 years since I recognized Cathy's picture. She had been my teacher?!

It was unusual for people to see me this out of control, so Jess and Ryan were frantically trying to help in whatever way they could. As they looked more closely at the card, they said it must have been another nun who took the same saint's name, which is a common practice among religious orders. They assumed this because the dates on the report card were 1969-1970, and Cathy was not teaching at Keough during that year. The thought that we had made a mistake helped me calm down. I then laid my report cards on the table and noticed that there was an error. The dates on the cards stated: freshman 1967-1968, sophomore 1969-1970, junior 1969-1970, senior 1970-1971.[95] The dates on my sophomore card should have been 1968-1969. Cathy had approached me at the end of my sophomore year, which was her last year at Keough. So, this 'Sister Joanita' on my report card was in fact Cathy Cesnik and the indicated dates were wrong. Once again, I began panicking. Not knowing what to do, Jess and Ryan just stayed with me until I calmed down.

For days after discovering I had Cathy as a teacher, I walked around in a state of shock. On June 1, 2016, working to move forward and come out from the fog and confusion, I created a mandala or a sacred space to pour all of my paralyzing feelings into. Solid purple represented those feelings, along with the thick dense confusion I now felt. Under the mandala I wrote, "Defusing those feelings helped lift the numbing shock."

Through the next few months, more memories opened that had been locked away. They came in that pattern of my involuntarily remembering one after another. Three were of me coming late to her class. The first time she asked, "Where have you been?" and when I did not answer she looked at me and asked, "Are you okay?" and when I still did not answer she said, "take a seat." The second time Cathy said, "This cannot go on. Why are you late?" When I did not answer, she said, "Are you sure you're okay?" No answer, then "Take a seat, but this has to stop." The third time she did not go through all of that. She asked, "Are you okay?" and when I did not answer, she said, "I want to see you after class." After class, she asked me for the real reason I was late, but I still did not answer. She then asked again, "Are you okay?" and when I once again did not answer she said, "You need to be at class on time. So please, make a point to do that."[96] Now, I can see that Cathy was trying to get me into a setting where I would confide in her.

The fourth memory was some time before Cathy approached me at the end of my sophomore year. I was knocking on the Chaplain's door. Suddenly, Sister Cathy was behind me saying, "Jeannie, I didn't know you needed these services." My body became as stiff as the door I was knocking on. I stared straight ahead, terrified that Maskell would see her, and think I had talked to her. Every fiber in my being was screaming "Go away!" Maskell opened the door, stared down at me, then moved aside so I could enter the room. Cathy said, "I didn't know Jeannie needed counseling." He responded, "Yes, it's been very beneficial...very effective." and closed the door with Sister Cathy still standing there.[97]

Remembering these personal experiences from school is extremely important to me. With all the work I had already done regarding Cathy, I still had no internal foundational knowledge of her. I did not know her as a teacher, mentor, or friend, and I had no recollection of being in her classroom other than this handful of memories.

While still piecemeal, these new memories helped make more sense of my past. I knew Maskell told me to be at his office at a certain time on a recurring day. Because I remember coming late to her class so often, I now suspect that my time for 'counseling' with Maskell was right before Cathy's class. I was also able to understand more clearly my exchange with Cathy on that last day of school.[98] I could

---

96   Journal entry dated July 5, 2016.
97   Journal entry dated July 5, 2016.
98   See "The Keough Years," page 17.

never figure out why I went into that classroom to get a book, but now I know it was my classroom for the year.

Cathy had knowledge of things that I thought nobody knew about. She was asking me questions on that day because she had been watching me and trying to figure out what was going on. So, when she started to ask why I did not like school and I did not want to answer, she said that was fine: "I'll ask questions and you nod your head yes or no." Sister Cathy knew I was not going to say a word. She had tried that all year, so she cared enough that she was willing to approach the situation differently. By asking the questions in a new way, I could nod my head, and in a roundabout way ask for help.

Then I remembered something else from early in my junior year. I was standing at my locker in the middle of a crowded hallway. As I looked over, I saw Cathy at the far end of the hall, surrounded by girls. Cathy was looking at me. I can only assume she came back to Keough to visit or retrieve some of her belongings. I stood at the locker, feeling disappointed and rejected. I had already begun pushing down the pain of being abandoned and fooled by Cathy. Seeing her standing in the hall, enjoying the other girls, brought these feelings up with a force that made me turn and run. I had to get away from her prying eyes.

To this day I only know Cathy by piecing together what others have shared, and what I have remembered since 1993. For years, I could only tell my family, the police, church officials and the public somewhat disjointed and quite painful memories of Sister Cathy. The memories come at their own pace, sometimes triggered by external stimuli, or touched into during my inner work. With this trigger, everything shifts, memories surface, become focused, and I have a moment of clarity.

While my classmates, as well as Cathy's friends and family, began talking more about their fun and inspiring memories of her, I felt disconnected from the friendly and talented woman they spoke about. At first, I felt embarrassed and ashamed that I could not remember this side of her. But I now understand that I was just as connected to Cathy, even though we all met her through different experiences.

To survive, I repressed not only my experiences, but also a variety of emotions which I felt as a teenager toward her. Taking time to learn more about what I endured as an abuse victim at Keough helped me feel connected to my young self. I needed to feel that connection to understand the anger I held as a teen toward Cathy for naïvely confronting Maskell by herself.

Even today, I can feel that young girl's love for Cathy, but it is intertwined with terror and anger—anger at her for recklessly exposing me to an even more enraged and out of control Maskell. When he punished me for talking to 'someone' after I had disclosed the abuse to Cathy, it only got worse, and I had to fend for myself.[99] I understand that Cathy thought by addressing Maskell he would stop his abusive activities. My persona, Jeannie, knew from experience that she was wrong.

During my junior year, Maskell took me to see Cathy Cesnik's dead body. As this horrific memory unfolded in my adult body in 1993, I felt overwhelmed with the weight of indescribable emotions.[100] There I was, kneeling before the body of the woman who was going to save me, and the man breathing down my neck was the person who stopped her. In those moments, a part of myself laid down beside Cathy. That child stayed paralyzed in that spot until I could eventually go back to get her.

My work at finding and integrating Jeannie into myself has made it possible for me to sort out the emotions that are connected to my recovered memories. The pain and anger of Jeannie's feelings of abandonment and deception still surface in me today. But those feelings are now mixed with appreciation, sadness, and guilt. In September 2016, I journaled this moment of awareness from the heart of Jeannie:

---

99 See "The Keough Years," page 17.
100 Journal entry dated February 14, 1993.

How Was I to Know

If it weren't for her
I wouldn't be here.
If she had stayed quiet
I wouldn't be here.
If she intended to leave me in the dark
I wouldn't be here.
Leave me alone!
Go away!
Mind your own business!
Save me, please...
How was I to know, I was her business?
Too intense after she was gone.
They were so afraid of the light.
"Stamp out every ember."
Nothing left to do
but go deep,
deep within.
How was I to know, the depth would save me?
If it weren't for her
I wouldn't be here.

As an adult I see that uncovering and carefully piecing together these segments of my past has helped me appreciate Cathy's presence in my life. I now understand that Cathy was observant, courageous, determined, extremely creative, and most importantly, she cared. She was with me in those moments immediately after I was abused. She was not afraid to look into my dazed eyes, pull me to the side, and ask the hard questions. I was not invisible to Cathy Cesnik. I am sure she was not the only teacher who had girls come into their classroom looking spaced out—girls like me who had dissociated and could not pull themselves together in time for the next thing on their schedule. The difference was Cathy not only saw me and cared about me, but she had the courage to try and help. By doing this, she planted a seed of truth deep within me that would lay dormant for many years.

In 1992, when I began to remember the abuse, that tiny seed began to germinate, stirring a faint memory that someone once thought that what others were doing to me was not right, that I did not deserve to be treated this way, and that there was something about me worth caring for. This faint awareness brought an ember of hope that this just might be true.

CHAPTER TWENTY

Mediation or Nothing Changes

I learned in 2015, through Teresa Lancaster's interview on Inside Baltimore with Tom Nugent, that the Church was willing to mediate cases of the survivors of the Keough abuse. My first thought was to use this opportunity to take my power back. That power was taken from me during high school by the clergy, and by Church officials and the courts after I came forward in 1992. I hoped that by mediating, I could finally shake the dust off my feet and walk away feeling a bit more empowered. I thought I was done with them when I left Keough, and then again after the court case.

But here was an opportunity for me to tell the Church how my life, and the lives of so many around me, had been ruined or dramatically and negatively shaken. I saw the process as a chance for the priests and bishops to take responsibility for what happened on their watch at Keough. After Teresa and I lost our appeal in 1997, the Church had virtually no legal exposure because the statute of limitations would bar any suit, so their coming clean seemed like a possibility. I thought that if the Church hierarchy wanted to mediate, then perhaps they were looking to the survivors for ideas as to what would be of benefit to them and their families. I thought of the Catholic moms, who had approached me through the years, that had Maskell baptize their babies. They were very worried that their children's souls were not pure, causing some to have their grown children rebaptized.[101] I thought the Church was ready to

---

101 Baptism serves as the first sacrament one receives when entering the Catholic faith. It is a sacrament of initiation (which you can only receive one time), meaning once you received it, you officially enter into the body of Christ, the Catholic Church.

be accountable to their parishioners and openly help them with these soulful burdens they now carried.

I wanted the Church to take out an ad in our local newspapers taking responsibility for what happened at Keough and stating that Joseph Maskell is 'known' by the Church to have been a sexual predator of children—not just 'credibly accused' as first stated in the 2002 Bishop's Accountability list.[102] This list, made public in 2002, included Joseph Maskell, who had died on May 7, 2001.

For the mediations, I retained Joanne Suder and Sheldon Jacobs, the same attorneys that represented many of the Keough survivors. Nine of my close friends and family shared how all of this had affected them in letters forwarded to the Archbishop, Church lawyers, and the mediator. Not one of us has heard anything pertaining to those letters, leaving us to wonder if anyone ever actually read them.

There were two parts to the mediation. At the preliminary meeting, I spent two hours outlining what I suffered at Keough, as well as what my experience was in 1992 when I went to the Church for help, overwhelmed with abusive memories. By sharing all my experiences, and naming the people involved during my years at Keough, I thought I might corroborate the statements of the survivors of Maskell who were also mediating. Unfortunately, as the process unfolded, it became clear to me that the Archdiocese was not interested in what I had to say.

When I completed my statement, one of the Archdiocesan lawyers had two or three questions or statements for me. One thing he stated was that in 1992 I was encouraged to report the abuse to the police, and I chose not to. I told him I had no recollection of that occurring. What I did remember was the Church representatives strongly encouraging me to

---

The recipient receives justifying and sanctifying grace when baptized, and the Holy Spirit begins to dwell within them. "The Ultimate Guide to Catholic Baptism," by Shelby Mayer, *Ascension: The Faith Formation Leader*, November 7, 2020; https://media.ascensionpress.com/2020/11/07/the-ultimate-guide-to-catholic-baptism/.

102 *The Baltimore Sun*, Sept. 2002; https://www.bishop-accountability.org/resources/resource-files/databases/BaltimorePriests.htm.

make a formal statement to the Archdiocese, but absolutely nothing about contacting the police.[103]

Here is the statement which I gave at the end of the preliminary meeting on April 27, 2016:

> I believe the Archdiocese was harboring a crime ring headed by a master criminal. Maskell, Magnus and others were free to do these evil, dehumanizing, and despicable acts under the umbrella of the Archdiocese. These sex abuse crimes happened on the Archdiocese's watch, so that institution or corporation should be held accountable.
>
> Twenty-four years ago, while Maskell was still an active priest, the church had a chance to bring these atrocities to light. They had a choice to:
>
> (1) Shine a light on this evil by going public, begging all the victims (families included) for forgiveness, do penance, and create the environment for reconciliation; or
> (2) Not shine a light on the truth, keep the horrors contained, instill fear, hide behind the law, spend millions to keep the statute of limitations intact to avoid spending millions to help heal the past harm to the innocent victims and the community of believers, thereby continuing the silence.
>
> Silence is just a tool to keep the secrets. It is extremely powerful and effective.
>
> Martin Luther King said, "In the end we will remember not the words of our enemies but the Silence of our friends."

---

103 I later checked with my sister Kass, who was at those early meetings with me and Mike. She too had no memory of Woy or Ms. Hoskins, the Church lawyer, suggesting I talk to the police. We agreed that if that had been suggested we would have talked with our dad, a retired police officer. In 1992, he was aware of the memories I was experiencing pertaining to Magnus and Maskell.

In 1992 I believed the church I knew would choose to shine light on the truth. I was devastated when the big business, or the power behind the church, chose to stay in the shadows. Because of that choice, I hold the Archdiocese totally responsible for all of the pain and suffering each innocent victim, myself included, has endured.

What may have started at the hands of Joseph Maskell and others, has been allowed to continue into the present.

After the preliminary meeting, I felt uplifted and proud of myself. Internally, I was shouting, "I did it!" My kids and I went to visit Mike's gravesite to celebrate with him. He would have been so proud of me!

The second meeting was the actual mediation when the Church would decide, among other things, how much money they were willing to give me—and I would decide if I would accept it. A mediator was present at this meeting. I intentionally agreed to meet on November 1, All Saint's Day, which is a Catholic holy day. I did so in honor of Cathy Cesnik. I expected nothing, but I hoped the Church would be open to thinking of compassionate ways to comfort the survivors, and not just throw token money at us.

At both meetings I sat across from two Archdiocesan lawyers, while a Church representative sat at the end of the table away from me. They began by saying Archbishop Lori sent his personal apology, and he would meet with me if I desired.

Later, after signing the mediation agreement, I wondered why Lori was apologizing.[104] Was he just apologizing that

---

104 Although common language in legal agreements, referring to the abuse as merely 'alleged', was used 21 times in the *Settlement and Release Agreement*, I, as a survivor, took this as another denial of accountability.

Maskell had done what I alleged? Well, that was not the issue at that point in time; the issue was the Church's actions. In 1992, when I met with the Church representatives, they told me they had no corroboration, but we now know they did. Maskell had a history of perpetrating child sexual abuse, and the Church knew he was a predator. Despite having this knowledge, the Church:

- discarded me and my family, providing no pastoral counseling after I began disclosing the breadth of the criminal sexual abuse ring at Keough;
- destroyed the spiritual foundation supporting me, my parents, and my siblings;
- publicly portrayed me as being somehow 'confused' about what I alleged; and
- allowed their lawyers to mock me as not only confused, but possibly crazy.

The issue here was not Maskell. The issue here was that the Church allowed Maskell to do what he did, and they covered up his predatory actions while moving him from position to position. They silenced, discredited, or ignored those who tried to expose him. They were complicit.

But Lori was not apologizing for the actions of the Church. He stood behind the veil of referencing Maskell as just a bad apple. He was portraying himself and the Archdiocese as compassionate and generous parties, giving their time and limited funds, even though they would like us to believe they did not know about Maskell's years of predatory activities until much later. According to them, other than employing Maskell, they had no idea of what happened to me or all the other survivors. Apologize only for Maskell and not for what the Archdiocese did to me and so many other victims? That is a hollow apology, akin to 'Mistakes were made'. I did not want, nor could I stomach, such an apology.

The two matters the Church lawyers would discuss at the mediation were the amount to be paid for the settlement, and funds for therapy. As we moved into our fifth hour of negotiating, it was becoming obvious that any additions to the final agreement were being earmarked for payments for therapy. I told my lawyer I would prefer the funds be put into a lump amount, but it was apparent this was not the way these mediations worked. Instead, it felt as if we had reached the Archdiocese's maximum settlement amount and there was no changing it.

I then decided to accept the church's final financial offer if Archbishop Lori said a mass in honor of Cathy Cesnik. I thought her family and the Facebook grassroots community might want that opportunity. The Church lawyers responded that they do not negotiate masses. I could not believe my ears and asked the mediator to readdress it with their lawyers. I told him to tell the lawyers this was a clear sign that these mediations were devoid of a true pastoral presence and accented the emptiness of the Archbishop's apology. The lawyers finally agreed to ask the Archbishop to say a mass and I agreed to their final amount.[105]

The Archdiocese refused to accept my request that they run an ad in the newspapers about Joseph Maskell, which I believed could have compassionately brought about accountability and reconciliation. Their only goal appeared to be in keeping their pre-determined range of a payout to a minimum.

After a five-and-a-half-hour mediation, my children and I were exhausted and disheartened. We agreed that the amount to be paid was sad and insulting. The least the Archdiocese could have done was suggest, or not shut down, a discussion of ways it could show genuine atonement and reconciliation. That would have made the tedious exchange with their lawyers over this amount of money somewhat more tolerable. We went home deflated.

---

105 The Archdiocesan representative asked Cathy's family if they wanted a mass and they said no. There was a mass said in honor of Cathy's 70th birthday; it was orchestrated by her family and friends, not the Archdiocese.

The next day I went to Mike and Matthew's gravesite with John, the cameraperson, to read Mike my final mediation statement since it appeared to fall on deaf ears at the meeting. John went into the trees to film, while I sat on Mike's grave. I began to read to him: "I entered into this mediation with the Archdiocese with two of my heart's desires in mind. One was justice for all innocent victims, me and Cathy Cesnik included. The other was to take back the power the Church took from me—not 45 years ago (that is ongoing), but 24 years ago, when I began remembering this crime against me at Joseph Maskell's and other perpetrators' hands."

As I continued to read to Mike, I began to cry, feeling a multitude of emotions washing through me. Sitting against his gravestone and holding a very wet paper in my hands, I finished my statement to Mike, saying, "Innocent victims of your congregations and their families need to hear their church officials simply say publicly that these accusations against Joseph Maskell are true. They need to hear their church leaders take some responsibility for these sex offenders, considering as their employers, these atrocities happened on your watch."

I sobbed through the entire reading, now understanding that my message summarized what my past and present hopes had been for truth and reconciliation within the Church I once knew. Because of the Church leaders' lack of presence, accountability, and compassion, I was finally shaking the dust from my feet and walking away from the Catholic Church.[106] As I ended this part of my health walk, I was grieving and needed to be with Mike, the man who lovingly encouraged me to trust myself.

When I thought I had no more tears to cry, I walked to the car. John, who had witnessed my raw grief from a distance, put his camera down, turned to me, and hugged me. More tears flowed while, like Mike, John held me up until I could

---

106 "And if any place will not welcome you or listen to you, leave that place, and shake the dust off your feet as a testimony against them." (Mark 6:11 NIV.)

feel the ground back under my feet. The compassion this man showed me in those few minutes was greater than anything I experienced over the years with the Archdiocese and the legal system.

Later that day I journaled:

> Today is the day after the final part of mediating with the AOB. I thought I'd feel light, airy, and relieved. Instead, I feel sad, dirty, devalued, and disappointed. I can't really say fully what I feel or how it came to this kind of end. I knew all along it would be very empty on the AOB's part, but I didn't realize I would feel completely empty inside. I don't know what to do to change this. I can only let this feeling move through me at its own pace.

> I always think I'll feel better, less stressed, whenever I do these things outside of my safe space that take a lot of energy, strength, and courage. It never does. This was no different. I have to work with how I feel, so it can make more sense and I can feel lighter down the road. I'm doing the best I can and will continue, one step at a time. Right now, the numbness is wearing off and the emotions are releasing and moving through me. My mind is also beginning to engage with aspects of myself, thinking through what I feel and think on a body, mind, and spirit level about what just occurred. I'm exhausted!

One final detail to be negotiated within the few days after the mediation was the transfer of the allotted money negotiated for therapy. I wanted the therapy amount to be added to the total settlement amount or placed into a health savings account. The Church denied my request. They wanted to handle the disbursement of the funds and approve any payments to be made. This was unacceptable to me and contrary to the Church's explicitly stated position. The communications director for the Archdiocese at that time had specifically said that one option for survivors "who wish to have nothing to do with the Church and/or who would prefer to be in control of their own healing, [was to] offer them a one-time financial payment..."[107] I wanted the Church out of my life, and I did not want them being involved in my healing process this late in the game, and implicitly taking credit for my therapy. The Archdiocese would not agree; so, I took the final settlement amount, but left future therapy money on the table. I also left on the table any hope for true reconciliation.

I was naïve when I went to the Church for counseling and comfort in 1992. I was primarily seen by the Archdiocese as the person providing an opportunity for the Church to get Maskell out of its hair, thereby minimizing any further potential damage to the institution. Unfortunately, things have not changed. The Archbishop and his minions used the mediations as a public relations ploy, attempting to show how generous they were in doling out what amounted to a pittance compared to the trauma inflicted on so many women, men, and their families. Everything to them— everything—is still transactional, and reducible to a crass exchange of token money to the devastated victims so the Church can avoid moral and legal responsibility.

And not once did they ask us what we, the survivors, wanted. Yet when survivors demand transparency, open records, and accountability, we are met with silence. It sickens and angers me.

But this anger feels healthy. While I still feel terror at the memories of what happened in Maskell's office, I am not intimidated by the Church because I know I have told the truth and they have not. Nevertheless, after being on the opposite side of the Church, I also have a healthy fear of its hierarchy, the big business behind the altar.

They had an opportunity in 1992 to do the right thing and confess their part in knowingly allowing a predatory pedophile free access with their charge, the children of the

---

107 "Baltimore Archdiocese agrees to $50,000 Settlement with Clergy Sex-Abuse Victim Who Said She Was Shown Body of Murdered Nun," by Tom Nugent, *Inside Baltimore*, January 2017; https://insidebaltimore.org/.

Church. Unfortunately, they chose to stay silent. By staying silent, they are responsible for all the victims abused by Maskell before and after 1992.

CHAPTER TWENTY-ONE

Forgiveness

The Catechism of the Catholic Church taught us that the Apostles' Creed was our statement of faith, which was said at every mass and at the start of each rosary. In the Apostles' Creed, Catholics express their faith in, among other things:

> the holy Catholic Church,
> the communion of saints,
> the forgiveness of sins,
> the resurrection of the body,
> and life everlasting.

According to the Vatican, this prayer "associates faith in the forgiveness of sins...with faith in the...Church and in the communion of saints. It was when Jesus gave the Holy Spirit to his apostles that the risen Christ conferred on them his own divine power to forgive sins: 'Receive the Holy Spirit. If you forgive the sins of any, they are forgiven; if you retain the sins of any, they are retained.'"[108]

Forgiveness is an action that can bring great peace, but it can also be used as a weapon wielding guilt. It was rooted in my faith system, and seeking forgiveness was the beginning of the abuse I suffered throughout high school. I went to confession with Magnus as I was taught by the Church. Unfortunately, Maskell and Magnus, the so-called 'apostles of Christ', decided they would rather use my guilt and shame against me, instead of freeing me from it, telling me I was unforgivable.

---

108 Catechism of the Catholic Church, quoting and explaining the Gospel of John the Apostle, 20:21-23; https://www.vatican.va/archive/ENG0015/__P2D.HTM.

And when I disclosed the abusive acts in 1992, nothing about the process felt like representatives of the Catholic Church saw a need to be forgiven for harboring such men as Maskell and Magnus. Rather, I felt like I was seen as a liar, or possibly crazy, until I could prove differently. The authorities' insensitive skepticism, at times wrapped in silence, only served to widen the schism between the adult me and my inner child. I believed that others who heard the disgusting acts that had been buried deep within me would also believe I was unforgivable.

There was no room to consider forgiving myself, much less anyone else, like my abusers. It has taken me decades to accomplish some level of forgiveness, not for the perpetrators but for myself. I think this is the most important and hardest part of my healing.

As I struggled to forgive the child within me who did literally whatever she had to do to survive, I simultaneously felt no need to forgive Maskell for anything he did to me. As a young girl, Maskell held a place of power in my life and in my community because he was a priest. I believed I was the one at fault and deserved everything done to me. My faith system placed him in that position of power, but it was Maskell who used that power and our mutual Catholic faith to make me believe I was at fault. This was only intensified as he proceeded to rape my body, mind, and soul.

After my story came out in *The Keepers*, a few strangers and acquaintances wondered if I had forgiven Maskell and other perpetrators and the Church, sounding at times as if that was more important than the horrors done to me. My response was straightforward and honest: "I hate Maskell and Tom, and I am mainly concerned with forgiving the young child within me."

This response regarding Tom came about in the early 1980s once I remembered him sexually assaulting me as a little girl. I was Catholic when I remembered this. I struggled with the question of how I was to forgive a man whom I deeply hated, especially since this was the first time I felt hate for another person. But I was also numb with blame, shame, and disgust toward myself for letting those things happen to me. I discovered that saying the words, 'I forgive' did not make forgiveness happen.

These memories of Tom surfaced out of my quiet, when I ardently prayed for a miracle to free me from the nightmare I was living. Unfortunately, I experienced a difficult process of remembering, feeling, and working through what happened when I was very young. At that time, I could not conceive of forgiving Tom, so I chose to let God know that I hated Tom and if that meant I would go to hell, I was fine with that. That was the only way I could move beyond the wall of guilt I hit when I discovered the strong feelings I had buried against another person and myself.

However, ten years later, when I began to remember the abuse at the hands of Maskell and Magnus, I lost my faith in a god and any of the religious guidelines constructed by the male-dominated Catholic hierarchy. I was in the middle of processing horrific memories and was focused on the perpetrators who had embraced cruelty and their calculated torture. It seemed absurd to even entertain the idea of forgiveness.

Some encouraged me to forgive the abusers since many of the abusers were dead, and I might find peace through forgiveness. This is a nice sentiment. However, Tom, Maskell and other predators who are dead and buried continue to take up space in my body and mind. The freedom that is evolving, through the integration process within my soul, has brought about an awakening of righteous anger—not forgiveness. Instead of spending wasteful energy on trying to forgive abusers and criminals, I continue to choose to work on forgiving the little girl within me.

In 2009, while in the middle of a writing sabbatical, my persona, Frances, freely shared her feelings about forgiveness, through journaling:

I Forgive Myself

I forgive myself for…
What others did to me.
What others made me feel like.
What others made me believe.
What others made me do.
What I have done to survive.
What others did to silence me.

I forgive myself for…
Being afraid~
Being very afraid~
when I needed to be strong
for me.

I forgive myself
for being human.

I remember as the adult being surprised by these words. I felt what I said at that time seemed ridiculous given what had happened to me and what I had done. But even if the words were just an inner longing at that time, I feel the truth of them even more so now.

The more I embraced the truth of what happened, the more I could forgive myself. And as I learn to accept my past and love myself, Tom's and Maskell's presence and power in my life diminishes. I can disengage from them and chisel away at the boulder of guilt their actions put on my shoulders. Eventually, I understood what Frances was writing; I realized there was no need to forgive myself for anything done to me. I recalled Maya Angelou's words, "At fifteen, life had taught me undeniably that surrender, in its place, was as honorable as resistance, especially if one had no choice."[109] But that was different from forgiving those

---

109 "300 Maya Angelou Quotes That Will Blow Your Mind by Maxime Lagace," November 3, 2017; https://wisdomquotes.com/maya-angelou-quotes/#courage.

who abused me and those who covered up the abuse and shirked their responsibility.

Forgiveness does not flow from faith, as stated in the Catechism; rather, forgiveness flows from truth. Just as I needed to understand the truth of what happened before reaching the question of forgiving myself, so too does the Church need to come to its own reckoning with the truth and be held accountable before it can expect any discussion of forgiveness.

For example, the Church has been resisting full disclosure of the records pertaining to clerical sexual predators, including Joseph Maskell. If a pedophile priest's records are not disclosed, and his confession of a sexual crime against the child is exempt "due to regard for the seal of the Sacrament of Penance" as specified at the U.S. Conference of Catholic Bishops, survivors are likely to remain silent out of guilt and fear.[110] More importantly, communities would be safer if the names of hidden clerical predators, pedophiles who never stop abusing children, like Maskell, were revealed and given a registered sex offender's status.[111] This lack of transparency is strengthened by the Church's continual support of the statute of limitations pertaining to victims of child sexual abuse.[112] Until all the obstacles are removed, the truth will not be known, and it is the truth that allows us as a society to hold the parties responsible and accountable.

The Church should open its records and bring the clerical abusers and the Church itself to justice. This can only occur when we determine the truth and assess accountability. Forgiveness, justice, and accountability all flow from truth.

---

110 "Is the Clergy Required to Report Child Sex Abuse? Not in Some States," by Elaine Povich, *Governing: The Future of States and Localities*, January 2019; https://www.governing.com/archive/sl-clergy-sex-abuse-reporting-states.html.

111 See for example, United States Dept. of Justice: National Sex Offender Public Website; https://www.nsopw.gov/.

112 "In the past ten years, The U.S. Catholic Church spent $10.6 million on lobbyists to prevent victims of clerical sex abuse from suing for damages." NBC News (Digital), June 4, 2019; https://www.nbcnews.com/news/us-news/catholic-church-spent-10-million-lobbyists-fight-stymie-priest-sex-n1013776.

Without justice there can be no reconciliation for all, or forgiveness for the perpetrator or the enabling Church. When this process starts with truth, we begin to repair the systemic damage caused by others' abusive actions and lies, thereby finding communal peace.

In early 2020, I was at a hearing in the Maryland Legislature on a bill to abolish the statute of limitations for civil suits involving child sexual abuse. During the hearing, an expert witness, who also happened to be a survivor of child sexual abuse, was testifying in favor of the bill. One of the delegates asked if she saw room for forgiveness for perpetrators and their enablers. The delegate further asked why there was no sense of forgiveness and 'moving on'. I was stunned, not being sure if the question was more ignorant than insulting, as though it is up to the victims to be strong and compassionate enough to put this all behind us. I felt it was a revictimizing question.

But the witness calmly responded, asking the delegate how survivors were to forgive the abusers and the Church when no one was even acknowledging they did anything wrong. She added that to forgive an abuser does not eliminate a survivor's right to hold a perpetrator accountable for their crime.

We cannot begin the process toward forgiveness until we all accept that clergy child sex abuse is a systemic problem and acknowledge the truth of what happened and who is responsible, then and now. Unless we as a community do this, no one can know the real harm that perpetrators' actions cause the victims, their families, and their extended communities.

Some survivors may need to take their claims of abuse to the court system in order to realize justice. There has also been, and will continue to be, outrage from the community over the actions, or lack of actions, by the Church. For survivors and their families, there is actually a type of justice that occurs when the community shows its outrage at the way religious and civil institutions respond to the victims of clergy sexual abuse. Their reactions validate our painful truth and in turn justify survivors' demands for accountability. This ultimately is what we are looking for from the Church. Whether that decree of accountability and the justice rendered comes from the court or the community, there will not be total justice until all the known facts are revealed.

I am grateful that my process of finding, acknowledging, and working with my own truth is bringing about a deeply transformative forgiveness within myself. Through this process I have learned a valuable lesson: I am responsible for my actions and others are responsible for theirs.

CHAPTER TWENTY-TWO

Mom

During those Silent Years, before I even identified myself as Jane Doe or participated in *The Keepers*, I decided to bring my mother to live with me. In 2012 and 2013, my mother lived in an assisted living facility. Because the facility's assessment of her condition differed from ours, Kass and I knew their effectiveness had come to an end. I offered to bring her into my home if the whole family agreed that it was the best thing to do for her.

In late 2013, we had a family meeting with all ten siblings and spouses. I told them the reason I would offer my home was that Kass and I thought it was best for Mom. Since Mike died, I had more space than I needed for myself, and

Mom could have some privacy given the layout of the condominium. My mother would never have expected or asked for us to do this. She was not the kind of person who made you feel guilty if you did not come to one of the hundreds of meals served at her house.

All my siblings and their spouses agreed to move her to my home and to work together to provide the best care for her. Mom cried with joy when Kass went to her little room at the facility and asked if she wanted to move in with me. She said "Yes! Today?"

Truth is, I loved my mother very much, but I could not feel it. Deep within me, I knew I kept a distance between us, like a moat around a castle. I would do anything for her, yet the emotional space was just something I felt and accepted as normal, like my feelings for Mike during the first years of our marriage.

We moved my mother to my condominium in January 2014. We were told by the medical staff at the assisted living facility that with her 'rapid decline' she may have six months to live. However, immersed in a sea of loving care and surrounded by family and friends, Mom was able to enjoy two years of quality time. We all took shifts to be with her.

For me, having been severely abused and misused by my mother's uncle and the priests of our faith community, there was something simultaneously shifting in me. Once Mom moved in, I slowly became aware of the distance between us on a more conscious level. I liken these times to the process of the stages of a pimple, this being the beginning stage; and it hurts the most. Now that she was on my turf, I gently told her that she might hear me talking directly about what was happening in my life and what had happened in my past pertaining to the abuse. Before this, I seldom spoke about the abuse around her. I knew it upset her. We agreed that I would be respectful, and Mom could always go to her room if she did not want to be a part of a discussion.

My mother thrived on the excellent care she was receiving, but what surprised me was how all that positive energy was also supporting me. I was now having more meaningful conversations with siblings who were coming to the house regularly to help with her care. I continued working at my business, my therapies, and my inner healing work. But it was while my mother was with me that I:

- Heard about the Facebook page created by Gemma Hoskins and Abbie Schaub focusing on who killed Cathy Cesnik;
- Spoke to the police about "Brother Bob";
- Identified myself as Jane Doe in an interview with Tom Nugent; and
- Agreed to participate in *The Huffington Post* article and *The Keepers*.

As 2015 unfolded, I continued to practice using my voice to speak my truth. As I expected, these outer experiences caused tremendous movement within me. By October 2015, as Mom continued to decline, I was becoming uncomfortable with the distance between us. I realized that no matter what I did, I could not breach that divide. This moved me to write my first piece on the Keough Facebook page, posted by Abbie:

October 1, 2015, Post:

Hi! This is my first posting on this wonderful Grassroots site. Between the years of 1967-1971 I was the recipient of a horrible crime, committed by Joseph Maskell. He robbed my body, mind & spirit! The sex abuse, spiritual abuse, terrorizing, conditioning/brainwashing, threatening and physical abuse have ended. We make neat explanations so we can sleep at night...I made it happen, it was so long ago, no worse for wear, still alive, he was celibate and denied sex, etc. He's thought of as lover, protector, father figure, torturer, spiritual counselor, priest, pervert. All the explanations disguise the truth that Joseph Maskell was a criminal. As I care for my

88-year-old mother, 45 years later, I am painfully aware of something very precious that he also robbed me of. He took, deliberately and methodically, my God given right to a deep, trusting relationship with my mom and her right to be there for me. This is something I wrote to try and explain the depth of this horrible crime...

Where Were You?

Tiny + frail, lost in a bed of pillows + "stuff"
"1, 2, 3 up...I got you.
Turn, turn, turn...are you on the pot?"
Where were you?
"You need your nourishment, build energy, that's it...
sleep."
Where were you?
He said you'd disown me.
He said you'd throw me away,
"Out on the street!"
Why couldn't you see beyond my wall of fear?
So much distance, anger + longing
Even as I change you, bathe you, feed you
I feel the wall he created between us.
Each brick a lie, a betrayal, deliberate and connived.
I know it the same as,
I know you're not asleep...just too tired to hold your
eyelids open.
Yet as I still stand behind this wall I ask,
Where were you?
Would you have discarded me like these half-used
tissues + straws?
Would you have believed his lies?
How could you not, I did!
We'll never know, We'll never know...
Turning you on your side, your leg is stiff + sore.
Heating Pad, Tylenol, Sleep
You can't leave me!
How can you leave me standing behind this wall,
Yelling...
Where were you?!

My inner work pertaining to my relationship with Mom was intensifying, like that pimple, now too sore to touch but crying out for relief. Some weeks later, Mom was resting as I took my quiet time. I was suddenly struck with the realization that I was not angry at my mother for not being there for me. I was angry at Maskell. The infectious pimple burst! That was a powerful shift in my consciousness. Until that moment I could not feel anger at Maskell. On a victim level, I had been totally locked into the belief that he was my protector, and my parents were the villains. Realizing this, I burst into tears. I went right to my mom, sat on her bed, and told her I forgave her. She was not to blame, Maskell was. She broke down in tears. As we both cried and hugged, I told her she could go now, I'd be ok.

On Sunday, February 7, 2016, I was settling down to watch a TCM movie with Mom, expecting someone to stop by later in the day. By now she was not responding, and we were basically keeping her comfortable. With the movie playing, I watched my mother sleep that deep, unending sleep. I placed my hand on her heart. Her eyes opened, looking straight up and ahead. I think my dad came to get her. I was startled, and keeping my hand on her heart said, "That's it, just rest." Her breathing slowed. She closed her eyes as I whispered over and over, "Be at peace Mom, it's time to be at peace." Within minutes, she took her last breath with my hand on her heart. She truly was at peace.

At first, I was shocked—did my mom just die? Then slowly I was overwhelmed with the beauty and power of what happened. I have had a lot of time to process that experience. I know my mother and I were connected when I came into this world, but I would never have imagined we would have been so connected as she exited. I have come to believe no matter how the abuse affected my relationship with my mother through the years, in the end Tom, Maskell and the Church would not be a permanent wedge separating the love that bound me and my mother.[113] The moat had disappeared.

---

113 See "Going Back for Frances (Vignette)," page 230.

CHAPTER TWENTY-THREE

Meeting Jeannie (Vignette)

In 2009, I made a commitment to begin writing again. I was going to take a six-month 'sabbatical' to resume journaling and to take my quiet time on a daily basis. On and off since the late 1990s, I felt there was something that I needed to write about, and now that feeling had surfaced again. The abuse at Keough was not widely known, except for what was revealed in the 1995 court trial. I felt a need to share the spiritual and psychological journey I had been on. But since the whole story had not been made public, this was difficult, especially when memories of my own personal experience continued to surface and unfold in bits and pieces.

I began writing daily. I did so with some trepidation; the last time I journaled regularly, the trial court ordered that I turn over my journals to the Church's lawyers. After that experience, I never again felt safe writing from that sacred space. Nevertheless, I felt like I needed to do something to make public what happened to me at Keough and somehow hold all these abusers accountable.

I also felt the familiar inner stirring pertaining to Cathy Cesnik. I was never sure if this meant Cathy was not at peace or I had more inner work to do around our relationship. I found myself thinking, "Cathy has something to say and that's why she's on my mind so much."

The first time I had that feeling was in early 1993, after being triggered by the yearbook picture of Cathy. I was sitting in my sunroom where I saw clients for spiritual direction. As my very first client, Barbara, and I were praying, I felt overwhelmed with what I had been remembering. While in prayer, I felt Cathy place her hand on my left cheek and say, "I told you I would take care of this." With tears in my eyes, I told her, "I didn't think you meant 20 years later." That prayer session in 1993 was the start of my feeling that Cathy Cesnik was not done disclosing the abuse at Keough.

So, in 2009, I decided my writing would be focused on connecting with Cathy. Once I began journaling, I had a clear and direct dialogue with the younger aspects of myself who experienced the abuse in high school. This was surprising, and emotionally stirring. I was the adult talking and listening to myself as a girl as young as 14. The words flowed until I knew we were finished with the dialogue. In fact, the young aspects of myself were dialoguing and struggling with each other as they talked these issues through. I felt at times that I as the adult was a participant, and at other times I was the facilitator. Whichever it was, I just kept moving with it. The talking was more akin to poetry than prose; a young persona wrote through me in late 2009:

As I sit by the chair
I look with eyes
that do not see.
I have fooled them again.
They think they are
looking at me.
Little do they know
I'm not even here.
I've left quite
sometime ago.
My eyes are just
empty pools of jelly
trying not to be found out.
If they knew
they would eat them too.

As the words flowed, I felt the pain, separation, and terror that I had experienced sitting in that room with those perpetrators.

After a couple months of writing, I began to feel the presence of a new aspect of myself as an older high school student. I realized from what she said that this was the part of myself that survived after Cathy Cesnik was murdered.

This new persona taking form told me her name was 'Jeannie'. I was aware, as Jeannie continued to speak, that she sounded angry and petulant, like she was still in high school. She said, "I know you don't like me. Just get on board with the idea that I am in love with him." She was speaking of the man who said he killed Cathy. (Using a certain tone, Jeannie called the man by a nickname, implying familiarity. It stunned and disgusted me. I, however, will continue to refer to him by his pseudonym, "Brother Bob".) Jeannie said that "Brother Bob" told her that he had been in love with her. This teenager told me that she/I had seen this man more than I had currently remembered. She said "Brother Bob" also told her he loved her—ME!—and that I should just get used to that fact. I wanted to throw up.

I thought, "What was this all about? I was in love with the man who told me he killed Cathy Cesnik?! What the hell was I doing? Was I really making up stories?" I was so upset with this revelation that I did not want to go any further.

Up to this point, I intentionally did not search for repressed memories, especially those of being shown Cathy's dead body. I was intent on avoiding any memories of myself after Cathy's death. But with the unexpected entry of my persona, Jeannie, into my life, a door was being pushed open to my memories of the period after Cathy died. I immediately shut that door and ceased dialoguing with Jeannie. I stopped journaling. My writing sabbatical ended in early 2010.

Feeling the impact of Jeannie's words, I took this experience to my therapist. I worked on how I could have possibly thought I was in love with "Brother Bob". The idea that I was anything other than the pure victim upset me most. I was condemning myself for my feelings as a 16 to 17-year-old teenager. My therapist tried to help me understand what some victims may experience after going through extreme trauma. They may find later that they bonded with their abuser. This is commonly known as the Stockholm Syndrome. My therapist also tried to help me see that even though I was being severely abused, I was still a girl in high school who experienced crushes or feelings of love. I could not get my brain around it all and refused to reengage with Jeannie.

Ironically, I began my sabbatical with the feeling that the spirit of the late Cathy Cesnik had something she wanted expressed, and that I was her 'transcriber'. Instead, Cathy knew I had something to reveal to myself; it was Cathy who was the conduit from me to myself.

CHAPTER TWENTY-FOUR

Birth of a Warrior (Vignette)

After Maskell took me to see Cathy's body, he intensified his efforts to brainwash me. His efforts literally imprinted on my tormented mind, heart, and soul the belief that I was not only responsible for Cathy's death, but that I killed her. On some level, I felt responsible. I had acknowledged to Cathy that the priests were hurting me; she then promised she would take care of it. Next, I was confronted by one of the priests who Cathy apparently questioned. Then, she wound up murdered. Maskell took my guilt and bludgeoned me into feeling fully responsible for her death. His torturous mind games got much worse.

Shortly after being shown Cathy's body, Maskell took me to a house. We walked into the foyer, and he put his gloves in the pocket of his coat and hung it up. I did not want to take off my pea coat. We went upstairs and entered a room, where I saw "Brother Bob". He was sitting in a chair, waiting.[114]

Prior to that date, when an adult was abusing me, Maskell would stand next to the door, appearing to be guarding the room. Because this was his reenactment of what Tom did in the back of The Green Door, I saw it as an act of protection. In fact, he was standing there watching everything that was going on, being sure the 'Johns' behaved and that I acted willingly. He was conditioning me to believe that he cared, and that he was watching over the situation in

---

114 The 'room' refers to any room where I was being sexually abused. I started remembering the abuse at Keough and could only accept that what I remembered happened in the Chaplain's office, which is where a lot of abuse occurred. The more I remembered, the more I realized I was taken to other locations as well.

case I needed help. I still feel on some level that he was my protector, a distortion I am working out in therapy.

This time, Maskell surprised me and left the room. I now stood in front of this man who had previously raped me, without my 'protector'. I was terrified!

As I stood there shivering with fear, wrapped in my coat, "Brother Bob" told me he killed Sister Cathy. As he said this, he showed me a Polaroid picture of her lying on the ground in the same position in which I had seen her with Maskell. He told me he did not mean to kill her; Cathy said she was going to go to the police, and he hit her.

I was completely paralyzed. This man proceeded to tell me why it should have been me dead on the ground. He said Cathy was as pure as the driven snow and that I was the daughter of the devil, lower than dirt. As he continued to attack me with his words, he made me perform fellatio. Afterwards, I remember standing there thinking that this ordeal was over.

Then "Brother Bob" said, "Oh no, no, it's far from over." He had me take off all my clothes and proceeded to pull out the vibrator. Until that point, only Maskell had threatened me with or used that weapon. I now was frightened that another person had this tool in his hand, this tool that would bring about a physical reaction that showed how evil I was.

At this point, I had been abused at Keough for about two years and that abuse had been at the hands of various clergy and other adults. I had confided in Cathy, she was found murdered, and I was taken to her body. Now I realize that, as intense as these incidents were, I was still able to dissociate my body from my mind. But the vibrator would cause a physical reaction in my body, an orgasm, from which I could not separate. Not understanding what an orgasm was, it only confirmed in my mind what Maskell and this man said: "I was the daughter of the devil and a whore, and I liked it." I still cannot imagine why any person would do this to me or any child.

"Brother Bob", using a vibrator and intimidation, raped my body and soul. As he forced me to an orgasm I did not welcome, he said, "Look me in the eyes." Maskell had always warned me not to look in the eyes of an abuser. But I looked in "Brother Bob's" eyes as I climaxed. He then forced his penis into my mouth. Maskell came in the room, looked at me lying naked in a fetal position on the floor, and asked "Brother Bob" if I was going to 'say anything'. While putting his pants on and still physically excited, he said, "You're right, she really does like it!"

As the adult, I was shocked to see my younger self naked and curled up on the floor of a grown man's bedroom. Maskell told me to get up and go pray for forgiveness. As my zombie body walked naked to the crucifix on the wall, he grabbed my privates and made some crude remark about my being a real money-maker. He again asked "Brother Bob" if I was going to say anything. "Brother Bob" said he did not think so. Maskell responded, "I don't want to know what you think. I want to know will she talk!" With that, "Brother Bob" said, "No she's not going to say a word."

After "Brother Bob" tortured me, the spirit of my 16-year-old persona Frances was done. If I was ever at the point of suicide or a mental breakdown, it was now. After all I had endured, I could no longer separate from what had just happened in that room with "Brother Bob". I felt totally exposed, my 'evil nature' laid bare for anyone to see. I now believed what I was being told: I was evil. With Frances crumpled on the floor at their feet, I felt my spirit had died. It took years of inner work to finally bring this part of me out of that room.

As this memory of that young girl on the floor continued to unfold over time, I stayed with my journaling and meditation. This is how I would handle any experience I had when relating to my child-self being abused. I would go into my quiet, journal, and meditate with no sense that I was directing what was going to happen, frequently resulting in memories of the experiences awakening in my everyday reality. At some point they just flowed, no matter where I was or what I was doing. I was essentially in two realities at the same time.

These inner children became paralyzed under the weight of the abusive acts perpetrated on me, which is what saved me, and I was on a spiritual quest to find and reconnect with them. Each child, a part of myself, was a persona who carried various traumas that occurred throughout my life. I somehow knew their names when they presented themselves to me.

The inner child who endured the torture at the hands of Maskell and "Brother Bob" on this day was 'Frances'. Frances was a tough teenager who had been protecting me since Magnus and Maskell began abusing me. She was 'born' in order to allow 'Beth' to rest. Beth, along with the younger 'Little Jeannie', were the aspects of myself who had dealt with the abuse at the hands of Tom. When the priests started abusing me, it was too much for Beth to take on, so Frances, being older with more spitfire, gathered the wounded younger one, Beth, into herself and pushed forward.

After "Brother Bob" raped me in Maskell's bedroom, I knelt before the crucifix as Maskell had directed, and listened to those men talking above my head. My soul was as exposed as my bare body. I was done.

Then, my survival instincts kicked in. Out of that spot of death, a new persona named 'Jeannie' spontaneously formed, dressed in full armor. 'Jeannie' was seemingly 'the whore' born from Maskell's lies, which I believed. Until 2015, I wanted nothing more to do with her and the pain she held. I

came to know her as 'Jeannie', which contrasts with 'Little
Jeannie', the persona from when I was around four and
coping with the abuse by my uncle.[115] Just as Frances had
supported Little Jeannie and Beth when the abuse by the
priests began, now Jeannie was arising to support Frances.

Jeannie's attitude was, "I have to get out of here. You
aren't taking me down; I won't let you do it." She gathered
up Frances, and all the other broken, younger parts of
myself who had through the years done what they could
to help me survive. They were all under that armor. This
courageous part of myself came forth asserting with determination: "You tell me what to do and I'll do it. You want me
to stand on my head in the corner? I'll do it. I'll do whatever
I have to do to get the hell out of here!"

And she was true to her word.

---

115 See "Little Jeannie (Vignette)," page 50.

CHAPTER TWENTY-FIVE

Jeannie Returns (Vignette)

Between the court's decision in 1996 and identifying myself as 'Jane Doe' in 2014, I made a conscious decision not to look at any photos pertaining to my high school years. In 2015, once people knew who I was, I thought I could handle a couple photos which were sent to my e-mail account. One of the first pictures was of a present-day individual, which meant there were a lot of years that had passed since the Keough days. Even so, for days I struggled with myself about what I should do. After debating my options, and talking this through with my therapist, I finally told myself, "Come on Jean, it's an old man. There is no way you would recognize him. Get a grip and just look at the damn picture. You've got yourself unnecessarily whipped up. Just get it done."

On January 6, 2015, at 11:30 at night, I made the decision to look at that picture. I sat down, opened the computer, opened the e-mail, and looked at the photo. I then found myself on the floor in the corner of my bedroom, curled up in a ball, rocking back and forth and crying, "He's alive! He's alive!" I could not calm down. I was in a panic and shaking—shocked that I recognized him. A part of me wished he were dead while another part was surprised that he was alive. I did not know until that experience just how much I hoped he was dead and gone. I did not know why this man was upsetting me so much. I was amazed that I knew him...I knew his eyes! I knew him as "Brother Bob"! These were the same eyes of the man who had admitted to killing Cathy. After his admission, he raped me, leaving my spirit decimated and crumpled on the floor. That crumpled self was my persona, Frances.[116]

As the adult rocking in the corner of my bedroom, I was aware that I was totally out of control. The younger parts of myself had been triggered and my adult self was now within their experience. We were all in my body looking out and exclaiming "He's alive!" As the adult, I had been hoping that the man who terrified me the most, "Brother Bob", was dead so I would not have to 'do' anything about him. Frances was bent over, cowering, and screaming in fear, "He's alive!" Jeannie, my teenage persona who I last met in 2010, was responding, "He's alive!" I was not sure if she was glad or not. To be honest, after our last conversation, I immediately thought she was glad, but I was confused by the emotions I saw cross her face. I thought I noticed sadness or disappointment.[117] I felt an unexpected twinge of compassion; that feeling threw me through an inner door and into a room which did not seem like Maskell's office. It had two windows with a desk under one of them. There was also a couch, a bed, and a door to a small bathroom.

As my whole being was engrossed in this multi-layered experience, I knew I needed help immediately. Even though it was midnight, I managed to get myself up off the floor and call my therapist. Thank goodness she answered! For the next half hour, I shook, feeling so outside of myself, while my therapist talked me off that ledge. She did not hang up until I stopped shaking. I did what my therapist advised: had a chamomile tea with honey

116 See "Birth of the Warrior (Vignette)," page 190.

117 I later remembered, after "Brother Bob" told me he killed Cathy, that Jeannie would get excited when Maskell would tell her he was taking her to see "Brother Bob". When they arrived, someone else was there, and Jeannie would be extremely disappointed. Maskell used that lie to get me to go calmly. He later told me that "Brother Bob" had been killed in a car crash. Hearing that he was dead had a major psychological impact on Jeannie. See "Buried in Despair (Vignette)," page 246. Now that Cathy and "Brother Bob" were both dead, Jeannie felt totally alone. Her surprise in 2015 at him being alive came from a deeper realization: If he loved her like he said, and he was alive, why hadn't he come for her.

and wrapped myself in an Afghan blanket. I eventually fell asleep.[118]

One thing that lingered for me was the compassion I felt as I was thrown through the door and into that room that night. Using meditation and journaling, I slowly began to work on what happened and its impact on me.

During subsequent periods of quiet, I discovered that in the middle of the room where I landed stood Jeannie, dressed in full armor—the same girl I was disgusted with, yet afraid of in 2010. She was like a frozen knight in armor, standing guard. After five years of working to avoid this aspect of myself, I was now not only standing next to her but looking her in the eyes and feeling an inkling of care for her. We stood in the middle of the room for a long time—Jeannie in the armor and me as the adult, not sure what to do.

Why was I feeling compassion? I could barely feel compassion toward myself, much less this older teenager who had previously repulsed me with her behavior. Something undeniably happened the night I looked into the eyes of the photograph of "Brother Bob", simultaneously touching what Frances and Jeannie held: terror and pure vulnerability.

The door I was thrust through that night had separated me from Jeannie for many years—with her standing on the other side the whole time. I would never have walked through that door on my own, fearful there was a monster behind it. I had to be thrown through it by looking into the eyes of "Brother Bob". That forced me to begin interacting with Jeannie in some way.

As I stood with her, I noticed that from the inside of the room, there were at least 30 different locks on the door. With the passing of time, I began to talk to Jeannie, apologizing for believing Maskell when he told me I was a whore, a horrible person, the daughter of the devil. I assured her

---

118 After this triggering experience, I promised my therapist I would not look at any photos pertaining to that time without them being in a sealed envelope and with her being present.

I was staying and wanted to help her take off the armor so she could sit down. Days passed and we agreed to remove all but three locks on the door. Jeannie was fearful that someone was going to re-enter. She also was intent on not leaving the room since she had needed to stay locked up for me to begin a new life after Keough. The armor and the locks were put in place to keep 'the whore' contained within Jeannie.

As she began to see I was not going anywhere, she let me help her remove the suit of armor. I slowly and methodically removed parts of the suit, observing horrible sores all over her body. I cried as I removed each piece of that heavy suit. I then noticed that Jesus was in the room, so I asked him to help hold her up. She was so weak; she had only been able to stand because of the stiffness of the armor. Watching her fall in on herself as each piece was removed, I was grateful that Jesus was there for her to lean against. As I removed the last piece, Jeannie passed out and crumbled to the floor. This poor child's body was covered in sores. With the help of Jesus, I picked Jeannie up from the floor and carried her rag doll, sore-infected body to the bed. I was not sure that she would live, but I felt a newfound determination to do something to help her.

Jeannie held all the pain and suffering for me, so I could leave that school and have a chance at life. I began to care for her within my spirit. I washed her body, put healing ointment on her wounds, then gently wrapped her in a clean white cotton cloth. Now I waited, not sure if Jeannie would survive the wounds and horrible neglect she had endured for so many years. I was extremely relieved when, after what felt like several days of agony, Jeannie stirred. She was alive!

CHAPTER TWENTY-SIX

My Inner Garden (Vignette)

For many years, my practice was to sit quietly in prayer and meditation, including some journaling and dialogues with Jesus. Of course, the normal chatter was in my brain, and the thoughts seemed like they would not stop, but with time I got beyond that.

The 'Jesus' I dialogue with today is different than the 'Jesus' I knew before 1993. Before 1993, Jesus was my personal, heartfelt connection to God. He was God and a friend. After 1993, as the sexual abuse at priests' hands resurfaced within me, I wanted nothing to do with Jesus. However, no matter how I tried to break up with him, he continued to hang around. I eventually made a spiritual contract with Jesus which I wrote out on paper. It stated that he could stay male within my inner walk, helping me along my spiritual path as my advisor and guide, not my God. Since then, he has become a spiritual guide, and a mentor who I trust.

In my meditation, Jesus would invariably ask if I wanted to go for a walk. During these walks, I would either pick up from a spot we had been in a previous meditation, or I would find myself in a new location, heading in a new direction. We often ended up walking down a path within a beautiful forest.

Whenever Jesus asked me to take a walk with him, part of me would take up the invitation to go into the unknown, while another part cautiously observed what was unfolding. My prayer experiences over the years have been a mix of good and bad outcomes. Because of this, I have learned that discernment of these spiritual occurrences is especially important. What I mean by discernment is dropping judgement, taking my time, using my head and heart, cautiously assessing the situation to obtain spiritual guidance and understanding, and at times talking with a friend. The nature of this experience in my quiet becomes an indicator of the fruits I experience in my life because of the therapeutic, spiritual, and emotional work I do.

On these walks along my inner path, Jesus would normally say, "What do you see?" This prompted me to look more intently at what was around me. On one occasion around 2003, while walking with him in the forest, he said he wanted to show me my garden.

Along our path, I saw a rusty, broken gate which was the entrance to a barren area within the forest. Jesus then told me that this decrepit gate was the entrance to my garden. I thought, "Oh my god. THIS is my garden?!" With time, I pushed the gate aside and went into an area that felt like death. The trees were dead, the ground was hard and there was no sign of life anywhere—no birds, no animals, no green, no nothing. There was a little stream bed with no water running. And there we stood...

As my health walk continued and I moved through my regular days, I would sense this garden within my spirit. It could be days or months between visits, but I would periodically find myself back in this sacred space and aware that there was new growth. This often correlated with some breakthrough or an inner shift I was experiencing in my everyday life. For example, while in the space, a small trickle of water began to flow in my stream, and I realized that there was some life coming into my garden. These images helped me stop and reflect on what was going on in my body, mind, and spirit. I knew the trickling stream was symbolic of the grief work I was finally doing pertaining to Cathy Cesnik's death. That inner work was brought on by a Death and Dying college course I was attending. These meditations were powerful visual tools for me.

I remember one time, Jesus asked me to lay in the stream with this tiny trickle of water, and I did. I felt the water move around me and through me. Whenever I returned there, I would find myself in the water. With time, my stream began to flow, and my garden became alive with bees, butterflies, and birds, reflecting the healing that was going on within me.

After Mike died in 2007, I would find him sitting on one of the rocks by the side of the stream. Great Grey would be sitting across the stream on another rock. The water was bathing me and washing through me, feeding every cell in my body. As I lay in this nurturing stream, trusting my safe space, Jesus would show up sitting on another rock.

Mike, Jesus, and Great Grey were my protectors; I trusted them. I could play openly and freely here. It was all mine, and no one was allowed in without my permission.

My beautiful garden became a reflection of the deep healing that was unfolding in my life. It was like being wrapped in Great Grey's wings or Mike's loving embrace at Big Sur. The image of my garden would fill me with a sense of strength and peace. These benefits were accessible in my day-to-day life, but I could also draw on them, even in my other periods of quiet.

For example, after seeing the photograph of "Brother Bob" in 2015, I was thrust into the room with my persona Jeannie in armor. I did not know how to interact with this aspect of myself, who I felt had betrayed me. I saw her as a whore because she had decided to acquiesce in the abuse. As she stood stiffly in armor, I looked in her eyes and felt compassion for her. I was afraid, did not know what to do, and did not want to be there. I struggled for a month with these simultaneous feelings of betrayal and compassion.

At the same time, in another period of quiet, I found myself in my garden in its lush and beautiful state, and as always, I was lying in the flowing stream. I saw Mike, Great Grey and Jesus sitting on rocks surrounding the stream bed. Amid the inner struggle I was having with meeting

Jeannie, I sensed Jesus had drawn me here in order to somehow help me with this complex situation.

Jesus began by asking what animal I needed to protect me. When I asked him why I needed protection, he said to cushion and shield me from the pain that I kept at a distance. The armor Jeannie wore in that room was the armor I wore as an adult. It was terrifying to think about removing Jeannie's armor, leaving myself completely exposed to my past, and those who might hurt me in my present.

Sitting up and looking around, I became aware that every kind of animal you could think of filled the whole garden, all forms, shapes, colors, and species of animals. I did not even know what some of them were as they all stood facing me. I asked if there was a certain animal for this time in my health walk. From the crowd of animals came the most gorgeous, beautiful, and graceful tiger I could have ever imagined.

For the first time since entering the garden, I now emerged from the flowing stream which had grown from the trickle of water. Feeling a bit nervous with this animal's size, I asked if I should ride her. Following the Tiger's lead, I just walked cautiously alongside her. Before exiting the garden through the now repaired white, gold-hinged gate, I went over to pet the Tiger. As the Tiger and I were leaving the garden, Jesus told me to pay attention to tigers in my dreams and in my everyday life. Once out of the garden, we began walking down a path through the woods. I was not sure what to do, so I just continued walking at her side.

I believed the Tiger was to be my support, helping me navigate my way through the pain contained within the part of me standing in armor within that room. But I did not know what was next. Where were we headed? Should I get on her back? Should I just walk? When I turned to ask the Tiger what I should do, she came toward me. I was afraid she was going to eat me. She began to take me into her mouth, feet first and down into her belly. I thought, "She is eating me!"

But when she took me into her massive body, my head remained pointing out of her mouth. She was not eating me; she was protecting me. She was to be my full-blown protection as I dealt with the pain and suffering that would come from unlocking Jeannie's armor.

The day after this experience, I had an appointment with my therapist. I told her that I felt I was in the great Tiger's body and her body would now be my armor. I shared that I knew this Tiger, my protectress, was to be the spirit guide who would support me through whatever was about to unfold on my health walk. The next day, my therapist came across a photo she then e-mailed to me.

The picture was of a bronze ceremonial vessel in the form of a tiger shielding a man in its mouth. This Chinese figurine was made during the Shang period, more than 3,000 years ago. Apparently, in China, the tiger is identified as the protector of souls and guardian of graves.

I then remembered Jesus telling me, as I left my garden, "Pay attention to your dreams and what shows up in your regular life that has to do with a tiger." I wondered if that same ancient Chinese tiger spirit would protect me as I cautiously proceeded to learn who Jeannie was, what she had hidden under her armor, and how I might reconnect with her.

CHAPTER TWENTY-SEVEN

The Council Gathered in the Cellar (Vignette)

After reengaging with my persona, Jeannie, in 2015, I was hopeful that when her armor was removed and she recovered from her sores, we would be ready to leave the room that had been her prison for 34 years.[119] Unfortunately, in the spring of 2015, as I was preparing to exit, Jeannie began telling me about the cellar. She pulled the rug back and there in the floor was a trap door. I did not want to spend another minute in this place, much less go down into its cellar. What the hell was buried deep within my subconscious that I needed to go down a ladder into that scary place to find?

Jeannie was not ready to leave the house, so I told Jesus I would go into the cellar if he went first. I was disappointed when he agreed. We had to enter the cellar backwards, holding on to the ladder—Jesus first, then Jeannie, and then me. Once we were standing on the floor, I took some time to look around. There was a lot of stuff down there which I had no interest in exploring. I was only there to look at what Jeannie wanted me to see, and nothing more. This was her idea and her mission.

In real time, these experiences would extend into weeks and months of prayer and remembering. I had to attend to my regular routine and responsibilities.

Eventually we ended up sitting in the middle of the room with a box containing pictures, jewelry, and other trinkets in the center of where we sat. Jeannie wanted me to look at

---

119 See "Jeannie Returns (Vignette)," page 196.

the contents in the box. While I decided if and why I would do this, I became aware that my other personas, Frances and Little Jeannie, were there with Sister Cathy. Little Jeannie was resting on Jesus's lap, Frances was sitting in a chair, and Cathy was sitting next to a young girl. As I looked toward the box, I watched Jesus take a ring from the box and hand it to me.

The ring was not familiar to my adult self; however, just by holding it in my hand I was immediately taken on a journey to discover another part of my past. As I have explained, I can have different levels of inner and physical movement go on at similar times in my life. While the ring revealed areas of my past that I needed to remember and research for my own peace of mind, I continued reflecting on what Jeannie needed me to see in order for us to finally leave the cellar.[120]

When I reconnected with those gathered in the cellar, I wondered who the teenage girl was sitting beside Cathy. In time, I realized that she was 'Little Cathy', another aspect of myself. She was a part of myself who held a lot of the experiences that caused me great pain after Cathy went missing in 1969. She held that pain so my persona Jeannie could move forward as she had resolved after Frances was beaten down and left in Maskell's room.[121]

Sometimes Maskell would call me 'Little Cathy'. That was Maskell's way of keeping Cathy's death front and center in my mind. He was creating terror and confusion, a form of brainwashing. The pain was unbearable. I had been referred to as 'Little Cathy', treated like I was taking Cathy's place, told I was the one who should have died, told I was the reason she was killed, and told I was the one who killed her. After Cathy's death, I needed to create another part of myself to hold the horrors, and the responsibility for her death. Jeannie's job was to get out of Keough alive, so

---

120 This ring handed to me in my meditation ultimately revealed a major puzzle piece of my past. See "Girl with the Long Black Hair (Vignette)," page 207.
121 See "Birth of a Warrior (Vignette)," page 192.

Little Cathy was born to bear the brunt of the guilt associated with Cathy's murder.

Little Cathy was sitting in the circle next to Cathy Cesnik, who apparently was her spirit guide. I was amazed that these two were together since Jeannie told me in 2010 that Cathy was dead because "Brother Bob" wanted to be with Jeannie, which is what Jeannie was told and believed. As the adult, I thought Cathy would have hated me, yet here she sat as the protector of Little Cathy.

As I began to dialogue with Little Cathy, I felt her pain from holding all the responsibility Maskell had put on me after Cathy's murder. Already disgusted with these men's denigration of Cathy's death, I started getting angry as I slowly realized that by making me think I was responsible for her murder, they were not only separating me from myself, but from Cathy as well.

I could not continue calling this part of myself the name Maskell gave me while he manipulated and abused me. I said, "I'm not calling you Little Cathy; so what would you girls like to call her?" Frances and Little Jeannie agreed she was like a girlfriend. I said, "Okay, so her name is 'Girlfriend'?" I thought it was an awkward name to remember, but the girls were all tickled, so I went along.

As the two of them sat together in the circle, Girlfriend leaned against Cathy and Cathy kept a protective arm around her. I could tell there was a bond between them that was not going to be broken.

My attention was then drawn to Jesus. I wondered out loud why these young ones within me needed him here. I was still very confused and angry with his part in all of this. "He just silently sits there! I don't know why you guys want him here. You know he's no good to us. He's helpless." But they talked and told me he could stay, so he did.

While this deep 'cellar work' within me continued, a lot was happening in my daily life. I again heard that the man I remembered as "Brother Bob" was still alive, which threw me into a panic. All I wanted to do was run away. I immediately connected with my support network. I tried to convince my-self that these feelings were coming from my younger selves, but I was simultaneously experiencing the terror as an adult. I was genuinely afraid for my physical safety, and I knew I had to deal with these emotions with caution.

Meanwhile, in the circle, my younger selves were very afraid of "Brother Bob"—even more afraid than I was. Despite all the work I had done to connect with them, I saw the terror these perpetrators caused the child within me. I sensed that the deep-rooted fear this news triggered in the girls was more important than anything happening in my adult reality.

Finding it hard to comfort them, I determined it was im-portant to invite our spirit guides into the circle. We needed their protective presence to help calm the growing fear.

One by one our guides showed up. The beautiful Tiger came down the ladder, lumbered over to Frances and sat down beside her. Frances excit-edly put her arms around its neck, rubbing her face into the Tiger's fur. I now understood who this massive animal, whom I met in my inner gar-den, was here to protect.[122] Next the graceful White Mare, who helped me while experiencing the abuse by my uncle, walked down the ladder, and moseyed over to Jesus who in turn sat Little Jeannie on the White Mare's back.[123] The White Mare was followed by Great Grey, who flew into the cellar landing gracefully be-hind me.

I looked over at Jeannie and asked, "Did you have any kind of support that you felt you could lean on during that hellish time after Cathy's death?" She responded, "Yeah, well I did." I said, "You can invite it to join us."

---

122 See "My Inner Garden (Vignette)," page 200.
123 See "Little Jeannie (Vignette)," page 50.

With that, a huge, grey snake came slithering down the stairs into the cellar. As it moved off the steps, it continued to slink its way around the floor, stopping right in front of Jeannie. Then it slowly and methodically coiled its long thick body in front of her. It swayed hypnotically, with its black eyes scanning the room as its red tongue darted in and out, hissing its warning to stay away. This spirit guide could not have been more unexpected, but it made perfect sense. This teenage warrior's protector would not be a cute, fuzzy animal. It would be something that was cold blooded. There had to be nothing about her guide that would stir you to reach out and pet it. It was there to cause one to recoil in fear.

I felt as if an important Council had convened, and I was about to find out why.

CHAPTER TWENTY-EIGHT

Girl with the Long Black Hair (Vignette)

While the Council was gathering in the cellar, Jesus had asked me to look at a ring.[124] I was surprised to find that holding that ring had the same effect on me as when I looked at pictures of certain individuals; it stirred memories buried within my body.

The memory being triggered by that ring began with Maskell supposedly giving me a ride home.[125] Maskell said he first had to stop at his residence at St. Clément's to get something. This made me wonder, "Did I go there often? Was this a tactic he used to get me to go there? Where else might he have taken me under the guise of giving me a ride home?"

When we got to his house, he told me there was a girl waiting for him in his room. He wanted to play a prank on her and wanted me to go along with it. He said he would hand me a cup of Coke which I was to hand to her. Then I was to turn away and look at a picture on the wall. He said she would not think it was funny at first, but later she would. I followed him into his room and saw a girl with long black hair standing there. She appeared older than me, wearing a white blouse and a plaid skirt, but not a Keough uniform. She was obviously angry at Maskell yelling, "Give

---

124 See "The Council Gathered in the Cellar (Vignette)," page 203.

125 I should note that in all my recovered memories, I never actually got a ride from Maskell directly to my home. He would drop me off two or three blocks from my house, usually after I was abused. I do not remember a lot of times this occurred, but I suspect Maskell gave me rides more times than I remember, considering that these triggered memories drop into my consciousness without direction or full context.

me back the ring! You had no right to take that from my sister. She had no right to give it to you. It was my grandmother's. You need to give me that ring back!" Maskell was telling her to calm down. He nonchalantly walked over and poured a glass of Coke, which he turned and handed to me. The girl had sat down, so I handed her the glass, then walked over to look at one of Maskell's pictures on the wall.

I heard a thump, and when I turned around the girl was lying on the floor. Maskell surprised me by focusing on getting me out of there, not seeming to notice the girl on the floor. He was telling me he had to make sure no one found out what I had done, especially since he was already working so hard to keep what I did to Sister Cathy secret. While he hurried me out of his room, Maskell kept repeating that he had to get me home right away, while leaving the girl with the long black hair crumpled on the floor. I was in a state of shock. I had no idea what Maskell and the girl were talking about, nor why she was now lying on his floor. All I knew was they argued about a ring, I handed her a glass of Coke, which was now splattered on the floor beside her.

As usual, I took this new memory both into my therapies and in my inner work while taking my quiet. As I sat with Jesus and the others in the cellar, I wanted Jesus to tell me what in the world went on back then. He reached into the box and handed me a black and white photo of a young girl lying in a hole in the ground. That picture stirred more buried memories.

I remembered Maskell showing me the same black and white picture of the girl with the long black hair lying in a freshly dug grave. She was on her left side, knees bent, wearing the same uniform she had on the day I saw her. Maskell told me I killed her.

Going through that experience as if for the first time, I felt the same deep despair that I experienced after Cathy was murdered—despair that was so intense that I was numb. Jeannie was certain that she/I killed that girl and Sister Cathy, and that Maskell was our sole protector.

In 2015, that upsetting memory drove me to discreetly inquire whether anyone knew of any girls that went missing or were found dead after Cathy died and before 1972. None of the missing girls I was told about matched the description of the girl with the long black hair.

Meanwhile my psychotherapist was trying to help me look at this terrifying experience from a different angle. She suggested that with all the tools Maskell used to apparently brainwash his victims, maybe the girl was drugged. It took me a few years to seriously consider that possibility.

While I dealt with these memories and the impact of them on me, filming for *The Keepers* was progressing. An important piece of information that Ryan White was investigating pertained to the two locations where it was suspected that Cathy's body may have been found. Whenever I talked about or reflected on Maskell taking me to see Cathy's body, I always thought, 'it was far, far away,' so even though I was scared, I asked Ryan if they would take me to those locations. I really did not believe Maskell took me anywhere near Keough.

In preparation for that outing, I drove from Keough to two different locations—St. Clement's, the place where that girl crumbled to the floor, and the area around Monumental Avenue where Cathy was supposedly found. I wanted to compare the actual distance to the 'far, far away' feeling within me. I later realized that both locations were no more than 15 minutes from Keough, and within blocks of one another.

The day I went with Sarah, Ryan, and Jess to pay my respects to Cathy at the two possible discovery sites near Monumental Avenue, I brought three bouquets of flowers. There was one for each of the possible locations, and the third one for that young girl with long black hair, and anyone else who may have died because of the abuse by Maskell and others.

After parking the car on that hot summer day, we began hiking through the woods. Ryan led me and Sarah to the two locations. At each spot, I took a moment to say a prayer, and laid the flowers there in honor of Cathy. Along the way I found myself paying close attention to my surroundings in case something triggered a familiar feeling. Even though we were hot and sweaty, we continued to hike along train tracks, climbing over a freight train at one point to get to the other side of the tracks. I was excited to be actively exploring my past, finding a level of peace by physically being in the area and doing my prayer rituals. Continuing down the train tracks, just a couple blocks from St. Clement's, I began scattering roses in honor of the girl with long black hair, and any other victims who did not survive, whether at Maskell's hands or their own.

I felt safe with Sarah present, and secure knowing that Ryan and Jess knew where we were, and that Ryan had his camera with him. That camera, my witness, came along to reveal to others what my journey was all about.

We continued to walk until I was almost out of flowers. Feeling content, I walked over to the chain link fence that ran the length of the train tracks to put my last flower into the fence. Walking a short way past that spot, I looked up and saw the side of a building in a place that suddenly looked familiar. My heart began to race as I told the others, "I need to go over there." With the fence between me and the property, I asked, "Can we get over there?" With that, we turned around and headed back to the car.

Once we were in the car, they directed me to the area I had seen through the fence, which appeared to be some sort of factory at the end of Monumental Avenue.[126] I felt wobbly with the feeling that I knew this place. Ryan asked if I wanted to stop and walk the site. Acting calm, while feeling a fear beginning to grow, I told him I did not want to stop. Turning the car around, I said, "I'm fine, I just needed to see that area."

As I drove my car away from that place, I began to feel the blind panic of a memory start to overtake me. I told

---

126 See Map of Majestic Distilling Co. Inc., page 263.

Sarah she needed to drive as I jumped out of the car. Sarah immediately came around and got in the driver's side. As she continued up the street, I felt myself go into a full-fledged panic, yelling repeatedly, "Stop the car! Stop the car!" She quickly pulled over into a parking lot at the other end of Monumental Avenue, about a quarter mile from the factory building where we turned around. Sobbing, I bolted from the car and began blindly moving in any direction, with Sarah running after me. I literally ran into the side of a building, stood with my head against the wall, and cried.

Ryan and Jess stayed at a distance while Sarah stood protectively behind me. Thrown back in time, I felt like a terrified 16-year-old girl who was figuratively and now literally up against a wall. I was extremely vulnerable, and totally out of control.

My brain turned to mush. I became exhausted, unfocused, and spacey. I was embarrassed because this happened in front of others since I was usually alone when experiencing memories. Once I calmed down, I did what I do best as a survivor; I began to pull myself together.

I was determined to be normal with Ryan, Jess and Sarah, and I insisted I was fine. Out of concern, they asked if I should go home. I restated that I was fine and said we should proceed to the next stop we had planned to make while they were in town. What we did not do was talk about what just happened since I was still in shock, and they dared not bring it up again.

Later, I began to process what happened on that early August day. Wanting to be at peace with the death of Cathy and the girl with long black hair, I found myself in the vicinity where I last saw each of them, Cathy's body lying in those woods and the girl's body just blocks away at St. Clement's.

When we dead-ended at that property on Monumental Avenue, there was a long brick wall to my left, and a small clearing, which would have felt much bigger in 1969 without the fence breaking the view. I knew this spot, and I could tell something was coming and I needed to run. Every cell in my body seemed to know what my brain did not. But I could not escape the truth: this was the place Maskell took me to see Cathy's body. My body could not stop shaking with this knowledge, even while my mind struggled to catch up. This was a painful awakening, while simultaneously healing and freeing.

For a couple months afterward, I worked on different aspects of that breakthrough. I became aware that another aspect of myself, fractured when faced with Cathy's dead body, was still stuck in that traumatic experience. I began the work of bringing her away from that sadness and reconnecting with her.

I also began to understand that the box Jesus asked me to look at was another tool created by my mind to help me remember myself. My mind was both integrating and healing me along a path, that path being:

- I was handed a ring;
- My mind took me from that ring to the girl with long black hair;
- A photo presented by Jesus in my quiet revealed a hidden belief that I killed the girl, like when I first remembered Cathy Cesnik;
- Life's events provided opportunities for me to pay my respects to Cathy and that unknown girl; and
- Seeking peace with those two individuals led me straight to the goal of the whole journey, to recover another aspect of my teen self, left for dead on the ground where Sister Cathy's body lay.

I was beginning to understand that one of the ongoing themes of my health walk was that when finding Cathy, I found and connected with more of myself. On October 7, 2015, I wrote this in my journal:

On Saturday I will take flowers to the place I believe I saw Sister Cathy's dead body. It has been two months since I stumbled upon it. I know I need to pay real respect to the spot where my teenaged self was forced to leave Cathy behind. I have calmed down from the shock and extreme emotional upset I experienced connected with that 'find'. Sarah, Greg, Ryan, Jess, Ed and his wife, Val, will go with me. I will pick up yellow roses to take. I feel like I want to say something, so I am taking time to reflect and write what comes...

Like a dream,
my saving Hope
crumpled on the ground before me.
I don't know at what point
my hands knew they were touching
death.
That the maggots were not on you
but in you.
That death was you.
All I know, at that moment,
part of me died too.
As I fell to the ground beside you,
the cold stench of death
crept into my body
like breath itself.
Looking like me, leaving with him.
No hope of waking from this nightmare.
I know now you kept that
young part of me safe, for my return.
You were taking care of me, like you promised,
by holding that broken, beaten down,
left for dead, little girl.
But death could not contain you.
I had to find you
to find me.
There could be no peace
until I woke from my death sleep,
until the nightmare ended.
I am awake!

I am alive!
I am hopeful!
Rest now...in peace.

 On October 10, 2015, I placed yellow roses in memory of Cathy Cesnik at the spot where I believe I was shown Cathy's body. Once again, I hoped this was the final time I would be letting go of Cathy.

Postscripts

On October 10, 2016, I visited the area where Cathy's remains were ultimately disposed of and later discovered. It was around the corner, on the same street, from where I was taken by Maskell. Sarah, Greg, Ed, Val, and *The Keepers'* team went with me to put plaques on two trees in honor of Cathy and the life she lived.[127]

At the end of 2018, a survivor of Maskell contacted me. Because of my extreme cautiousness, I responded a year later. We began an exchange of messages. In one of her emails, she spontaneously shared a memory where she had been drugged and heard Maskell say, "Make her look like she's dead." I was stunned when I read that. She had no idea that I remembered the girl lying in a shallow grave, and that my therapist believed she most likely was drugged. By sharing her painful experience with me, I found I could more fully embrace Jeannie's innocence.

My Daughter Sarah's Reflections

"Growing up with my mom I can't count the number of times I've seen her have a trauma response. She comes across something unexpected like an image on TV, someone surprising her from behind, or an image of an abuser. Suddenly she's in crisis mode; upset, overwhelmed, and working to

---

127 See The Plaque to Honor and Thank Cathy Cesnik, page 261.

remove herself from the experience. She might make a star-tled sound and is often shivering, covering her face, moving away. As I've gotten older and learned more about trauma, while discovering that other people I care about also react to trauma in this same way, I understand it more. Her mind is rational and clear; whatever this upsetting thing is can't hurt her and she's safe; but the body is having a totally different experience.

When we sat together to watch a screening of part of *The Keepers* she hadn't seen, I was there in case she might recognize another man in the film. Mom was so confident that she would not know him or have a reaction that she in-sisted we watch it instead of looking at a picture of him with her therapist. So...the face popped up on the screen with his voice and suddenly she was reacting. Mom was visibly shaken and telling us to make it stop. We couldn't pause the video fast enough, so she got up and closed herself in the bathroom. She seemed to feel completely out of control and needed to get safe fast. If anyone had any question that she 'recognized' this man, the answer became pretty clear. She had to get away and protect herself from even the image. This is what a trauma response looks like.

One of the things Mom wanted to do was take flowers to the places identified as locations Sister Cathy's body may have been found. Now there's a red flag of an outing! She had the thought to bring me for safety and support. But when she recognized something along the way, there was nothing I could do to stop it. She was suddenly gone, upset, panicked. She needed to get out of that place, and then she needed to get out of the car, and then she needed to get away from me. And when it was all done, she was determined to do the next thing on that day's list. Maybe to prove she was fine, maybe to get back control, or maybe because she was still shaken up.

A challenge I have as someone who loves my mom and wants to protect her from feeling that kind of fear, is antici-pating what might cause it. I want to try to get her to avoid it all together or take extra precautions to feel safe and in control when it might happen. Unfortunately, she has a hard time anticipating that something will set her body reacting because her mind is so clear that she'll be safe. The TV can't hurt her, a space in the woods can't possibly hurt her, etc.

I am gentler with myself now that I understand that no matter what I do I can't stop Mom from feeling so scared and out of control. She does try to appease me by putting more protections in place when she thinks she might see something that takes her back to a past trauma. That's progress."

CHAPTER TWENTY-NINE

The Lightness of Love (Vignette)

I wish my memories followed a certain timeline and made logical sense. That would make it easier to explain or express these experiences to others. Unfortunately, there is no linear approach to this memory recovery process. It cannot be explained through logic. I have no control over which memories surface, when they surface, or how much of an experience reveals itself. An example of this would be my remembering in 2016 that I had Sister Cathy as a teacher. I was asked if she had been my teacher in 1993. My brain was blank, and I really did not know. Twenty-three years later, when I found out that 'Sister Joanita', my sophomore English teacher, was the given name for Cathy Cesnik, I was emotionally and physically shaken.[128] I found it best not to force memories that have not surfaced. My former therapist, Dr. Bradford, cautioned me to trust my instincts.

So, the memories and the experiences may seem somewhat garbled and temporally non-linear. I may contemplate an experience with one of my young personas, thinking I am at peace with that part of my young self, only to find I am having a similar experience months or years later. But that is the way these contemplations come to me. With time, perseverance, more memories, and more information, I have been able to piece together a clearer picture of what happened to me in high school.

In 2015 and 2016, after identifying myself as Jane Doe, the events in my adult life were occurring at an almost dizzying pace. I participated in *The Keepers*, cared for my mom in my home before she peacefully passed away, recognized the

128 See "Piecing Cathy Together," page 155.

man I knew as "Brother Bob", realized that Cathy Cesnik was my teacher the same year she went missing, discovered the place Maskell took me to view Cathy's body, culminating in my honoring Cathy by placing a memorial plaque at the site where her body was discovered. On top of this, I was preparing to mediate my dispute with the Archdiocese.

The pace in my periods of quiet and meditation was no less hectic. I had discovered that Jeannie, my teenaged persona, had been locked away for years as if in a prison. I could feel the fear of "Brother Bob" steadily rising in my personas, and for as much as that fear may have been inexplicable to somebody detached from the situation, what terrified my personas terrified me. My spirit guides were on high alert, protecting me and my personas.

The accumulation of so much movement in my life was causing inner pressure, pushing more buried memories and feelings to the surface. Aware of what was going on in my life, my friend, Barbara, offered me the gift of a six-day Reiki healing workshop at Omega Institute in New York. I readily accepted.

The day before I was to go to Omega, I was driving to work when I asked my personas, 'the girls', what they thought about what I had done to honor Sister Cathy. There was no response, which concerned me, so I asked, "Why can't I see you? Why can't I hear you?" My immediate thought was they were upset with my actions. I then realized I could not hear them because they were outside the cellar of the house, in the backyard.

I was delighted they were outside. Since we began to gather in the cellar, and despite my desire to escape, no one had left there before then. As a matter of fact, there was a feeling of safety with the cellar door blocked by boxes and other stuff. I took this change in the girls' environment as a sign of how pleased they were due to my posting the plaques in memory of Sister Cathy. I realized their feeling of freedom to go outside was a big step in my integration work. I was becoming aware that my personas trusted me more as

I outwardly expressed my belief in what I remember, and what they shared with me.

Focusing on the interior of the cellar, I noticed that Jesus, Cathy, and I were sitting there. The spirit guides had helped clear the back door so the girls could go out. I looked into Jesus's eyes and felt love and pure joy. Cathy was next to me, and I wondered if we needed to stay in the cellar or if we too could go out. I sensed Cathy wanted the three of us to stay put. She told me she had something to show me. I knew the girls were in good hands and Jesus also seemed to think that staying there was necessary. Nevertheless, I persisted and asked Cathy if we could look at what she had to show me outside. She said it was in the box of photos and trinkets still in front of us on the floor, and those items were to stay in the cellar.

As I looked at her, I found myself wondering if she was the living spirit of Cathy Cesnik or a part of myself. As if hearing my question, Jesus responded, "What does it matter?"

As we sat close together in a circle, I took an 8 x 10 black and white glossy photo out of the box. It was a picture of Cathy's decayed body when she was found in 1970. In 1993, I told the police and my lawyers that I remembered being shown these 'crime scene' photos by Maskell, as he repeatedly told me that I was responsible for Cathy's death. To this day, I cannot allow my eyes and brain to again see and experience those pictures shown to me.

However, in my quiet meditation and reflection, I knew Cathy as a courageously caring person, especially after I humbly stood where her body was found. I was sitting next to her in the cellar, looking at a horrific photo that no one should ever be made to look at, much less a young girl. Now I understood why the girls were playing outside.[129]

Some context to this cellar experience would be helpful here. On a psychological and spiritual level, I was sitting with Jesus and Cathy in my inner cellar and holding a crime

---

129 Journal entry dated October 17, 2016 and October 18, 2016.

scene photo. In real time, Barbara was driving us to the Omega Institute.

Arriving at Omega, we were pleased to find that we would have plenty of opportunities for quiet reflection. While meditating during one of the early course sessions, I discovered a large, beautiful bird that appeared to be from the tropics; it sat in a palm tree within my mind's eye. Its vibrant blue, green, yellow, and red feathers reminded me of a parrot. It had a strong, powerful presence accompanied by loud bird noises. I felt I was being introduced to another spirit guide. Similar to when I met Great Grey, I had no idea why this guide showed up, nor what kind of bird it was. After doing some research that evening, I came across a photo of the exact bird I saw in my meditation; it was a macaw. I learned that macaws are bright rainbow-colored birds, usually found in the tropics. I was right in that they are a part of the parrot family, and they mate for life.

As I reflected on the beauty and presence of this bird, I sensed Macaw would inspire something much different than the gifts Great Grey helped me embrace within myself. Some areas within me that came to mind were to see myself standing fearless and beautiful in any situation, to speak my truth with confidence, and to explore my creativity. What I was learning to trust was that these two bird guides were instinctively committed to me. Great greys are 'devoted parents', and macaws 'mate for life'. Even though I knew it would take time to learn more about my relationship with Macaw, I believed I had taken the first step.[130]

As the week unfolded, I found myself also reflecting on my relationship with Cathy. I was proud of the insights and healing that had occurred between the wounded child within me and her. I felt that this recent experience of visiting the place where her body was found may have finally brought closure to our search for peace. There were a few

---

130 While Macaw has been a part of my personal growth since meeting her, I am presenting just the primary guides needed to explain this memoir.

other times since I first remembered Cathy when I believed the inner work on our relationship was over, only to discover we were not done.

After a massage one evening at Omega, I decided to focus on Cathy and what she needed in order to finally rest in peace. In our workshop session the next day, we were to spend time drumming while reflecting on an intention. As I drummed, I invited Cathy to let me know if she needed anything else. I was surprised when she asked to "hold Little Cathy." (I found it interesting that Cathy referred to her by the name Maskell gave me, not 'Girlfriend', the one I changed it to.) Little Cathy and I said yes.

As my emotions intensified, Jesus asked if he could be of help. I agreed, and he told me to look through his eyes. I was immediately reminded of how much love I saw looking into his eyes right before I headed to this workshop. As I drummed, I felt one with Jesus. I was immersed in the drumming, and acutely aware that while I felt alone, I was sitting in a room full of people who were also drumming their way along their own personal paths.

Within my quiet, I saw Little Cathy sitting next to Sister Cathy's dead body, which was in the same condition as portrayed in the 8 x 10 photo I saw earlier in the cellar with her and Jesus. Little Cathy was crying. Cathy walked over, sat down, put Little Cathy on her lap and while rocking her said, "You did not do this to me. I am not there." Feeling one with Little Cathy, I too felt her rocking me as I sobbed on her shoulder.

As I continued to drum, the tears poured down my cheeks. Cathy comforted Little Cathy by saying, "I never meant for this to happen. You should never have seen this." I felt as if I were being emptied of all those feelings of guilt and responsibility. I drummed and cried, drummed and cried. As the heavy weight of shame and guilt lifted, my raw grief released, shaking my body. Eventually, Little Cathy began to feel calmer. I noticed a lightness within me. I found myself thinking, "I'm OK!" with real joy.

Once the tears ended, Cathy said, "Great Grey has been with you all the time." I was a bit taken aback by this change in focus, but then I noticed my Protector standing off to the side. Feeling empty of all the lies, guilt, and labels forced on me after her death, Cathy said, "I want to take you away from here for good."

Cathy lifted Little Cathy/me onto the back of Great Grey. She then joined me. As we flew, I was aware of all forms of animals following on the ground beneath us—all heading to the edge of the ocean. As I drummed, I was lost in the flight and the wonder of what was unfolding.

Great Grey landed on the beach, and we walked to the ocean's edge. Once again, I found my adult self, sitting on the floor at Omega, sobbing as I drummed. I was now aware that Little Cathy not only carried the guilt and burdens thrust on her by Maskell and "Brother Bob", but she simultaneously was the part of me allowing space for Cathy to rest. Cathy Cesnik looked at me/Little Cathy and said, "You are ready. I can go. You are in good hands." All the animals gathered around as I tearfully said my good-byes. I was encircled by my ancestors and spirit guides, along with all of my young personas. Cathy walked out into the ocean saying, "The Mother is waiting and ready." As the ocean waves engulfed her, I drummed, repeating... "I let you go..." Everyone gathered around Little Cathy, hugging, and absorbing this moment.

Still looking through Jesus's eyes, he said, "You have journeyed the path of letting go and I hold you in my heart. Stay here and take in all the love and care for you." As I continued looking into his eyes, I saw the beach illuminated with light, caused by the intensity of love being focused on me.[131] In a normal situation, I would have been absorbed in the emotions and ended feeling spent. By looking through Jesus's eyes, I was able to be more present and observe what was happening. I felt the full emotional impact of the

131 Journal entry dated October 20, 2016.

release of the guilt and grief around Cathy's death, but the experience was energizing rather than draining.

When I returned home from my retreat, I took time to see if my inner girls had anything to say about our recent experience. They/I wrote a response right from of my heart onto the journal page of October 27, 2016:

> There was a wind that blew through and carried me on the wings of a beautiful bird. My sister was with me and I felt safe and free! The smell of death was washed from my nostrils with pure fresh air. I felt my sister's warmth and the soft feathers of this magnificent bird. I was in heaven!
>
> Then we came to a place where the ocean meets the earth and the bird landed. We walked to the edge of the powerful waters. My sister turned to me and said she must leave. I could not bear this. She said I would be in good hands and that she would not be far if I ever needed her. My heart felt like it would burst with sadness. I realized I've never really grieved the passing of my sister. So, this is how it feels.

Soon after the amazing workshop at Omega, my daughter and I went away for a weekend. One day we went for massages followed by a delicious meal. I had a special ritual in mind, so that evening we made a fire outside of the cabin. Since being triggered by the photo of the man I remembered as "Brother Bob", I had made two decisions. First, I would never look at any pictures of men connected to Maskell or Keough without my therapist present. And second, I would begin to take my power back by starting to ask for pictures of individuals. I slowly began to put faces on some of the faceless perpetrators in my memories, instead of waiting for their photo to blindside me. I took a number of those pictures with me to throw in the fire.

I decided we would have a 'Grandfather Fire' like the one we had at Omega. Sarah and I lit candles and placed them toward the four directions representing earth, fire, air, and water. One by one, I put all the pictures into the fire, sending them back to themselves. I asked the fire to transform the energy into something good and positive for me and others.

I had taken a photograph of Cathy to Omega, which I now offered to the 'Grandfather Fire'. I thanked Cathy and sent her off into peace and love. It was a wonderful ritual, very freeing and uplifting.

Prior to going to the cabin, I e-mailed pictures of our plaque honoring Cathy to Gemma and Abbie. The morning after the Grandfather Fire, I read Gemma's response to my e-mail about the memorial. She said it was appropriate that I did this at this time of year. Curious as to what Gemma meant, I researched and discovered that the night Cathy Cesnik went missing was November 7, 1969, with November 7 being the date of the fire ritual. Exactly 47 years after Cathy went missing, wrapped in a feeling of complete awe, I wrote this in my journal:

On the night she was betrayed
the fire was prepared.
The Great Spirits were called.

Candles were placed in 4 directions
acknowledging
Earth, Air, Water and Fire.
The circle was complete.

I called upon those who had gone before me.
'Help me face my fear.'
'Help me send these abusers back to themselves.'
One, then another, then another
let go into the fire.
Heavy Fear changing to Light Freedom.

Finally, my last intention.
Holding the picture of the one who was wounded,
thought stopped,

I said, 'Be at peace. Know I am at peace.
You have accomplished what you headed out to do.
I have found my voice.
I am taking my power back.'

When I next returned to the cellar in my quiet, I found everyone was now gathered inside, Cathy and Girlfriend included. The feeling in the room was lighter. A burden was lifted, and I felt freer. I had let go of the guilt and responsibility for Cathy's death. I could tell Cathy would continue to be Girlfriend's spiritual guide in dealing with any obstacles toward full integration and peace, such as the deep-rooted terror that "Brother Bob" was coming to get me.[132]

---

132 See "The Council Gathered in the Cellar (Vignette)," page 205.

CHAPTER THIRTY

The Council and the Mandala (Vignette)

While everyone was reuniting in the cellar, I became aware that the aspect of myself that was feeling most terrified of "Brother Bob" was Frances. Over the years, I spent many hours working to reclaim and integrate with her. She had been degraded, manipulated, raped on multiple occasions, and forced to see Cathy's corpse lying in the woods. The last time Frances was raped by "Brother Bob", she was gathered off the floor by Jeannie, who took over to keep Frances from being crushed by the weight of the unbearable pain.[133] But she was still shattered and needed help. I knew in my gut that we were gathered to deal with the fear that she/I still deeply held. I had a sick sense that what was coming might entail going back into the room where "Brother Bob" told me he killed Cathy.

As the adult, the mere thought that he was still alive and could hurt me was terrifying. I had work to do in my quiet, but I was anxious about what that might be.

I continued to take this combination of feelings and inner movement into my therapy, journaling, and meditation. One helpful process that I had worked with through the years was the 'mandala'. 'Mandala' is a Sanskrit term that means circle. In various spiritual traditions, mandalas may be employed for a variety of reasons, one being to establish a sacred space. As more traumatic memories emerged within me, my therapist suggested I try to use a mandala. She instructed me to draw a circle on a piece of paper. Then,

---

133 See "Birth of a Warrior (Vignette)," page 192.

as I reflected on what scared, worried, or angered me, I would direct the thought or emotion into the circle through the crayon in my hand. The goal was to do this until I had no more energy or emotion left to place into that sacred space. By decreasing the intensity of the situation, I could look more clearly at what I was dealing with. I also would remind myself that the overwhelming emotion was now contained in that circle, not in me.

Meanwhile, in my quiet, Jesus had shown me the ring from the box of trinkets, which stirred me to remember my encounter with the girl with the long black hair. That meditation distracted me from the anxiety building within me and my young personas. When, after a period of time I returned my attention to my inner children, I panicked when I heard Jesus ask, "Why not invite 'Brother Bob' into the cellar?"

Surprisingly, no matter how afraid I felt, this made sense. If I were ever going to break through the intense terror Frances held, we had to bring "Brother Bob" into the circle so all my personas could somehow see him and then contain him.

I knew to do this I first had to defuse some of the fear in me that could easily derail my efforts to move forward with my health work. As I journaled about this, I put the fear and nervousness I felt about meeting "Brother Bob" into a mandala. The black crayon in my hand covered the circle with a webby heaviness of the jumbled unknown to come. Then my hand reached for red, releasing blood pulsing fear all over the webbing. On December 17, 2016, I wrote under the mandala, "Here is my nervousness and fear of facing B. B.—my actual fear of facing him, as well as, letting go of any obstacles placed deliberately, or by my own survival process, to block my ability to see him or acknowledge him."

While preparing to bring "Brother Bob" into the circle, I sensed the younger aspects of myself were still in a panic. I watched as Cathy pulled Girlfriend closer to her, encircling her with two strong and protective arms. Then, just like my initial meeting with the Tiger in the garden, Frances was slowly taken into the Tiger's body through its mouth.[134] They stood as one with Frances looking out from its mouth through the tiger's sharp teeth, protected by its entire body. I watched the Snake move like a streak of lightning, coiling itself around Jeannie's body. The Snake quite literally became her armor. Its head faced forward from Jeannie's face protecting her entire body while hissing its threatening warning.

For my adult self, Great Grey, who had been standing regally behind me, wrapped its wings around me, as it would often do, providing me a deep sense of protection while facing fear of the unknown. Little Jeannie was carried off on the White Mare, away from all fear and harm.[135]

Now that everyone was in their protective stances, I became aware of the back door. When I first entered the cellar, that door had boxes and all kinds of junk blocking it. Thanks to the spirit guides' earlier help, the entrance way was cleared. The door opened, and I was surprised to see Mike and my father walking into the cellar with "Brother Bob".[136] I quickly did an assessment of how the girls were doing. Realizing they were protected, I felt cautiously okay having him there.

Mike and Dad stood on either side of him, each keeping a strong hand on his shoulders. As the three of them faced the circle of Spirit Guides and my personas, I wondered how we would contain him. I thought maybe a mandala would work. I drew a large circle on the floor right in front of where he stood. As I looked over at Mike and Dad, careful not to look at "Brother Bob's" face, I motioned them to the circle.

They walked him into the center of the mandala. Then they slowly pushed him down into the circle until he was contained. Now, with his squished face peering up and his

---

134 See "My Inner Garden (Vignette)," page 201.
135 See "Little Jeannie (Vignette)," page 50.
136 My father died on March 15, 2009.

hands and palms pushing out beside his face, he looked as though he were pressed up against a window. My anxiety began to lift, but I needed more assurance that he could not leave his container. With that, Mike and Dad began to chain him to the edges of the circle. Finally, he was controlled, and I could freely work with those aspects of myself who were still terrified of him.[137]

Once this experience was over, Mike and Dad asked me if I needed anything else. I told them, "Not right now." Their response was, "Anything you need let us know." They wanted to be sure "Brother Bob" was not a threat, so seeing that I was okay, they left through the cellar door.

The energy lightened as the young ones within me began to consider that "Brother Bob" may not be able to go anywhere. The girls relaxed; Frances made her way out from within the Tiger; the Snake unraveled from around Jeannie; Cathy released her hold on Girlfriend; Great Grey took his wings away from me; and the White Mare and Little Jeannie were back behind Jesus's chair.

Then I sat for a long time, taking in what just occurred, wondering if the young ones could trust that this perpetrator was totally contained. Surprisingly, he has stayed within that mandala to this very day.

---

137 See "Brother Bob" Contained (mandala), page 261.

CHAPTER THIRTY-ONE

Going Back for Frances (Vignette)

While I was working on the next level of fear, the filming of *The Keepers* was coming to an end. One evening, my son, Greg, presented Ryan and Jess with a carving he had made of Aletheia, the Greek Goddess of Truth. Greg said Aletheia is known to carry a mirror that faces outward to help us awaken to the truth that lies deep within ourselves. He felt Ryan and Jess were holding a mirror out for everyone to see; but the challenge was always for people to see that truth. I felt the gift of Aletheia was also being given to me, but I did not know why.[138]

Now, with "Brother Bob" contained, the Council could take a closer look at what we needed to totally sever from him. I needed to decrease the fear he instilled in me in high school, which continued to be with me for over 45 years. I looked at my teenage persona Frances with a heavy heart, feeling it was my job to determine what she needed. While I wanted to help her, I was not sure what to do. I sat with this dilemma for quite a while.

I began to think that Aletheia may be able to help, so I asked her to join us in the cellar. On entering the circle, she took a seat directly across from me.[139] Even though the mirror was resting in her lap, I sensed my image was in it and that made me uncomfortable. I was not aware of any reason I needed Aletheia's support, so I figured she was going to show

---

138 See "The Gift of Aletheia," page 135.

139 After inviting Aletheia to join the group in the cellar, I created a mandala. When I finished, I found light within the mandala circle, revealing a rainbow of myself under the brown feathery shreds of who I thought I was. On December 13, 2016, I wrote under the mandala, "I invited Aletheia into the basement circle. Light illuminates the Darkness and I find multi-colored issues, details, dimensions...NOT SO SCARY!"

Frances the truth of what those evil men did to her. When Aletheia finally held up the mirror, she looked straight at me, not at Frances. All I could see was my adult image.

On January 3, 2017, I recorded my interaction with Aletheia once I was aware that the mirror was intended for me:

> I looked in the mirror and said, "I know you." The Goddess asked me to go with her to what I saw in the mirror. I was then in the room with "Brother Bob", and I was saying, "I know you." Aletheia asked, "Know who?"—and I said, "Me." I saw the adult me who was reflected in the mirror, not Frances, looking at that man. Aletheia asked what I would like to do. So, I began hitting "Brother Bob", saying over and over, "Get off of me!'; then screaming, "I know you and I'm going to tell what you've done. Get off of me! I know you, and I will tell who you are." I pulled his penis out of my mouth saying, "Take this back. You won't keep me silent any longer. I will tell what you did to Cathy. Be afraid... Be very afraid." Aletheia asked, "What next?" After I pulled myself together, I pushed the door open and beat on Maskell saying, "You won't keep me locked up any longer. I am not staying a prisoner here any longer."
>
> When I looked up from my seat in the circle, the mirror was right across from me, and I saw myself—a 63-year-old woman who will not be silenced by them anymore. I will not be locked up in that room any longer.

I then knew Aletheia was there for me. I was the one who needed to go back into that room where Frances encountered "Brother Bob", to acknowledge to myself just how enraged and pained I felt. Once again, I faced the truth, which I tend to shy away from, that I am Frances, and she is me. As the adult, I was surprised and exhausted, releasing so many repressed emotions with my thoughts stumbling into my awareness and falling onto the paper of my journal.

Until then, I could not bring myself to feel anger toward Maskell. My display of rage, reflected in Aletheia's mirror of truth, was so unexpected I would need time to rest and reflect on what just occurred.[140]

As I continued to move toward integrating Frances, I became aware of the confused state "Brother Bob's" abuse created. In late January 2017, I wrote in my journal:

> I am now in the room with "Brother Bob" as a 16-year-old. I feel his hand on my left shoulder pushing me down to my knees. I hear him telling me to take my clothes off as he strips his black shirt and pants off. As he uses the vibrator to bring me to orgasm, he sits over me pushing his penis into my mouth. I am done, gone, dead. But then I get up, like a spirit/ghost from a dead body and walk away from myself, the me laying on the floor.
>
> I find myself crying in real time. Today I thought that I wasn't pinned under him anymore. I cried feeling like I don't like not being pinned under him. My emotions, which seem to be all over the place, are very sensitive and tender these days.

As I reflected on what I had written, the pain that Frances held within me could not be denied. The harder I worked to gather her back to myself, the more I connected. Because of this journaling, I realized something as disgusting as being pinned under a grown man helped this young girl feel secure and grounded. He was the weight that kept her from floating away for good. I not only felt her pain, but her fear as well. What would keep me connected to the ground if he were gone?

As I regained my energy, I knew there was still more work to be done. Aletheia was guiding me toward feeling the pain of Frances' experiences with "Brother Bob", and to do so as an integrated person. I did not want to do this. What made it possible was knowing "Brother Bob" was chained to his container, as well as having a supportive environment for myself.

---

140 See Rage and Pain Contained (mandala), page 262.

After taking time to decide if I would go with Frances into the unknown, I found myself with her, not in the cellar but back in the room. The intense fear I felt just being in this space helped me understand that a part of Frances was still stuck in that room; I was still stuck there. I wondered how many times I had been back here—to remember, to reconnect, to carry a part of myself out, to look more clearly at the truth and not the illusion created by lies or the actions that paralyzed me...to somehow let myself move beyond the point where the child within me stood frozen, like a block of ice.

I looked down at Frances, curled up on the floor in the same way Jeannie found her 47 years earlier.[141] But this time I felt something new; instead of feeling self-blame for being totally responsible for everything that had gone on in that room, I felt compassion for Frances. The ice was melting, but more love was needed for Frances to thaw. I had no idea what to do since I felt I had done everything possible. What happened in that experience with "Brother Bob" and Maskell was so horrific that Frances needed more than what I could provide. The ice around Frances was thawing into tears, as I felt her sobbing and pleading, "I want my mom, I want my mom!" I then heard my mother ask, "Can we help?"[142]

My mom had died shortly before my meditations regarding the council in the basement began, and my dad had been dead for eight years. Since the age of 27, when I first began remembering being sexually abused by a relative, I could not help but wonder, "Where were my parents during all this abuse? Why didn't they take care of me? Why did they let it continue?"

I sensed the only way to finally get Frances out of that room was to immerse myself in the pain she held, as well as in her longing for Mom and Dad's help and support. I was faced with the question of how I felt about them,

---

141 See "Birth of a Warrior (Vignette)," page 190.
142 Journal entry dated February 20, 2017.

already knowing the victimized kid in me felt abandoned, neglected, and ignored as if I were invisible. However, by this time in my life, I had already been able to confront these feelings and find some peace within myself, especially after working through a few issues before Mom died and after my dad passed. Nevertheless, their offer to help was surprising and ran counter to my lingering feeling that they did not care.

Still, I was not in the habit of requesting, much less expecting, my parents' help in the deeply personal matters about my abuse. I told Mom if she thought they could help get Frances out of this place, they were welcome to join me. Immediately, my parents came through the door, picked Frances off the floor, and we all sat on the couch. I sat on an end as an observer of them. They were sitting with Frances between them, with their arms around her. Holding their little girl and looking right at me my mom said, "Your dad would have killed him if he knew, and I would have let him!"[143]

As Frances began to cry, my adult self could feel tears running down my cheeks as I began to feel my parent's arms move around me. They gently said, "None of this was your fault. You do not need to stay here any longer. We're not leaving here without you."[144] They said the things I longed for them to say, but it was only when they said those words that I realized how much I needed them.

I was confused and surprised at myself. On some level, I was still dealing with my anger toward my parents and the chasm I had built over the years between us. If, in my present reality, they had somehow appeared and offered to help, I would have said it was too little too late.

However, in this interaction involving Frances, my adult feelings and defenses were put to the side. Frances had been longing for this to happen. She was hungry for their reassurance, and she was drinking up their acceptance of

143 Journal entry dated February 20, 2017.
144 Journal entry dated February 20, 2017.

her. I could feel my parents' love for me warming my whole being. This was just what I needed to get that little broken spirit within me off the floor and out of that horrible place.

At some point, as Frances was being comforted, cushioned, and coddled by Mom and Dad, they lovingly said, "Okay, it's time for us to leave here." Very gently, they stood up with me, as Frances, between them. Carefully, my parents walked me to the door and before I knew it, we were no longer in that room.

I could tell that something had been finalized, bringing with it a sense of freedom and connection at the same time. I took time to process the impact of this experience before I felt ready to reenter the cellar.

When I returned to the Council, I found that Frances and I were once again sitting in the circle. Aletheia was no longer present, and my parents were gone. Their work was done. "Brother Bob" was still contained within the mandala on the cellar floor. The spirit of the whole group had turned into a feeling of lightness, joy, and amazement.

This healing experience made me see that my personas not only carried the fear and the pain, but they also kept alive the longing and desire for my parents' love, acceptance, and protection. Frances helped me see that if I thought I did not matter to Mom and Dad, it would be impossible for me to trust them. This allowed me to genuinely feel that my parents loved and accepted me and would never have hurt me. I know now that if Mom and Dad had known what was happening at that school, they would have done something to stop it. They would have saved me because I did not deserve what was happening to me.

This rescue of Frances was another level of my letting go of my fear of "Brother Bob" who at one time had controlled me. I began to understand the fear had been rooted in the painful actions by that man, compounded by his statement that he killed someone. Going back for Frances awakened a truth within me; "Brother Bob" was just another pedophile. "Brother Bob's" power over me as Frances kept me so stuck, that it took my realization of my parents' unconditional love to rescue me. I needed them to show me I was so much more than what I thought of myself, and he was so much less.

Now, as we sat in the cellar, separated from the source of past fear, and resting in the lightness of the moment, I began to believe I was more.

CHAPTER THIRTY-TWO

Leaving the Cellar (Vignette)

Over the next few months, I could tell Frances and Jeannie were feeling more present, connected, and comfortable. Frances wanted to talk with Cathy before we left the cellar. After she moved over to sit next to Jeannie, they began to tell Cathy just what they felt about her, and why.[145]

Frances told Cathy that her death was upsetting. She explained that after Cathy left Keough, she felt tricked and alone. Cathy explained that she did visit after she left Keough, but I did not want anything to do with her; so, she thought it best to give me space. She also said she did not think Maskell would retaliate against me after she confronted him, nor did she know that he began abusing me again. Cathy's apologies touched Frances' heart, and Frances, obviously stronger since being rescued by me and my parents, was honestly, lovingly, and directly opening herself to Cathy. Frances was leaning against Jeannie, and as she softened to Cathy, I could feel the healing effects of this exchange within myself.

Now that the Council in the cellar felt calm, I hoped it was time for us to move on. It had been over a year since

---

145 I journaled on September 5, 2016 about one of the surprising insights gained from that intimate sharing between me and Cathy in the basement.

"Walking through the grocery store, buying ground turkey, I can feel Cathy in my heart. I am aware that I have invited her to sit with Frances, who said that is what she wanted before we leave the basement. I have been aware of Cathy's closeness for a couple days. Today, I lovingly asked Cathy to tell me what she needed me to know. Standing in the store, I was suddenly washed through with the feeling that she left me. Simultaneously, I thought, 'You left me; Mathew left me; Mike left me.' This feeling of loss was sudden and strong. I felt I would burst into tears right there in the middle of the seafood department, so pushing the overwhelming feelings down, I told Cathy, 'Not now...Later!'"

I began my quest for peace and another layer of healing sitting in the cellar, so I asked Jesus if it was time to go. With that we found ourselves in the yard of the house. The girls were playing, while the spirit guides stood around in a protective yet relaxed fashion. I was thrilled to feel the sun on my face and the breeze softly blowing against my skin. I looked at Jesus, not able to contain a smile, and asked, "Where to now? What still needs to be done?"

With that, I found us in the attic of the house I grew up in. I was carrying the mandala that contained "Brother Bob" like a suitcase. When I was certain we were in the attic, which was my bedroom as a teenager, I threw the mandala on the floor so everyone could see that "Brother Bob" could not hurt us.

The girls sat on the two single beds in my bedroom while the guides remained nearby. Although unsure of why we were there, I nevertheless felt relaxed being in what was a place of comfort, a haven during a very tumultuous time in my life.

From the fall of 2016 and well into the summer of 2017, my quiet sessions continued, but my focus was on the journey in my outer life more so than my inner path. This allowed me to rest on a spiritual level. With the airing of *The Keepers*, I found myself leaning on a strength that I was unaware existed in me. I spoke to the Baltimore City police and the State's Attorney's Office about the man I remembered as "Brother Bob".[146] I gave a number of talks and media interviews, and I worked through the impact of recognizing perpetrators from my past, which helped me become even more comfortable feeling anger. I was beginning to understand how the courage to do these scary things was a direct result of the inner healing that occurred in the cellar.

During the summer of 2017, I started to think about Beth, one of my earliest personas revealed to me in 1980.[147]

---

146 After *The Keepers* aired, I began to hear of other women who were now able to speak to authorities about abuse experienced by the man I refer to as "Brother Bob". Learning that I was not alone and that others were also keeping this secret due to fear helped me embrace my past more fully.

147 See "My Spiritual Path Begins," page 42.

Beth was an innocent little girl who was open, trusting, and extremely vulnerable. She was the aspect of myself who held the trauma resulting from the abuse by my uncle. Once the abuse by Magnus and Maskell began, she receded, and Frances pushed forward.

It was Beth who went into the confessional at Keough believing that it was the right thing to do. I thought about how horrible that moment must have been when she/I, ready to have the heavy weight of guilt lifted off my shoulders, hit the wall that Magnus presented. I felt compassion for Beth and found myself wondering where she was. This question concerned me since I had hoped I was done finding aspects of myself and reconnecting with them. For so long I had worked on this integration process successfully and was currently focused on my work with my persona Jeannie. Even though I wondered whether Beth was a distraction from moving forward, I continued to wonder where she was.

With this question in my heart, I asked myself, "What now?" Eventually, Jesus looked at me and, without saying a word, I found the two of us sitting in the chapel at Keough. As I sat with him, I slowly understood why we were there; this was where Beth was. She had come to the confessional to clear past obstacles but wound up stuck in the biggest obstacle of her short life.

Jesus and I began to discuss how to get Beth out of that institutional coffin.[148] As usual, he did not have a whole lot to say, so I told him, "I'm gonna figure this out." I went over to the confessional and asked Beth to come out. I told her everything was fine, she was safe, it was all over. There was no response or movement.

Standing outside the confessional, hoping to coax Beth out, I was thinking how different this felt from retrieving Frances' last bit of essence from Maskell's room. While Frances had been frozen in place, I knew she was stuck. So, I was relating on integrating with her well before I found her frozen in that room. However, with Beth, I had no idea

---

148 See "The Keough Years," page 19.

she was stuck anywhere, much less in this confessional. She appeared to be paralyzed, like a stone figure. She did not acknowledge that I was there or that she heard me.

Jesus walked over and stood with me at the entrance to the side of the confessional where Beth was. He suggested that I "go in on the priest's side." I quickly replied, "I am not going in on the priest's side! I will not enter that part of this confessional! I don't want any part of it! I'm not going in there!" Jesus said he just thought I would be closer to Beth and could better encourage her. I knew that statement was right since the priest in a confessional was only inches from the penitent's face. I begrudgingly went into the side of the confessional where Magnus would have been. After making a noisy fuss as I positioned myself, I looked at the little girl before me. I felt a deep sadness. I described my conversation with Beth in a journal entry:

> I moved into the priest's side of the confessional yesterday to speak to Beth. I first told her Magnus was dead... long gone, so it was time to get out of this place. Then I sat there telling her softly, over and over, "You did nothing wrong. The priest is dead...You did not make him do what he did. You were right to tell him what you felt guilty about. You did nothing wrong. He did. He never meant to help you, just hurt you."[149]

As time passed, Beth remained petrified despite my efforts, so I looked at Jesus and asked if he had any ideas. He said, "Let me try." His response really pissed me off. All I could think was, if Jesus knew all along that I was stuck in the confessional and how to get me out, why didn't he stop the abuse from happening. I was angry and curious at the same time. Interestingly, while I had no problem getting angry with Jesus, I had difficulty being angry with Maskell.

149 Journal entry dated December 22, 2017. As I wrote this exchange, I realized I was now in the position of a priestess for little Beth. I was doing for her what I originally looked to the priest for: acceptance, help to lift my burden, words of comfort and compassion.

As I looked over Beth's shoulder, I saw Jesus gently slip in next to her. Positioned beside Beth, Jesus looked up into my eyes and said, "Jean, it's time to leave this place." I was shaken to the core as he unexpectedly cut straight to the heart of the matter. Once again, the stark truth exposed something I spent years trying to deny—I am Beth, and she is me.

Jesus's powerful words reconnected me to the truth that Beth was a persona created by me when I was splitting into pieces due to the trauma caused by my uncle. I now understood that I blamed Beth for what happened in the confessional and afterward. It was innocent Beth's honesty that I needed in order to go into the confessional, and it was that which got me trapped in that cell. The awareness presented by Jesus filled me with love and compassion for myself. I felt wobbly; I was connecting with Beth.

I exited my side of the confessional and went around to help Jesus remove Beth from her 'coffin' of the last 49 years. We carried her stiff body to a bench, then sat her down with Jesus on one side and me on the other. We kept her safe and secure, guarded by our bodies and wrapped in our arms. Beth was not strong enough to move, and I had no idea where to go, so we just sat in a pew. My desire to get out of that place would have to wait a few days.

As each day passed in my physical life, my spirit grew more and more antsy. I needed to get out of the chapel and take Beth with me. No matter how weak she was, I could not stay there any longer. I looked over at Jesus and told him I was ready to go, but I wanted to destroy the confessional first. He responded, "That will have to wait."

While waiting to leave, I entered this in my journal on January 11, 2018:

> I hugged [Beth] and Jesus hugged us both. We are in a space without time or place. We are waiting to see where we will end up. I keep thinking of places we might land,

but nothing yet. I need to be patient. All I feel is relieved that this young part of myself is protected and safe.[150]

After a while, I realized we were on a path in the woods. Making sure my feet were planted solid on the ground and that Beth was secure between Jesus and me, I began to take in my surroundings. We were standing in the forest within my spirit, on a path I had walked on with Jesus many times before while meditating. I stood in the back of a dwelling I recognized from a previous meditation.[151] Confused as to why we were there, Jesus told me it was the best place to be and asked me to help him take Beth up the side of the house. I was comfortable in the situation, so I agreed to help him. Standing on either side of Beth, we helped her up the rocky walk along the side of the house. When we came around to the front, I was once again amazed at the beauty of the breathtaking view. This was indeed a good place for Beth to recuperate.

We walked along the front porch and decided we would sit on the wicker lounge where Beth could take in the view, put her feet up, and relax. After she sat down, I looked across the porch to see Great Grey perched on the railing. Cathy and my other guides sat lazily around my young

---

150 My integration was becoming noticeable in my journal entries and within myself. I began referring to the aspect of myself known to me as 'Beth' at times as 'Beth' and at other times as my nickname as a young girl.

151 About 18 years earlier, Jesus and I came across this house while on one of our many walks during my quiet. Jesus told me this modest home in the woods was for me. We discussed the meaning of this in relation to my spiritual life. Then, at his request, I followed him as we began climbing a rocky stairway up the side of the house. He got to what I assumed was the back of the building and moved aside. I had been watching my footing, so when I reached the top, I looked up and gasped at the magnificent scene before me.

I liken what I felt then to a deep spiritual experience. Staring out at endless beauty, I felt engulfed in childlike wonder and love, aware that it was not what my eyes were seeing or the quickening of my pulse that mattered. What mattered was what my heart observed, and my spirit felt. My soul knew this majestic place as The Great Unknown, which I can only describe as a mystical experience of God. (See "Brother Richard," page 44.) After I had some time to adjust my senses, I saw that we were on a beautiful porch that wrapped around the whole front of the house. I came to know this as my heart's dwelling place.

personas, Girlfriend, Little Jeannie, Frances, and Jeannie. I noticed the mandala containing "Brother Bob" was lying on the porch floor.

I told Jesus he could go over to sit with the girls, but he said he would stay with us. We stayed like this, on the front porch overlooking the Great Unknown, for five or six days. I was content listening to the chatting and giggling going on at the other end of the porch.

I slowly became aware that my persona, Jeannie, was staring at me, and it was making me uncomfortable. I eventually asked her if she had something to say. She told me she did, so I suggested we walk along the path in the woods. As we walked across the porch, I glanced toward Cathy with a look that said, "Will you keep an eye on things here?" Her nod said it all. By the time Jeannie and I were at the corner of the porch, we saw the Snake moving with us. Great Grey began flying around, the Tiger got up and stretched, and Jesus turned to follow. I asked Jesus to stay there in case Beth needed him. He said he would come with us. I responded with a quick "No, we don't need a parade! Stay here!" He just repeated that he was coming with us. I was frustrated with his insistence to come along, but more so because after so many years I could not figure out who he was and what he meant to me.

I decided to let go of my irritation with Jesus, so off we all headed, down the rocky walkway along the side of the house. On the path I walked next to Jeannie. Great Grey flew ahead, the Snake slithered down the path beside Jeannie, the Tiger lumbered along beside me, and Jesus walked behind us. I was glad the bird was guiding us since my sense of direction was so bad, and I needed to listen intently to Jeannie now that she wanted to talk to me.

We walked along the path for a few weeks in real time, with a good portion of the walk passing in silence. In time, Jeannie began to talk about how she felt when she discovered that "Brother Bob" was alive. She was devastated when Maskell told her that "Brother Bob", the man she thought she loved, was dead. Then, to discover in 2015 that he had not died, Jeannie was at first elated; then she was confused and hurt. If he really loved her like he said, why would he leave her to rot for over 45 years.

Yet, I continued to feel that something else was coming. As we walked, I would periodically say, as if obliged to do so, "Jeannie, what do you want to talk about? I'm listening." Eventually we stopped next to a bench positioned off the side of the path. We decided to sit there and continue our conversation. Jeannie sat to my right and Jesus sat to my left. The Snake curled around a low hanging branch overtop Jeannie, Great Grey perched on the back of the bench, and the Tiger spread out on the ground before us. There we sat in silence. As I enjoyed the beautiful scenery, I wondered if I would ever be comfortable talking to Jeannie.

CHAPTER THIRTY-THREE

Buried in Despair (Vignette)

Jesus, my adult self, and Jeannie sat on that bench, within my meditation, for a couple of weeks. I was waiting for Jeannie to tell me what she needed from me. I hoped I could do what I had to do for her, then finally move on from this awkward relationship. Despite feeling moments of compassion for Jeannie after 2015, I still wanted nothing to do with her since I could not accept that she was part of me.

I believed Jeannie liked the sexual activity going on at Keough after Cathy died. I was sickened with the mere thought that she could have been in love with "Brother Bob". I blamed her for everything that happened to me. Even after I had grown and healed so much, Jeannie continued to disgust me.

Here we sat, side by side, waiting. Eventually, I asked, "Jeannie what do you think...you want to talk?"

She quickly said, "I've been waiting for you to do just this—ask me to talk with you—and mean it. I want you to know what happened after Cathy died. It was hard on all of us. I don't know if the younger girls were as aware of how intense the abuse became after her death, but it got harder. Then, after Maskell told me that 'Brother Bob' died, I became uncaring. Nothing mattered. When I went with Maskell now, I didn't care what I was being asked or forced to do. I did anything and would try anything. I just didn't care."

Jeannie continued, "One day we were driving, and I thought we were going to his room at St. Clement's rectory. He suddenly pulled up in front of a building which reminded me of a school. He told me he had to pick up something, and I was to wait in the car. I sat there for some time before the door opened and a man got in. It wasn't Maskell. I was scared being closed in the car with this stranger. He told me he knew what I was, and that he was fine with it. He thought maybe I could help him. I saw his penis was exposed. I went to open the passenger door to leave, and Maskell came back. He was furious. He pulled the man out of the car, yelled at him, and hit him. Maskell told the man if he ever pulled anything like that again, he'd 'personally pull his prick off and feed it to him.' The man kept apologizing and handed Maskell money saying this was a sign of his good faith. He could be trusted not to do that again. The man turned to me and gave me an ugly smile, then walked away. I crouched down in my seat. Maskell got in and we left. He protected me from being out on the street with men like that doing whatever they wanted."

I asked Jeannie if she ever thought that might have been a set up for her to trust Maskell more, just like "Brother Bob" was not really dead? With a tone of despair, she said, "I don't know what to believe. I thought what they were telling me was true and now I'm finding out it's not. I just don't know what to believe..."

She then said, "Jean, another time Maskell parked on a street near Keough. He had me tell a man on the sidewalk that his fly was down. The man looked toward the car, smiled, then came closer. When the man got to the window, his penis exposed to me, Maskell told me what to do. I did as I was told. When the man was done, he went around to Maskell's window, leaned down, handed him money saying, 'I'm so glad you told me about her. She is wild and I'll be back.' He looked at me while licking his lips and walked away. That lasted all of five minutes, and no one even noticed. I was in a portable whore house. Maskell was my pimp, and I was his trained monkey."

As Jeannie relayed this incident to me, I became aware that Jesus, the adult me, and Jeannie were no longer on the bench in the forest; we were now sitting in the same order, in the front seat of Maskell's car. I thought I was about to vomit. I told Jeannie of my disgust after hearing what happened in that car with Maskell and asked her what she thought about all of this.

Quickly she responded, "I'm not sure what I think. I wasn't even aware that what he was doing was wrong. He was in charge, and I was to do as I was told, no questions asked."

I needed to be still and think about what I had just revealed to myself, but I also had to look away from those intensely upsetting images of what Jeannie just shared with me. I tried to quiet down.

Then, I looked at Jesus still sitting on the other side of me, and angrily said, "Jesus, actually I would like your input. This could not have gone on with no one noticing. How can you even sit there? You not only knew this happened; you did nothing to stop it. I really want to know if you felt anything while watching this disgusting behavior, performed in the middle of the day, on a public sidewalk, orchestrated by a priest. Tell me: What do *you* think about what she was doing?"

Jesus heard my question, but rather than look at me, he looked right past me to Jeannie, sitting next to the car window and asked, "How did you feel?"

She seemed to give this some serious thought before she answered, "I didn't feel much. He stunk. I felt pushed and pounded on. I wanted to bite down, but I was afraid of making Maskell mad, so I tried not to gag. I didn't want that man's stuff in my mouth; I was expected to swallow it, and I knew I had to because Maskell would get very angry if I spit it out. I didn't want to be there. I just didn't want to be there."

Jesus's response was direct and to the point. Continuing to look at my persona, Jeannie, but clearly speaking to me, he said, "You were trained to do what Maskell wanted—what he wanted, not what you wanted."

I cried, once again feeling compassion for this young part of myself. Her words and those of Jesus bypassed my brain and reached right into my soul. As she responded to Jesus, I heard her, felt her numbness, her fear—I was her.

What Jeannie was saying was quite different than my previous perception of her. This was not a teenager separate from me who was working as a prostitute, a willing participant. These were the actions of a younger part of me trained to do whatever her master told her to do. I had touched an unexpected pain beneath that horror and realized I *was* Maskell's trained monkey. I could not stop the river of tears washing through me.

With the ground of compassion established, Jeannie began to reveal more of herself. In response to the pain I was feeling for her, she said "At first it was hard to feel that pain and still do what I was expected to do. For me to feel sad, afraid, or lonely really got in the way of getting through what needed to be done, so the best thing to do was to get rid of the source of the pain, the source of the feelings."

She continued, "It took time, but me and the other girls finally got that little one into the cell and slowly and carefully chained her to the wall. I explained to her that for us to get out of this alive she needed to be separated from us because I was distracted by her sadness and fear for me—you. The other kids learned the hard way to stay quiet and numb; but she was so pure, sweet, and sensitive, we could only keep her contained and quiet."

My body was shaking as I hung on to Jeannie's every word. I was immediately reminded of the small child I discovered during a meditation, over 15 years prior, in a cell at the end of my bowels, the level deep within my subconscious.[152] Through the years, I tried to understand what the ruby was that sealed her mouth represented, how to communicate with this little aspect of myself, and how to get her out of the cell. I wanted to know who she was to me, and why I was so afraid of her. Since discovering her, I continued to work on different parts of this meditation in my therapies and in my quiet. Currently, because of that inner work, the scales had fallen away from the child's eyes and ears, she could move her limbs freely, and she was no longer hunched over. I became courageous enough to take her soft foods and she slowly began to eat. However, I could not get her out of the cell, whether due to her not wanting to budge, or my being afraid.

Now, I found myself wondering if she could have been put there to protect me? Did she agree to be isolated from the other personas in order for me/Jeannie to be able to do what had to be done to survive? Was my persona, Girlfriend, created to carry the guilt about Cathy's death so this little one could be shielded from that pain?[153]

I sat mesmerized as Jeannie continued to share, "The younger girls and I thought the best thing to do would be to cover her ears, so she couldn't hear what was being said by the adults or by me. Then we needed to be sure she could not see what was going on. Most importantly she needed to stay deep inside you, unable to speak or yell out. In case her feelings seeped through, I decided to bury her under the despair and hopelessness you felt. There was no way anything could be felt through that. Jesus gave us the red stone to put in her mouth. He also said he would stand guard in case anything went wrong."

---

152 See "Lantern in the Bowel (Vignette)," page 111.
153 See "The Council Gathered in the Cellar (Vignette)," page 204.

The guard is Jesus?![154]
My emotions were reeling and my head spinning with so many questions. This was so unexpected. I was torn between anger at Jesus and relief that he was the one watching over that precious child all these years. I felt such love for these young personas within me. While feeling so much appreciation, I had to ask Jeannie how Jesus could stay there and watch that child become like a caged animal. She told me, "He said she'd be okay because her heart was with him. I knew she'd be safe."

I asked, "Well, what did the little one think about this arrangement?"

Jeannie defensively responded, "She knew this was our last hope and she trusted me." I had to agree. After seeing firsthand what Maskell could do if you did not do as he said, it made sense that the only way out alive was to totally cooperate.

I was now exhausted, and it seemed like our conversation was coming to an end, but I felt I had to remind Jeannie that that child deep within me was still locked in a cell. I also asked her why she had a red stone plugging her mouth.

Jeannie said she was aware the little girl was still in the cell. Her explanation was direct: "It isn't time for her to leave that cell. You still need to understand that I'm you and she is the essence of love that connects us. It really hurts her to see you so fractured knowing there is nothing she can do. Without all of us safely connected, her pain would have you feeling overwhelmed with guilt and completely out of control. The more compassion you feel for me, and that means you, the freer that little one becomes. So, she stays where she is until you're ready to be more accepting of me. There is no hurry. She really is in good hands while we go at the pace we're going, and no one rushes us."

I knew this new awareness would take time for me to fully take in, reflect on and process. But I was now waiting

154 See "Lantern in the Bowel (Vignette)," page 112.

to hear what the red ruby was. Jeannie continued, "The red stone is the pure love the precious little one feels for all of us and you. She loves us all so much she was willing to be chained and caged like an animal to stay silent, still, and hidden, in order to save all of us."

Struck with how much confidence Jeannie had, I asked, "How did you end up with so much confidence when I have so little?" She replied, "You're the one isolated from the root, the foundation, the rest of us. As you reconnect, you become more of what you see in me and the others. You know it's true because it's already happening. It just takes time." And then our conversation came to an end, for now. I was deeply touched by this prayer experience, and I felt much lighter than when I started.

As difficult as this memory and conversation was for me, I realize I could not have faced it if I had not grown to accept and trust my spirit guides. Their presence was with the whole me on that path, not with different parts of my psyche. They provided a sense of protection I needed to see and feel Jeannie's and my innocence and vulnerability. While I knew it would take time to understand the impact of what just happened, I felt my desire to connect with Jeannie growing and my compassion for her intensifying. I had a new appreciation and understanding for the unconditional love my young personas have for me which was bringing about a feeling of love for myself. However, I still did not want to know all that Jeannie had to do to stay alive. I only wanted to hear what she needed me to know for us to reconnect and integrate more fully.

Reconnecting with my persona Jeannie is what I need for that young aspect of myself, the bearer of pure love, to leave her cage and be free in me.[155] I have no clear idea how that is going to happen or what more I will discover about my persona Jeannie. However, after this meditation, I do know I need to fully experience what is to come and let it unfold, just as I have done throughout my adult life.

---

155 See "Lantern in the Bowel (Vignette)," page 112.

Postscript

The bench, where I continue to sit with Jesus and Jeannie, has become a safe and sacred space for me. Sitting there, I have faced some of the hardest memories of abuse perpetrated on me after Cathy Cesnik's death. The memories continue to be revealed to me by my persona, Jeannie, and I find some sense of security in remembering what happened while on the bench, with Jeannie, Jesus, and my protective guides by my side.

CHAPTER THIRTY-FOUR

Fear and Courage

As someone who not only lived through intense sexual abuse as a child, but also repressed it until the age of 27 to survive, I believe I will be in some form of therapy for the rest of my life. New memories are triggered when I least expect them, and it may take months to work through their impact on me. I have found that it takes a certain level of courage and support for a survivor of sexual assault to venture into this deep psychological work. It takes just as much courage to speak of it to others.

Typically, when I begin remembering a perpetrator or an abusive situation, I process it on multiple levels within myself. And sometimes for years I watch to see how that one piece fits into the bigger puzzle of my time in high school. I do so because we all have a right to our past, and no matter how painful and disgusting it may be, it is still ours.

I am not only finding and integrating severed parts of myself, but I am also deprogramming. Each time I remember more of the abuse, I discover more of the lie. Simultaneously, I feel a kind of cellular shift accompanied by a natural reawakening and reconnection to the truth. An example of this would be when I look at a photo and it causes a body reaction—uncontrollable shaking of my head and body, scrunching and quick movements of my eyes, unexpected words like "Oh no!" or "He's alive!", a sudden feeling of dread, and/or sudden crying—all before my mind has any awareness of the person. I feel my body has held the memory on a cellular level and something like a photo triggers that memory to begin surfacing to my conscious mind. Aletheia once again holds up her mirror for me to see my experience more clearly.[156] That is when I can begin the work of distinguishing the lie from the truth.

My decision to stay awake and embrace the severed experience or part of myself, then integrate that memory with how it affected me on a physical, psychological, emotional, and spiritual level, is frankly exhausting. But it is worth it. I am relieved of expending so much energy to keep my past separate, while regaining my experiences and rooting my life in all of me.

Because of this work I am finally feeling what others have been encouraging me to do for years—appreciate what I have rather than focusing on what I could have been if perpetrators had kept their hands off me. I am now more consistently aware of what I am grateful for: a loving family including three wonderful grandchildren, close friends, my home, and my health.

I still grapple with fear and agree with Carl Jung's statement, "Where your fear is, there is your task." As I process my past and push forward in my present, I am working on defusing the fear within me that has the power to paralyze. Each time that fear overwhelms me, I slowly remember to address the fear and decide what it is connected to. For example, when I write, I realize the fear is frequently a deeper emotion pertaining to an experience I am writing about.

Fear can be a deeply limiting emotion. For me, it is a memory that was born out of Maskell's hunger for power and inexplicable hatred for me. I am learning how to deal with the triggered panic that hits me when an unexpected experience arises. Fear no longer suffocates me. I now experience it more like one would work with a recurring nightmare. There is a burst of terror and then a realization that this fear is rooted in my past experience, which I am more able to work with. But more times than I like to admit, I have decided I could not do a task due to fear. That is why I need to continue to remind myself that what matters most

---

156 See "Going Back for Frances (Vignette)," page 231.

is my finding the courage to at least do some of the things my heart calls me to do, despite the fear Maskell and others instilled in me. I am pleased to say that the more I process this emotion, the easier it gets to discern what is worth putting my energy and effort into.

Writing this book is a prime example of facing my fear and moving forward in order to follow my heart's desire. As I work on this project, I periodically feel overwhelmed with fear due to a lack of confidence in myself and my ability to speak clearly to the issue of surviving traumatic experiences. I also continue to deal with the fear-fueled lie that I should not talk about abuse experiences or my interactions with intimidating institutions, lest people think I am lying or crazy. But I breathe and allow the physical sensations that grow out of that fear to calm down in my body. By doing this I have been able to move forward with my writing, enjoying the powerful benefits of this part of my journey.

I also need to converse with confidants so they can help me process the specific past or present experience which caused the feeling of fear. I allow them to reflect to me some perspective of what I am feeling, sometimes finding excitement or normal nervousness intermingled with what was immobilizing terror. Eventually, the fear dissipates, but it takes time.[157]

In 2020, after a great deal of thought and reflection, I decided to testify before the Maryland Legislature, speaking in favor of a bill that would abolish the statute of limitations in civil cases for childhood sexual abuse in my state. This bill had been introduced in prior years; but then I was too afraid to even hold a sign with a group of supporters, much less testify. The fact that I felt I was able to testify was a

---

157 My current relationship with my brother Ed is an example of how allowing others into my personal space to process the feeling of fear helps me. He has been my companion along this portion of my journey. Besides being a good editor with a well-honed listening skill, he continues to voice his support for me and my project while mirroring to me what confidence and belief in my ability looks like. So, with Ed's support, I continue to lean into my fear of writing, and take another step forward.

clear gauge of how far I had come in my health walk. I still had to do my preparation process, with the understanding that if I got too overwhelmed, I could always back out. However, I am proud to say yet again "I did it!" I had the courage to sit before the committee, use my voice, and tell them what I wanted for all survivors of childhood sexual abuse, myself included.

Unfortunately, shortly after I testified, I experienced a major meltdown. My whole body began to shake, tears flowed, my mind was numb and muddled. I was suffocating. I needed to escape. While the hearing continued, I ran for the door. My friends Maria and Nancy were immediately at my side. Once I was in the hall, I began to calm down. A man who also testified had followed me out of the hearing. He stood in front of me, looked me in the eyes and said, "I may never have a chance to meet you again, so I want you to know you saved me!" Instantly I knew he was referring to watching me in *The Keepers*.

This happened to me a lot following the premiere of the documentary. But here it was all coming together. I had just walked through and finished a terrifying but fulfilling experience. Standing heart to heart in that corridor of the Maryland Legislature, we hugged each other and sobbed. He said he was testifying to help other survivors. I said that's why I did it too. As surreal as these types of experiences have been for me over the years, they are also powerful affirmations that my desire to do the right thing is spot on with the impact it has on the public.

I am proud I was able to follow my heart and use my process to testify, which is:

- I realized I wanted to testify,
- I acknowledged the fear I felt,
- I discussed it with my therapists and close friends, and
- I began my process of leaning into that fear, which surprisingly is where I found the courage to finish.

I am learning that one of the more important parts of this process is my focus. This time instead of getting lost in how terrified I felt, I tried to focus on me as the young girl, who had been the victim of unbelievable trauma. I made a conscious decision to let her know that I have her best interest at heart, while placing her in the Great Mother's lap so I could accomplish the task before me.[158] When I testified, I did it with my younger self in mind. I was surprised that I did not consciously lean on my spirit guides as much as previous times. The more I continue to integrate with that young girl, the less I need my spirit guides' protection. However, I know in my heart that they will always be with me.

My spiritual life continues to change and expand as I grow; however, my spiritual practice will never be what it once was. In 1992, I was free falling into an abyss, terrified since my religious foundation was gone, and convinced I was doomed. But surprisingly, I experienced something much deeper and more powerful, like a great spiritual basin, which I call the Divine Oneness or the Great Unknown. Whatever it was, it cushioned my fall.

I say this with a smile since I no longer have the false certainty of a man-made belief system. Instead, throughout my journey, I find my personal faith to be rooted in the wisdom of the heart of the sacred feminine. It has taken me years to become comfortable enough to speak about this drastic change in my life. I feel like a student learning a new language and then trying to explain what my heart and soul are experiencing in that language. I value and hope to deepen my sense of compassion, empathy, inner peace, intuition, and personal empowerment. I have learned a lot from my past, but three major lessons have been:

1. Be cautiously open to what touches my heart, speaks to my spirit, or has a synchronistic feel about it, like my last exchange with my mother;

---

158 See "The Great Mother (Vignette)," page 107.

2. Value my personal space; and
3. Ask, "How will this benefit me?" before I go deeper into a memory or agree to do something publicly.

Moving forward on my health path, I continue to stretch, grow, and heal, feeling more like my natural self. Even though I have no one religion at this time, there is a truth I trust. Because of the ongoing loving interactions with Mike, Mom, Brother Richard, and many others, I learned that love is not only real, but also transformative. I can state this simple truth with certainty.

So, my journey continues, one step at a time.

"One does not become enlightened by imagining figures
of light, but by making the darkness conscious."
                                          – C. G. Jung

Appendix

My Personal Journals

The Vignettes in this book are taken from some of my journals, which were referred to as diaries by the lawyers for Joseph Maskell, the Archdiocese of Baltimore, and the School Sisters of Notre Dame in the 1995 lawsuit. They insisted I give my journals to them, for them to read with the hope of catching me in a lie or contradicting myself. I call them 'sacred' because they contain years of inner dialogues, written prayer experiences and reflections on my spiritual journey. After the court case, I destroyed two of my original journals, embarrassed and terrified that someone else would read them and think I was crazy. I no longer have the sense of trust which once allowed me to write freely in my journals. However, I am learning to respect my sacred space, and to trust my ability to just say, "NO!"

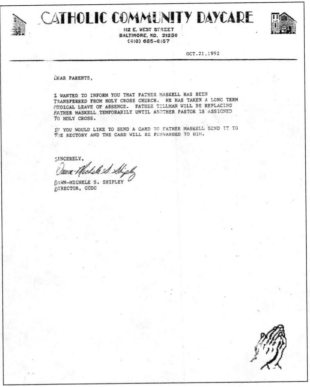

CATHOLIC COMMUNITY DAYCARE

112 E. WEST STREET
BALTIMORE, MD. 21230
(410) 685-6157

OCT.21,1992

DEAR PARENTS,

I WANTED TO INFORM YOU THAT FATHER MASKELL HAS BEEN TRANSFERRED FROM HOLY CROSS CHURCH. HE HAS TAKEN A LONG TERM MEDICAL LEAVE OF ABSENCE. FATHER TILLMAN WILL BE REPLACING FATHER MASKELL TEMPORARILY UNTIL ANOTHER PASTOR IS ASSIGNED TO HOLY CROSS.

IF YOU WOULD LIKE TO SEND A CARD TO FATHER MASKELL SEND IT TO THE RECTORY AND THE CARD WILL BE FORWARDED TO HIM.

SINCERELY,

DAWN-MICHELE S. SHIPLEY
DIRECTOR, CCDC

Joseph Maskell Removed from Holy Cross Parish.

Dear Jeannie, Mike, and Mrs. Hargadon,
I'm in a state of shock !!! Before this, I didn't know that there was such a thing as a joyful, elated, grateful state of shock. I'm almost traumatized by bliss; I can't fully believe it; I'm tempted to bite the check(s) to prove to myself it's real.

For the past hour, my mind has been racing with thoughts about what will I do with this incredible windfall. Shall I take a vacation to Florida? To my beloved Philippines? Should I pay off my Visa bill that I ran up while I was in the Philippines trying, unsuccessfully, to live on $12.50 a month. Oh yes, I'll do that and finally be free of monthly payment! Oh! I can buy some new shirts that actually fit and slacks too! And I'd like curtains in my bedroom! I can't believe it! Oh my God! Thank you, Thank you, thank you.

It's true, I know, that money don't buy happiness but now I know also that it's true that it certainly helps!

It's incredible! I can't possibly express my gratitude adequately. I feel so free knowing I won't have to punch pennies for a while – and I can also send some money to my friends in Africa and in the Philippines.

You are too kind and generous to me but oh how I thank God and you that you are !!!

(If I were an obedient religious, I would turn the money over to my community, but NO WAY, JOSE! Thank God, I accept myself as a sinner – and "disobedience" in this case, doesn't even begin to make me feel guilty). Seriously speaking, I am deeply grateful for your generosity, but I am forever grateful to God that I know you and that we are part of each other's lives. Love, Richard

Brother Richard's Thank You Note

Memorial Plaque posted where Cathy's body was found, November 2016

Mandala, "'Brother Bob' Contained," Journaled on January 11, 2017,
"I put B. B. in this mandala. He is chained in, cannot leave!!"

Mandala, "Rage and Pain Contained," Journaled on January 3, 2017.

"I see a wild woman with a penis stuffed in her mouth. She needs to keep it there to keep the rage and pain contained. I've had some very powerful releases over the years with the image of a penis being taken out of my throat. This is more stuffed in my mouth like a stopper in a tub. My face is exploding with the emotions stuffed in. I am suffocating myself by keeping this penis in place. It reminds me of the key held by the guard, at the bottom of my bowels, where I am chained to the wall of the cell. There a ruby stone is cemented in my mouth."
See Lantern in the Bowel (Vignette), page 112.

Map of Majestic Distilling Co. Inc.

The black X with the white dot at the right bottom corner of picture is the The Majestic Distilling Co., which is where Maskell took me to view Cathy Cesnik's dead body. The spot where Cathy's body was found is marked with a black X, to the left of the distillery, under the words "Cathy's Body".

Archbishop Keough High School

Front view of high school shows the exit doors and the brick wall of the convent are to the far right of the photo. The covered main entrance is to the far left of the building. End of breezeway, circled on photo, is where some Alumni remember a fire door for exiting the breezeway.

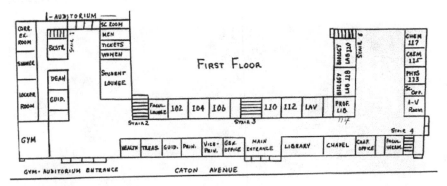

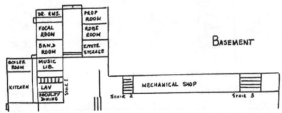

First floor, floor plan—chaplain's office at the far right of the building, near exit doors.

Door exiting chaplain's office into breezeway is visible through the concrete lattice. The breezeway was located between the school building and the latticed front of the school.

Dear _____ :

This office is conducting a highly confidential and sensitive investigation. I represent an individual who is an Archbishop Keough High School graduate, In this regard, I am seeking information concerning improper sexual conduct on the part of certain faculty and staff at the school during the period from 1969 to 1975.

It has come to my attention that you were a student at Archbishop Keough High School during this time period. If you have any information or know anyone who might have such information that would be helpful in this investigation, or if you were or know of one who was a victim of any type of abuse while at the school, please contact me or my investigator, Richard Bussey, at the number on this letterhead.

It should be understood that this is an independent investigation on behalf of a particular client and not an attempt to solicit additional clients.

Thank you for your attention to this matter.

Very Truly Yours,

DRAFT

Phillip G. Dantes

Draft Newspaper Ad:

Anyone with information concerning any improprieties of a sexual nature involving faculty or other staff of the Archbishop Keough High School during the years 1968-1975, please contact us at _____ .

DRAFT

Draft of Letter to Alumni and Draft of Newspaper Ad in 1993

Four Report Cards with Sister Joanita's Name and Wrong Dates

JEAN AGE 3

JEAN AGE 5

JEAN AGE 13

JEAN AGE 15

MOM & DAD 1970

Me with my siblings at mom and dad's 50th anniversary on August 1997.

Our wedding picture, January 19, 1974.

My immediate family, August 1997.

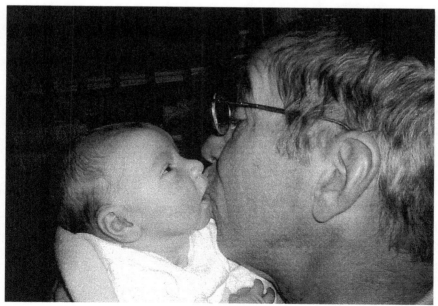

Mike

My entire family, August 1997.

Acknowledgments

I would like to acknowledge certain individuals who were an important part of my writing project:

- Without my younger brother and editor, Ed Hargadon, this book would never have been completed;
- I am thankful for a few friends and family who advised me about specific chapters or portions of the book. I am especially grateful to five individuals who were my readers and consultants for my manuscript while in progress and upon its completion: Valdone Kuciauskas, Marcella Biggins, Maria Rauser, Alex Kuciauskas Hargadon and Jim Casey;
- Maria Staub Goebel is the amazing artist who was able to take images that had been housed in my brain for years and put them to paper;
- Susan Yost's internal layout and cover design blew me away, and Rick Ramos was so patient and professional in mentoring me through the making of my audio book;
- Several friends and family met with me in August of 2018 to discuss if a book written by me, focused on surviving trauma, would be helpful. It was because of their encouragement that I began *Walking with Aletheia*;
- Ryan White and Jessica Hargrave created a foundation for my book with *The Keepers*. Their documentary broke the silence, providing survivors of Joseph Maskell and others the opportunity to deal with our past in order to grow. This is something the Church and the courts should have done many years ago;

- Kerch McConlogue at kerch@wefixbrokenwebsites. com did an excellent job designing my website, Steve and Krys Crimi, my new friends and publishers at Logosophia were wonderful to work with, and Bruce Mason was a great help in getting the word out about my book;
- Last but not least, I am grateful to the personas and spirit guides who continue to help me maneuverer my way through unfathomable terrain.

Resources

Psychology Today: Find a Therapist – detailed listings for mental health professionals in the United States. https://www.psychologytoday.com/us/therapists

SNAP (Survivors Network of those Abused by Priests)
Website: https://www.snapnetwork.org
Toll free phone: 1-877-SNAP-HEALS (1-877-762-7432)
General information: (314) 776-9277
**Include contact info for local chapters and for the State's Attorney General's office.

RAINN (Rape, Abuse and Incest National Network)
24 Hour Hotline: 1-800-656-4673
RAINN is a nonprofit and the nation's largest organization dealing with sexual assault.

National Suicide Prevention Lifeline
24 Hour Hotline: 1-800-273-8255

Maryland State Attorney General
(Investigation continuing from 2018 to present)

If you were a victim of an abuser associated with school or place of worship in Maryland, or you have knowledge of such abuse no matter when, please provide the information you want to share in an e-mail to: report@oag.state.md.us. If you do not feel comfortable using that e-mail address, you can e-mail or call Rich Wolf, the A. G. Justice Dept. investigator. Rich Wolf stated, "No story or life event is too small." Tel.: (310) 576-7290
E-mail: rwolf@oag.state.md.us

You can also contact Elizabeth Embry, the criminal lawyer for the investigation, at eembry@oag.state.md.us.

The Body Keeps the Score: Brain, Mind and Body in the Healing of Trauma, by Bessel Van der Kolk, M.D., Penguin, 2015.

Sexual Boundary Violations in Psychotherapy: Facing Therapists Indiscretions, Transgressions, and Misconduct, edited by Arlene (Lu) Steinberg, Judith L. Alpert, Christine C. Courtois, American Psychological Association, 2021.

ABOUT THE AUTHOR

Jean Hargadon Wehner, a survivor of childhood sexual abuse, is an advocate for sexual abuse survivors, their families and the people who work with them. Jean has experience working, educating, and communicating with diverse populations, including faith groups, student groups, and professional associations. She is also a contributor to the Emmy-nominated Netflix documentary series *The Keepers*. In addition to her advocacy work, Jean, originally trained as a Spiritual Director, is now a Nationally Certified Reflexologist, Certified Life Coach and Reiki Practitioner. Her website is https://walkingwithaletheia.com.

CPSIA information can be obtained
at www.ICGtesting.com
Printed in the USA
FSHW010937050122

9 781735 043241